IS OUR GOSPEL THE GOSPEL?

WHAT DID JESUS DO?

An observation of constructively critical examination and comparative analysis of our present understanding and presentation of the Gospel of our Lord and Savior Jesus Christ

BY DR. PRINCE MAURICE PARKER

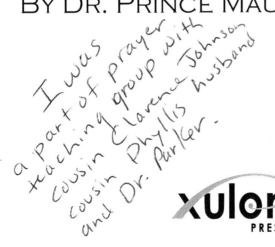

I was a part of prayer teaching group with cousin Clarence Johnson cousin Phyllis husband and Dr. Parker.

XULON PRESS

Reference Material:
Hebrew Old Testament (Tanach) (HOT)
LXX Septuagint Greek Old Testament
Hebrew Old Testament (Tanach) w/ Strong's Numbers
Brown-Driver-Briggs Hebrew-Greek Dictionary
Biblia Hebraica Stuttgartencia w/ Strong's Numbers

www.xulonpress.com

God bless you Abundantly!
Psalms 20:1-5
HMC

Dr. Prince M. Parker
08/29/2014

1) The LORD hear thee in the day of trouble;
the name of the God of Jacob defend thee;
2) Send thee help from the sanctuary, and
strengthen thee out of Zion;
3) Remember all offerings, and accept thy burnt
sacrifice; Selah
4) Grant thee according to thine own heart,
and fulfil all thy counsel.
5) We will rejoice in thy salvation, and in
the name of our God we will set up our
banners; the Lord fulfil all thy petitions.

CONTENTS

My Respectful Dedication and Thanks to:
To my Lord and Savior, Jesus Christ, the Son of God – my life.
To Guillermina (Gina) Olmos de Parker–my wife.
In addition, A Respectful Recognition To:
To Leonard Ravenhill – who has influenced and influenced my life
by his writings.
William MacDonald, Dr. Keith W. Phillips, Ray Comfort,
Winkie Pratney, Keith Green and Walter J. Chantry –
Fellow servants that have also written and taught masterfully on
this all-important subject.

Comments from Juan Carlos Escobar Carrasco - General Superintendent Federation of the Assemblies of God of Spain

<hr/>

I met Dr. Prince Parker more than twenty years ago. From the first moment that I saw him, I noticed a naturalness and a charm that made him stand out from other traditional evangelical ministers.

He has always proven to be easy-going and relaxed in his communication style, whether with other people or in communicating the Gospel. In a teaching and preaching context, his faithfulness to and grounding in the Gospel stand out, along with his creative style of instruction and his openness to all types of believers, whether young or old, whether well-versed in Scripture or just beginning in the faith.

Faithful to his own style, simple but convincing, he projects a genuine gospel in sharp contrast to certain evangelical formats that do little to reflect the central place that the very essence of the gospel ought to hold. I am certain that this book will give readers the opportunity to engage in a critical evaluation that will be both constructive and even entertaining.

Pastor Juan Carlos Escobar,
General Superintendent
Federation of the Assemblies of God of Spain

… … … …

Senior Pastor
Iglesia Celebración Cristiana
Arganda del Rey
Madrid, Spain

COMMENTS FROM ESTEBAN MUÑOZ DE MORALES ASSISTANT GENERAL SUPERINTENDENT - FEDERATION OF THE ASSEMBLIES OF GOD OF SPAIN

———∞∞∞———

We live in a time of a pure hedonism where people's main worry is the enjoyment of the here and now, without assuming responsibilities for their eternal well-being much less contemplating the certainty and reality of death. That is why I would like to thank the effort of ministries like that of Dr. Parker's, which investigate and go in depth in the Scriptures in order to find a complete sense of this last enemy to be defeated.

As Prince rightly says, *"Wisdom is the ability to see the relation between our problems and the principles of the Word of God"*, and death… is a big problem! If we want to understand life, we have to understand death and its consequences from a biblical perspective and then understand the purpose of its existence.

This is Prince's second book (or "Príncipe", as we call him in Spain), a man passionate about his pedagogy and with pastoral experience. In our country, along with his wife, Gina, he has pastored the congregations of Daimiel (Ciudad Real) and Caceres (Caceres). However, he has been doing missionary work since 1974, principally in Mexico and Spain. Now the time has come to show, in his books, his developed knowledge and his vast gathered experience arrives.

Esteban Muñoz de Morales
Assistant General Superintendent
Federation of the Assemblies of God of Spain
http://www.adenet.org/inicial.php

Senior Pastor
Comunidad de Amor Cristiano (Córdoba)
http://iglesiacac.es/

COMMENTS FROM MARIO ESCOBAR

※

D r. Prince Parker is a professor and academic that approaches us through his book on the essence of the Gospel with depth and precision. Only lives that have been transformed, as has his, are able to impact other lives.

Lic. Mario Escobar Golderos

Madrid, España (Spain)

January 2014

Historian and author of more than 20 books

COMMENTS FROM
ALEJANDRO ALONSO

———⁓———

W hen a person can speak more with his testimony than with his words, they are worthy of being heard. Dr. Parker and his wife Gina have been friends of mine for many years, and I must say that their lives demonstrate, to us, a healthy and enviable relationship with God.

Dr. Parker tell us about the deadly destruction of sin, which was introduced to the world by way of our father, Adam's disobedience. However, as Dr. Parker explains in his book, God, in His perfect plan, has provided the necessary elements for our resurrection. He has made us to be heirs of innumerable promises through his Son, Jesus Christ.

In this book, Dr. Parker shows us the most valuable guidelines to consider and apply for receiving the freedom that Jesus has for each of us.

Alejandro Alonso
Professional Musician/Songwriter
Pioneer of CCM (*in Spanish*)
http://www.alejandroalonso.com/
Pastor
Maranatha Chapel
1915 N. Twin Oaks Valley Road,
San Marcos, CA 92069
http://www.iglesiamaranathachapel.org/Mapa.html

A Preludial Note from the Author for the English Version

———— ∞∞∞ ————

This book is written for those fellow servants who are in the trenches as pastors, missionaries and plain faithful believers fulfilling their indispensable duties in the church in the manifestation of their unquenchable love for our Lord. My hat is off in respect to all of you. So as a note to my fellow academics and theologians: Though I cover theological themes and indulge in some academia, this is not a book written to be a theological or academic treatise, nor was it written for theologians per se. I do pray, however, that you will enjoy the reading for some of the stimulating and thought-provoking insights that I hope to present.

I am a career cross-cultural missionary and have been for well over 40 years at the time of this writing. I was born in the United States on an army base and was raised an army brat. My dad was career military personnel (20-plus years of service). As a result, moving and travel were the norm and I spent many of my preadolescent years in Europe. As a missionary, I have also lived in Europe as well as several other countries a majority of my adult life and frequently find myself traveling around the world because of our ministerial endeavors. Therefore, though I am an English-speaking native (both American and British English), I have spent most of my life communicating in other languages and living in foreign environments.

User-Friendly Theology

For this reason, many years ago, I wrote this book originally in Castilian (Spanish). The primary purpose of the original book was to minister to the countless thousands of pastors and workers in the Lord's vineyard in Spanish-speaking countries. The majority of these faithful servants, though highly intelligent and duly prepared for their ministries, are not scholars. The flow the book was geared to minister to the spectrum of the Christian populace, from the studied academic minister to the simple faithful local church worker. The idiomatic flow and feel of the English version is set to follow the Castilian style that was written to cover a wide swing of academic needs and levels and comprehension.

That being said, be it noted that I am also a theologian. Because of this, combined with my experience on the mission field, I refer to myself as the "Indiana Jones" of theologians. The mission field has also kept me in touch with both practicality and the folks outside of the realm of academia. Therefore, I will attempt to cover both light and somewhat complicated theological themes in a user-friendly manner. As a professor at the seminary where I teach, I employ an elementary teaching philosophy in that I first set before my students, concepts that I feel they can comprehend with minimal effort. I then progress to take them to concepts that seem far out of their reach so that they might know that there is so much more that they must learn. On a less aggressive scale, will also attempt to do so here in a comprehensive manner. Thus, I will attempt to embrace an educational pendulum that swings from the easy to understand, to the somewhat challenging and thought provoking concepts of our subject matter. In the same fashion, the vocabulary utilized in this version swings between humorously colloquial Californian American English and polysyllabic academia.

FYI

Just so that you know and can understand something else about my background, back "B.C." (Before Christ), I was a college prep student, artist, wannabe rock musician and a pacifistic "hippy". My dad retired at Fort Ord, California, in the beautiful Monterey Bay area, during the war in Viet Nam in the late 1960s. It was there that I spent the remainder of my preteen and youth years. If you're a Baby Boomer, you remember the era and perhaps you also remember the Monterey Pop Festival? My mother was on the executive board of the Monterey Jazz Festival, so it was natural that I was able to get close when Hendrix and all the greats of the 60s came to Monterey.

As an inspiring musician, I was able to work with or hang around many of the rock groups of that day and some impressive names were in that line-up. But, I was on a dark dirigible to destruction while wondering, *Am I having fun yet?* Thank God, that although there was much evil that I never touched, sin still wound its barbed tendrils through my soul and I knew that I was lost and headed to hell. That was until I was gloriously saved with the Jesus People in 1971.

Because of this varied and colorful background, when I illustrate various points, it is easy for me to employ folksy anecdotes and colloquialisms in what my adult children lovingly call, "Dad's horrible sense of humor". In many ways or in all, I do so pray that this book becomes an edifying factor and positive influence in your life and ministry. May God continue to bless you as we serve Him together!

H.M.S.,
Prince Maurice Parker, Th.D.
Professor of Exegetics and Old Testament History
Assemblies of God Theological Seminary
La Carlota, Córdoba,
Spain

Is OUR Gospel THE Gospel?
Part One

Recognizing the Problem

Psychologists know that in order to help a person with a psychological problem it is necessary for the person to understand and clearly recognize that they indeed, do have a problem. A person that suffers from alcoholism or drug addiction will remain in their hopeless state until they recognize that they have a serious problem that has dominated and is destroying their life. Recognition is the first step to recovery; denial always leads to desolation.

In the same way, God's people must recognize that deep problems exist in our churches in reference to our ideological concepts. The first part of this book is written to help us to understand that such problems truly exist. This is where we want to identify and explain them. The second part of the book is written to resolve the identified maladies.

The victory is ours in Christ Jesus; we are more than conquerors. The church is the chosen people of God and the gates of Hell shall not prevail against her! When we recognize these problems and strive to correct them, we will close the doors to the enemy and then the God of peace shall bruise Satan under your feet shortly. The grace of our Lord Jesus Christ be with you. Amen.

CHAPTER 1
LEARNING FROM PAST ERRORS

———— ∞∞∞ ————

A Good Story

There are two things that I really like–the study of history, and a good story. That good story could be a testimony or a novel. I like it much more when I find a good story based on historical facts. They absolutely fascinate me; I just love them. This is simply one of the thousands of reasons that I love the Bible so much; it's full of good stories about historical events.

Speaking of history, someone once said that the only thing that man has learned from history is that man has learned absolutely nothing from history. Some else said that if we don't learn from our past errors we are condemned to repeat them.

My Big Brother

When I was a kid, I learned from my big brother's mistakes and saved myself a lot of the butt whippings that our dad gave him. If he got into some kind of mischief and my father caught him and he got it, I always reasoned: Look, if he did that and it didn't fare him well, why in the world would I every want to do it? The worse thing about it is that my brother repeatedly challenged my father by getting into the same mischief over and over again.

The incredible thing is that my dad was U.S. military Special Forces who was assigned to hold a high post in King Haile Selassie's palace training his security guards in Ethiopia during the Cold War. He was a man with an extremely fine mind, perfect physical condition and a sterling steel personal discipline. When we moved back to the States, he had to register his body as a lethal weapon. I would think, "Dude, can't you see that this man is three times bigger than you and a thousand times stronger? My brother was a rhino chaser. He would say that I was a coward; but what he called cowardice, I called intelligence. His adventures and challenges never had a happy ending.

Bruce Lee versus Rambo

This is the reason that when I see a movie by Bruce Lee, Chuck Norris or some kind of monster like that, I always think that sometimes people can be really stupid! This huge guy is fighting with Bruce. Bruce beat him up so bad he turned him into a crossword puzzle (the dude entered the room vertical and left horizontal). There's another dude who had seen how his friend just got knocked into the twilight zone- and he still wanted to fight with this guy?

Or, we can take another case with one of those *Rambo* movies. Ten guys have gone through this door and Rambo has killed them all with that famous machine gun that NEVER runs out of ammo. Now why the heck would I want to go out that door? But, not everybody thinks like me... The young playboy has used and abused dozens of young ladies; yet the girls are still lining up thinking, "He'll be different with me". They stay in line until they receive their own personal experience of being chewed up and spit out when the sugar is gone. I don't get it.

More Shrewd?

Jesus said that the people of this world are much shrewder in handling their affairs than the people who belong to the light (Luke 16:8b). If the examples that I have mentioned are things the people of this world do, where does that leave the children of Light? If the Children of Darkness have learned nothing from history, what is to become of us with all of the problems and terrible doctrinal detours that we have had in the history of the church? Help us, Lord!

A Sure Guarantee

This is why it is great to know that God is the Savior of His church and that He has not left us orphans or without guidance and counsel. God Himself jealously guards the honor and purity of His Word. Jeremiah 1:12 says, "*… for I watch over my word to perform it*" (ASV). Psalms 138:2 says, "*… for you have exalted above all things your name and your word*" (ESV). This means that God has placed the honor of His Word at the same level of His Name.

Now we all know that the Bible solemnly warns us in Exodus 20:7, "*Thou shalt not take the name of the LORD thy God in vain; for the LORD will not hold him guiltless that taketh his name in vain*" (*KJV*). That's something that God doesn't play around with. He will never condone an abusive use of His Name or His Word. It's a mockery; and we all know what the Word warns us about that.

- Be not deceived; God is not mocked: for whatsoever a man soweth, that shall he also reap (Galatians 6:7 KJV).

He gave us His Word. He also gave us His Holy Spirit and ministerial gifts like prophets and teachers, so that we would stay firmly guided on the course that Jesus Christ marked out for us from the beginning.

Nonetheless, man always has a bag of tricks up his sleeve and is always seeking how to get his own way. Even in the letters that the Apostles wrote, we can see the human predisposition to seek detours from the way that Christ indicated for us to follow. This has even occurred with very sincere churches and individuals like the Corinthians and the churches of Galatia. This truth is graphically explained in a case that involved the Apostles in Galatians 2:11-14 (KJV),

- *But when Peter was come to Antioch, I withstood him to the face, because he was to be blamed. For before that certain came from James, he did eat with the Gentiles: but when they were come, he withdrew and separated himself, fearing them which were of the circumcision. And the other Jews dissembled likewise with him; insomuch that Barnabas also was carried away with their dissimulation. But when I saw that they walked not uprightly according to the truth of the gospel, I said unto Peter before them all, If thou, being a Jew, livest after the manner of Gentiles, and not as do the Jews, why compellest thou the Gentiles to live as do the Jews?*

Can you imagine that! The Apostles weren't walking uprightly according to the truth of the Gospel! Well, taking that into consideration, there yet remains hope for us. The truth be told, almost all of the apostolic letters were corrections of errors that had entered the congregations of first Christians.

But They Are So Sincere

The problem is not one of sincerity, zeal or dedication; a person can be sincere, zealous or dedicated and still be wrong. History is full of such cases; I've already mentioned an incident with the very apostles. Rather, it's simply a matter of whether we are walking in the truth or not. Hear me out; I'm not saying that it's necessary to have all of the minute details on point in order to be saved. I quite actually don't believe that any one group or individual has a complete understanding of all biblical truth. There are many that I believe that are very accurate in their assessment, understanding and handling of a wide array of biblical understanding. Nonetheless, I believe that we all err at some point or another in the countless details of the Bible. I think that, in some degree, God meant for it to be that way. Because, as Jack Nicholson said, "You can't handle the truth!" In a way, Jesus said the same thing when He said, *"I have much more to tell you, but now it would be too much for you to bear"* (John 16:12 GNB).

Let's take, for example, the study of eschatology and the time of the Second Coming of Christ. One brother aptly said that concerning the timing of the rapture, we should pray for the pre and prepare for the post. But honestly, we can always learn something from brethren who hold to different criteria than we embrace when it comes to such subjects.

Then Where Lies the Danger?

There is not the slightest doubt that the doctrine of the Second Coming is of grave importance for the church. One in every thirty verses of the New Testament refers to it. Nevertheless, our eternal salvation does not depend on whether we believe one or another position concerning this great biblical truth or other similar doctrines. The danger of entering into heresy begins when we stray on one of three non-dismissible points of the Scriptures. In this, we are talking about three basic truths:

- The person of Christ – who is he?
- The Word of God and the doctrine of salvation; exactly how we can be saved.

- How we should present this incalculable valuable message to the world.

Let us break it down a bit:

1. The Person of Christ:

   a. Is He the only begotten Son of God or not?

      1. Is He the only way of salvation or a way of salvation?

      2. Is He the Savior or a savior?

      3. What place or role does He have in the salvation of our souls?

   b. Is He God manifest in the flesh or not?

   c. What place does Christ hold among all of the other people who have ever lived on the face of the earth?

2. What about the "saints" or "virgins"?

3. The vicarious death of Christ.

   a. What role does the death and blood of Christ hold in the salvation of the souls of mankind?

4. Is there another agent of cleansing and forgiveness apart from these?

5. What place do dogmas, sacraments, and traditions hold in the soul's salvation?

   a. Did Jesus really—literally rise from the dead or not?

6. Is it really important to believe that Jesus physically rose from the dead?

7. The Bible:

   a. Is the Bible (I am referring to the "*autographs*"—the Hebrew, Aramaic and Koine Greek Scriptures) the perfect and infallible Word of God totally inspired by the Holy Spirit?

      1. The Scriptures came directly from the very mouth of God.

- But he answered and said, It is written, Man shall not live by bread alone, but by every word that proceedeth out of the mouth of God (Matthew 4:4 KJV).

b.) Is the Bible *The* Truth or does it contain the truth?

   1.) Is the Bible complete or do we need other books in order to know all truth about God?

c.) Is the Bible the maximum authority for the life of the Believer or not?

d.) Every cult attacks the Bible as an insufficient revelation. According to their assessment, you always need another book, experience or revelation in order to understand it. Whenever it is necessary to have dogmas and traditions, the words of a leader, a non-biblical prophecy, an angelic visitation or something of that nature so that one can see this "new and additional truth", beware!

Everything that the Bible teaches us is important. We must understand this. Never the less, our eternal salvation really depends on these three points—what we believe and how we answer these basic questions. Why is this? This is so because these basic points deal directly with the way of the salvation of man's soul.

I have contemplated this deeply because I'm a person that does not enjoy polemical doctrines and subjects. This is why it's somewhat ironic that my first book is one that deals with a subject that some would debate. The saddest thing for me is the fact that this absolutely indispensable doctrine, the doctrine of salvation, has degenerated to such an extent that now it actually IS a matter of debate.

Thermodynamics and Biblical Truth

Stating it simply, the second law of thermodynamics says that molecules always seek stability. This is a law that reigns over this present world and it tells us that the universe is in a constant state of deterioration. Every star will one day nova and die. Every new car and every new building will one day be rubble and scrap metal. Everything that exists in the material world be it organic or synthetic, will degenerate. It seems to me that the same thing happens to humankind's understanding of eternal truths. An idea, perhaps originally true, is passed down from one generation to the next. Yet unfortunately, it seems as if it becomes more and more distorted as it is passed on just like an image that's a copy of a photocopy of a copy that was sent by a really bad fax machine… not good. If biblical Truths were simply passed down to us by word of mouth, we might be able to say that such is an excusable and understandable state of affairs with us today. However, such is not our situation, for we have the verifiable, written Word of God ever accessible and at our disposal.

A good teacher of the Word[1] said something that is applicable here. He said, "That which parents permit in moderation, the children will abuse with excess." I've personally come to the conclusion that, that which is sin today, is tomorrow's subject of debate as to whether it is acceptable or not. That which is a subject of debatable acceptability today is tomorrow's norm. Like dominoes falling in line, things tend to degenerate, and this presents us with a grievous problem when it comes to the presentation of the pure Eternal Gospel.

How?

Several years ago, a cult had a split. This cult had a newspaper called, *The Truth*. Well, the splinter group came out with their periodical and they called it, *New and Improved Truth*! Now come on, if it's true, it's not new, and if it's new, it's not true. I admit that there can be, for us, undiscovered truth. However, there is no "new truth". Solomon said, *"The thing that hath been, it is that which shall be; and that which is done is that which shall be done: and there is no new thing under the sun"* (Ecclesiastes 1:9 *KJV*). We must understand that truth is immutable. Time cannot change it and if it has changed over time, it only goes to show that it was never really true. This is so because truth is eternal. Two plus two will always be four. I will admit that there might arise values in another generation that people will espouse as true, but that does not make them true. It just made them acceptable to that generation.

It's like value and worth; something that is truly valuable will always be valuable … if it was truly valuable in the first place. Let us follow the fluctuating values of our lives.

- As children, we value our little plastic toys that we wanted so much. Someone takes them from us and we cry.
- The size and cost of our toys increase as we grow and … *"mature"*. Yet they continue to be mere toys.
- Then, in our adolescence we begin to value our, all-important–defend at all cost–vanity and ego.
- Then comes career and more toys (whatever happened to our original *have-or-die* toys of our infancy?).
- Then comes the deathbed—whatever happened to everything else?

Think about it: If something is truly valuable and important – it will still be so 110 years from now also. In fact, some things that we do not esteem as valuable now, will be extremely valuable 110 years from now. (I use the figure of 110 years because it is pretty much a sealed guarantee that if you are reading this, 110 years from now you will have already personally faced your eternal fate.)

Different Kinds of Gospels

It's interesting to note that the word *gospel* (εὐαγγέλιον) appears in the Greek New Testament 77 times in 74 verses. It almost always appears with the articles "the" (ἧν) or "this" (τοῦτο) before the word "gospel" saying, "*the* gospel" or "*this* gospel" in reference to the truth. In I Timothy 1:11, Paul calls it the *glorious* gospel and said that he had been placed in charge to care for it, "*According to the glorious gospel of the blessed God, which was committed to my trust*" (*KJV*). He received the Gospel as it really is—a sacred trust. He committed himself to zealously guard and defend its purity.

Paul knew the truth of the "*glorious*" Gospel with such confidence and taught this truth with such preciseness that three times in his writings he could refer to his preaching and teaching as "*my* gospel" in Romans 2:16 (*KJV*) "*In the day when God shall judge the secrets of men by Jesus Christ according to my gospel.*"

- (Romans 16:25 *ASV*) "*Now to him that is able to establish you according to my gospel and the preaching of Jesus Christ, according to the revelation of the mystery which hath been kept in silence through times eternal,*"
- (II Timothy 2:8 *ESV*) "*Remember Jesus Christ, risen from the dead, the offspring of David, as preached in my gospel.*"

In II Timothy 2:2, Paul emphasized the importance of faithfully passing the precious truth of the Gospel to others. He said, *"Take the teachings that you heard me proclaim in the presence of many witnesses, and entrust them to reliable people, who will be able to teach others also"* (II Timothy 2:2 *GNB*). He knew just how to teach them the precise way in which they should accurately share the Gospel with such exactness that two times he actually called it *"our gospel"*. He had the privilege of taking this liberty because he and his disciples taught the same word that Christ manifested during His earthly life.

- But if our gospel be hid, it is hid to them that are lost (II Corinthians 4:3 KJV).
- For our gospel came not unto you in word only, but also in power, and in the Holy Ghost, and in much assurance; as ye know what manner of men we were among you for your sake (1 Thessalonians 1:5 KJV).

On the other hand, Paul always referred to a perversion of the Gospel as "*a* gospel" or "*another* gospel".

- For if he that cometh preacheth another Jesus, whom we have not preached, or if ye receive another spirit, which ye have not received, or another gospel, which ye have not accepted, ye might well bear with him (II Corinthians 11:4 KJV).
- I marvel that ye are so soon removed from him that called you into the grace of Christ unto another gospel: Which is not another; but there be some that trouble you, and would pervert the gospel of Christ. But though we, or an angel from heaven, preach any other gospel unto you than that which we have preached unto you, let him be accursed. As

we said before, so say I now again, if any man preach any other gospel unto you than that ye have received, let him be accursed (Galatians 1:6-9 KJV).

Think about the gospel that Paul taught. Think about his words in II Timothy 2:2 (ISV), *"What you have heard from me through many witnesses entrust to faithful people who will be able to teach others as well"*. We can see that Paul thought that discipleship proved itself efficaciously after four [spiritual] generations of carrying the truth.

Let's look at this in his life then we will look at one of his disciples after we consider Paul. Now we know that Paul was not one of the original twelve. He was not one of the 120. He was not one of the 500 (I Corinthians 15:6). He was not one of the eight thousand (Acts 2:41; 4:4). We are informed confidently, by Luke's account in Acts that many more were saved in those days besides those major blocks that I have mentioned. Nonetheless, just to give you a general idea of the just how the Gospel maintained its original purity though it was communicated through several spiritual generations. Considering this, we must take into consideration that he was saved in Damascus and received his first discipleship via Ananias, a Believer that was most probably one of those who were part of the diaspora that came about is a result of the persecution after the martyrdom of Stephen (Acts 8:1). We are talking at least five spiritual generations of the communication of the Gospel from the original fountain – the twelve.

Paul grows, develops his ministry, becomes one of the most effective communicators of the Gospel of his day and we see that (very possibly) he leads Luke to Christ in Troas (Acts 16:8-10). Paul disciples Luke and develops him to become one of his most faithful disciples. Luke is a sixth generation believer – but Luke writes a

Synoptic Gospel! A gospel so pure that is fits seamlessly with Mark and Matthew and happens to be the longest and most complete Gospel of the four (knowing that all are intrinsically indispensable to the testimony of the other three). The Gospel that was passed to Paul was *"the"* GOSPEL, not *"a"* gospel. What I want to know is; is the teaching of today's gospel in its majority, *"the"* Gospel or *"a"* gospel? If it is not *"the"* Gospel, then it is synthetic, not genuine but artificial.

CHAPTER 2
HE RAN WITHOUT THE CORRECT MESSAGE

—∞∞∞—

A Problem in the Family

A s I said, I like a good story. We can learn a lot from them, especially is if the stories are found in the Bible. In II Samuel 18:5-33 we find one of these stories. This story will help us to understand what has happened to our churches and the message of today's gospel.

- *And the king commanded Joab and Abishai and Ittai, saying, Deal gently for my sake with the young man, even with Absalom. And all the people heard when the king gave all the captains charge concerning Absalom. So the people went out into the field against Israel: and the battle was in the wood of Ephraim; where the people of Israel were slain before the servants of David, and there was there a great slaughter that day of twenty thousand men. For the battle was there scattered over the face of all the country: and the wood devoured more people that day than the sword devoured. (II Samuel 18:5-8 KJV).*

We really have a problem here. I have seen people that have had family arguments that ended up rolling out into the street and becoming a public spectacle. But here, what started out as a family problem escalated until it became everybody's problem; it became a literal war involving the entire nation! Absalom, King David's son, had risen up in sedition against him. Now Absalom's name means, "Father of Peace", but this guy was anything but peaceful! Worse still, a great multitude was committed to following him in his rebellion. They truly believed that he offered and could deliver peace. The same thing happens to people in today's world. People are following other people in search of the solution to their problems; yet these people can't resolve their own problems!

Many years ago, I worked as a vocational counselor in a technical school for adults in Salinas, California. The great Hispanic civil rights leader, Cesar Chavez was active in the area and most of our students were people that he was helping in a great way. One of my fellow counselors was a psychologist; we'll call him, "Dr. Manny". I spent quite a bit of time talking to him and on many occasions, I was able to share the Gospel with him clearly explaining about the state of his eternal soul and his need for salvation. He always rejected the Gospel saying the psychology had all of the answers that people needed.

Manny was also a great cook and was the owner of his own Mexican restaurant that I would frequent. One day I entered and found him slightly inebriated and crying in his beer because he felt overwhelmed by his many problems. I didn't want to be mean, but I asked him exactly what it was that he was offering the people with psychology if it was unable to solve his problems- and he was the expert? "Is that all you have to offer them?" I asked. (Okay, I confess. I was being mean.) This time, when I shared the Gospel with him, all of his arrogance and pride had dissolved and he admitted that his psychology had nothing to do with the solution of the problems that he had. I helped him to see that the real cause of his problems was the existence of sin in his life and the lives of his loved ones. Only Jesus Christ has the solution for this malady. The Bible says, *"While they promise them liberty, they themselves are the servants of corruption: for of whom a man is overcome, of the same is he brought in bondage"* (II Peter 2:19 *KJV*).

The Blind Leading the Blind

I used to teach at a Bible school in Mexico in the early '80s where a young brother named Fernando studied. He had been blind since early childhood. One day he came to class with a very attractive young lady, also a believer, who was visiting the area; she was also sightless. We were all very happy to see him so happy and so well accompanied.

About two weeks later, I asked him about his girlfriend. He told me that they had to break up because things just weren't working out for them. "Why?" I asked. "Well", he replied, "the relationship just wasn't biblical". "How in the world do you figure that? You're both believers," I said unable to hide my surprise at his answer. He went on to explain that one day the other young people of the Bible school left them alone and they got totally lost. Once they even fell into a big rose bush in the school's garden area. He concluded by saying that they would have been the blind leading the blind.

Well, that exactly what happened to Absalom and his followers, and that is also what occurs when people want to lead and counsel others without submitting to the counsel of the Word of God! *"Don't worry about them! They are blind leaders of the blind; and when one blind man leads another, both fall into a ditch"* (Matthew 15:14 *GNB*).

Fallen with Your Eyes Open

In many ways, the war between David and Absalom is just like the war between Satan and God. People are following Satan believing that he can give them peace and many die in the process as a result of their deception. What's more, just as in this case, even nature testifies against these rebels "...*and more men died in the forest than were killed in battle.*" (II Samuel 18:8) Romans 1:20 *GNV* says, "*Ever since God created the world, his invisible qualities, both his eternal power and his divine nature, have been clearly seen; they are perceived in the things that God has made. So those people have no excuse at all!*"

It's also like the war between man and God. People have follow man's disoriented teachings and ideas believing that these can give him peace and many are destroyed in the process. It reminds me of a bumper sticker I saw once. It said, "Don't follow me, I'm lost!" The results of these things are very similar to what we see happening in the church today. People are following ideas and philosophies that are mere fabrications of sometimes sincere, yet misguided men. Unfortunately, their well-intentioned ideas will never guide people to peace or salvation.

Worse still are people like Balaam. The Bible speaks of those who "... *have left the straight path and have lost their way; they have followed the path taken by Balaam son of Beor, who loved the money he would get for doing wrong*" (II Peter 2:15 *GNB*). The man, after having known the truth, sold it to serve the lie. The Scriptures warn us about this in Proverbs 23:23, "*Buy the truth, and sell it not; also wisdom, and instruction, and understanding*". During his prophecies, he would mention himself saying, "... *Balaam the son of Beor hath said, and the man whose eyes are open hath said:*" (Numbers 24:3

KJV). He repeated the same description of himself in Numbers 24:16 (*ASV*) "*He saith, who heareth the words of God, and knoweth the knowledge of the Most High, Who seeth the vision of the Almighty, <u>Falling down, and having his eyes open</u>*".

Balaam's perversions were not occasioned by the ignorance of a sincere, but misguided person. He was completely aware of what he was doing and for the love of money, he was willing to lead thousands of people towards deception, destruction and death. Well said are the words, "<u>*Falling down, and having his eyes open*</u>". I would say that this kind of deceiver is, beyond a doubt, the most despicable.

Time for Some Fruit Inspection

Comparing this kind of people with trees, Jesus said,

- *Be on your guard against false prophets; they come to you looking like sheep on the outside, but on the inside they are really like wild wolves. You will know them by what they do. Thorn bushes do not bear grapes, and briers do not bear figs. A healthy tree bears good fruit, but a poor tree bears bad fruit. A healthy tree cannot bear bad fruit, and a poor tree cannot bear good fruit. And any tree that does not bear good fruit is cut down and thrown in the fire. So then, you will know the false prophets by what they do* (Matthew 7:15-20 *GNB*).

Much of the fruit of which I speak here is the result of what we hear today. Without any condemnation, I want to give a case in point – something to consider seriously. When I see the quantity of divorces in the church, even among our ministers, I recognize that it is the very same percentage that is found in the people of the world. This is a manifest evidence of the fruit of that which is preached in our churches. It is said that, in a sense, we are what we eat. In other words, in today's church, we are the result of the preaching and teaching that we are hearing, that which we spiritually consume. The Holy Spirit is shouting warnings at us that we are in the way of grave danger and that calamities yet await us on this present path.

What's more, as in the case of Absalom's followers, nature itself testifies against those who announce a synthetic gospel. Their own fruit betrays them. I'm not talking about the trees of the forest, but the natural results of the sermons and teachings. Human nature has manifested and flourished in the fertilizer of the synthetic gospel. The evidence is clear, because the disasters that we are seeing in our churches among our "converts" are not the results that God brings when the pure Gospel is preached. I repeat, these problems are warning signs and evidence that something is very wrong.

Seeing things in this lamentable state, we must ask ourselves the disconcerting question: "What's wrong with the Gospel?" Well, for me, it's easy to answer that question even in the face of such distressing situations. There is absolutely nothing wrong with the Gospel! I sincerely believe that this state of affairs is due to the fact that the gospel that is being preached in the majority of the cases is not the Gospel of the Bible.

We have taken the liberty to remove elements of the Gospel that we esteem nonessential, difficult or offensive and replaced them with human teachings. It's like a surgeon who discovers, after he has operated on and sutured the patient, that he has a few left over pieces lying around- pieces that turn out to be vital organs!

Watch Out for That Tree!

Speaking of trees, what's up with trees in the Bible? A tree was involved in the fall of man. Here trees are the cause of the death of Absalom and his followers and the Son of God was hung on a tree.

- *But by becoming a curse for us Christ has redeemed us from the curse that the Law brings; for the scripture says, "Anyone who is hanged on a tree is under God's curse."* (Galatians 3:13 *GNB*)

While we are at it, we might as well see where this verse comes from.

- *And if a man have committed a sin worthy of death, and he be to be put to death, and thou hang him on a tree. His body shall not remain all night upon the tree, but thou shalt in any wise bury him that day; (for he that is hanged is accursed of God). that thy land be not defiled, which the LORD thy God giveth thee for an inheritance* (Deuteronomy 21:22-23 *KJV*).

I think the trees represent the words that have come out of the mouth of God; the immutable words of the Bible. Doesn't the Bible tell us that if we are faithful in our obedience of the Word of God that we would be like trees?

- *"Happy are those who reject the advice of evil people, who do not follow the example of sinners or join those who have no use for God. Instead, they find joy in obeying the Law of the LORD, and they study it day and night. They are like trees that grow beside a stream, that bear fruit at the right time, and whose leaves do not dry up. They succeed in everything they do"* (Psalms 1:1-3 *GNB*).

It's just logical, because if believers take heed to the Word of God, it's a natural result that they would become more and more like that Word. Let me put it this way, when the believer brings forth good fruit, it simply shows what's going on in the inner being. These trees were fierce warriors in this war against Absalom. The fruit of the Spirit is love, but this love is so pure that it cannot abide perversions. In this sense, Jude, in his epistle counseled us as to how we should maintain pure our definition of faith.

- *"My dear friends, I was doing my best to write to you about the salvation we share in common, when I felt the need of writing at once to encourage you to fight on for the faith which once and for all God has given to his people"* (Jude 1:3 *GNB*).

Jude also compares those who announce a false gospel with trees.

- *"These are spots in your feasts of charity, when they feast with you, feeding themselves without fear: clouds they are without water, carried about of winds; trees whose fruit withereth, without fruit, twice dead, plucked up by the roots;"* (Jude 1:12 *KJV*).

Vanity of Vanities

- *"Suddenly Absalom met some of David's men. Absalom was riding a mule, and as it went under a large oak tree, Absalom's head got caught in the branches. The mule ran on and Absalom was left hanging in midair. One of David's men saw him and reported to Joab, "Sir, I saw Absalom hanging in an oak tree!" Joab answered, "If you saw him, why didn't you kill him on the spot? I myself would have given you ten pieces of silver and a belt." But the man answered, "Even if you gave me a thousand pieces of silver, I wouldn't lift a finger against the king's son. We all heard the king command you and Abishai and Ittai, 'For my sake don't harm the young man Absalom.' But if I had disobeyed the king and killed Absalom, the king would have heard about it—-he hears about everything—-and you would not have defended me"'* (II Samuel 18:9-13 *GNB*).

I don't think that there is anything wrong with a guy having long hair. I had mine long for about 30 years. Nevertheless, Absalom's hair is symbolic of his vanity – it was also a contributing factor of his death. In the same way, vanity will be the fall of all those who rebel against God. The Bible gives us a perfect definition of the word *vanity* in I Samuel 12:21 (ASV) *"and turn ye not aside; for then would ye go after vain things which cannot profit nor deliver, for they are vain."* That said, we can see that according to the Bible, a vanity is something that does not profit nor deliver; this means that a vanity is something that holds no true, lasting value. A vanity is something useless or worthless and without true purpose and that in the end will prove to have been a total waste of your time and life.

It's not that vanity is an easy thing to avoid and I am definitely not condemning people that want to grow their hair like Absalom. I don't consider this to be a point of great importance. We are all held captive by vanity in one form or another. It seems like it's a part of the curse of the fall and we will only be free when Jesus resurrects the redeemed from the dead. Meanwhile, trying to free ourselves is like trying to get chewing gum off the bottom of your shoe on a hot day.

Paul recognizes the role that vanity played in the fall, not only in humanity, but also in the entire creation. He spoke about our coming liberation in Romans 8:20-21, *"For the creation was subjected to vanity, not of its own will, but by reason of him who subjected it, in hope that the creation itself also shall be delivered from the bondage of corruption into the liberty of the glory of the children of God."* (*ASV*)

Jonah paid the ultimate Price because he followed a vain idea. He learned from his experience and God gave him a second chance teaching him the solemn truth that *"They that observe lying vanities forsake their own mercy"* (Jonah 2:8 *KJV*). Now there's a terrible tragedy for you. You lost your eternal soul following something that was totally worthless! What's worse is that it says that you forsook your OWN mercy to do it! Now... now that's just messed up! That being that the case with mankind, how much more should we pay rapt attention to the precious details of this message of salvation. Anyway, the story goes on to tell us about the evidence of the plague of sin also over the servants of the king.

- *"I'm not going to waste any more time with you," Joab said. He took three spears and plunged them into Absalom's chest while he was still alive, hanging in the oak tree. Then ten of Joab's soldiers closed in on Absalom and finished killing him. Joab had the trumpet blown to stop the fighting, and his troops came back from pursuing the Israelites. They took Absalom's body, threw it into a deep pit in the forest, and covered it with a huge pile of stones. All the Israelites fled to their own hometowns* (II Samuel 18:14-17 *GNB*).

Whose Witnesses?

Joab disobeyed a direct order and killed Absalom. The father loved his wayward son and wanted to deal with him at home. Joab was supposed to take him back to his father so that he might deal directly with this prodigal son. But that's how we are. Instead of winning with love one that has detoured from the truth, we usually react carnally and end up in aggressive and sometimes violent contentions. It proves true the old saying, "you won the argument, but lost a friend." The Bible says, *"let him know that whoever brings back a sinner from his wandering will save his soul from death and will cover a multitude of sins" (James 5:20 ESV).*

Joab, in his disobedience proved the truth of Romans 3:23, *"everyone has sinned and is far away from God's saving presence"*

(Romans 3:23 *GNB*). There is deliverance from this curse, but if people don't know how to find their way to obtain it, how will they ever be saved? If even the very servants of God err from the way that our Master indicated, as in this case, did Joab, what is ever to become of the ignorant? I Peter 4:17-18 (*ESV*) says,

- *For it is time for judgment to begin at the household of God; and if it begins with us, what will be the outcome for those who do not obey the gospel of God? And If the righteous is scarcely saved, what will become of the ungodly and the sinner?*

Brothers and Sisters, this is enough to send chills up and down your spine! After making that earth shattering declaration to believers, look at the question he presents saying, *"What, then, will become of godless sinners?"* The Scriptures put forth various provocative questions and comments such as this one, and all of them deal with our obligation to take the truth of the Gospel to the world. I just want to quote a few of the verses:

- *How then shall they call on him in whom they have not believed? And how shall they believe in him of whom they have not heard? And how shall they hear without a preacher?* (Romans 10:14 *KJV*)
- *Then said he to the multitude that came forth to be baptized of him, O generation of vipers, who hath warned you to flee from the wrath to come?* (Luke 3:7 *KJV*)
- *How shall we escape, if we neglect so great salvation;* (Hebrews 2:3 *KJV*)
- *But if our gospel be hid, it is hid to them that are lost: In whom the god of this world hath blinded the minds of them which believe not, lest the light of the glorious gospel of Christ, who is the image of God, should shine unto them* (II Corinthians 4:3-4 *KJV*).

Hey! That Me!

- *"During his lifetime Absalom had built a monument for himself in King's Valley, because he had no son to keep his name alive. So he named it after himself, and to this day it is known as Absalom's Monument"* (II Samuel 18:18 *GNB*).

This monument represents the desire that God has placed in our hearts to recover or obtain that which we lost in the fall, our immortality. This is a kind of a short cut that people think will take them to eternal life. It is taken as something about them that will be here forever; something, at least, by which they can be remembered. But alas, in reality this too, is a vanity and will take you nowhere good. Psalms says something incredibly succinct about this,

- *They that trust in their wealth, and boast themselves in the multitude of their riches; None of them can by any means redeem his brother, nor give to God a ransom for him: (For the redemption of their soul is precious, and it ceaseth for ever:) That he should still live forever, and not see corruption; for he seeth that wise men die, likewise the fool and the brutish person perish, and leave their wealth to others. Their inward thought is, that their houses shall continue forever, and their dwelling places to all generations; they call their lands after their own names. Nevertheless man being in honour abideth not: he is like the beasts that perish. This their way is their folly: yet their posterity approve their sayings. Selah* (Psalms 49:6-13 *KJV*).

This desire exists because God made man like this. "...*Also, he has put eternity into man's heart,* yet so that he cannot find out what God has done from the beginning to the end." (Ecclesiastes 3:11 *ESV*). Man was originally created to live forever! In our innermost being, we know this instinctively. Since man's fall into sin this organic understanding has been perverted by his altered nature and now a great part of this desire is the fruit of his vanity. Yet, though he doesn't quite know why, in one way or another man wants to regain his lost eternal life; though he now seeks it in his spiritual blindness and moral darkness.

For Sale

I once heard on the radio that now it was possible to buy a star and have it officially registered in all of the scientific astronomical archives in your own name. This way, when scientists study and chart the stars and come to your sector, they would have to call the star by your name. I thought that was a great idea and I asked my daughters to buy me a star for Father's Day. (I'm sure they were thinking, "Oh no, this is it. Dad has officially lost it." My wife talked them out of it, but they probably would have done it and given me the document along with a card with Acts 26:24 on it or something.) I heard later that it was a hoax.

Anyway, I think that the idea would have really caught on and sold well for the very reason that I mentioned. Man wants to be eternal like the stars. We all want to be eternal whether we admit it or not. It's a good thing to want eternal life. But people need to know how they can legitimately obtain this eternal life that they want so much. We, the believers in Jesus Christ, are the only ones that have the key to the truth. So if we do not correctly inform the people of this; woe unto us.

Once again I'll say it this way, that "by instinct", people know that death is not the end of life. Death was not God's original plan for man. Romans 5:12 tells us, *"Sin came into the world through one man, and his sin brought death with it. As a result, death has spread to the whole human race because everyone has sinned"* (*GNB*). If it were not for sin, death would never have entered the world. Man is an eternal being and in his innermost being he deeply desires to recuperate that which he as lost. This consciousness is found in every human being. The desire that Lucifer had is the same feeling that he utilized to trap all of humanity. Genesis 3:5 (*GNB*) says, *"God said that because he knows that when you eat it, you will be like God...".*

Two Messengers

- *"Then said Ahimaaz the son of Zadok, Let me now run, and bear the king tidings, how that Jehovah hath avenged him of his enemies. And Joab said unto him, Thou shalt not be the bearer of tidings this day, but thou shalt bear tidings another day; but this day thou shalt bear no tidings, because the king's son is dead. Then said Joab to the Cushite, Go, tell the king what thou hast seen. And the Cushite bowed himself unto Joab, and ran."* (II Samuel 18:19-21 *ASV*).

Now we've come to our focus point. There is a sincere servant of the King that has no desire to be idle. He wants to be occupied in faithful service to the king and desires to do something that will please him. Nothing wrong with that, but he was not chosen to carry this imperatively important message. His problem consisted in the fact that he only knew part of the message, and a half-truth can easily lead people into deception. He was not duly prepared and informed on the subject matter to be able to carry the message. The Bible says this of people like him, *"Depending on an unreliable person in a crisis is like trying to chew with a loose tooth or walk with a crippled foot"* (Proverbs 25:19 *GNB*). There was another runner more informed than he was; one that had the correct message and all of the truth of what happened to the king's son. He was the one Joab chose to carry the message. In other words, one servant was sent, but the other guy just went!

The Easy Road – A Short Cut

- *Then said Ahimaaz the son of Zadok yet again to Joab, But come what may, let me, I pray thee, also run after the Cushite. And Joab said, Wherefore wilt thou run, my son, seeing that thou wilt have no reward for the tidings? But come what may, said he, I will run. And he said unto him, Run. Then Ahimaaz ran by the way of the Plain, and outran the Cushite.* (II Samuel 18:22-23 *ASV*).

This zealous young man insisted on running with the message. He ran and did what it seems like always happens to those who do not take the truth of the complete message; he looked for a shortcut. A shortcut in the preaching of the Gospel is about as good an idea as putting an F15 jet's ejector seat in a helicopter.

Many want to remove details of God's message and the instruction of how to get back to Him. They think that these details are insignificant and superfluous minutiae. These inevitably seek for the easiest way to do things and almost always get there before the true Messenger does. Many years ago here in Spain, when we went to the streets to share the Gospel, everybody knew who the Catholics, Muslims and the Jehovah's Witnesses were, but painfully few had ever heard the Gospel or had known anything about Evangelicals. It seemed as if the false messenger had taken the shortcut, or *"the road through the Jordan Valley"*, and got there first. I want to point out here that the same thing happens with many Evangelicals when we take the Gospel; we take the road through the Jordan Valley.

<u>Poor Butterfly</u>

It makes me think of a kid that saw a butterfly struggling to come out of its cocoon. Half of its beautiful body was still in the cocoon. "Poor little thing", thought the child, "I'm going to help it". So with all of the sincerity and good intentions in his little heart he found some scissors and cut off the rest of the cocoon. To his shock and dismay, he discovered that instead of helping the butterfly, he had created a monster. The part of its wings that had yet to emerge in its struggle to escape the cocoon were wrinkled and deformed. The struggle to emerge from the cocoon demanded that the wings stretch and expand in such a way that they would have remained beautifully extended.

This story makes me thing about the straight gate that Jesus spoke about when he said, *"Enter ye in at the strait gate: for wide is the gate, and broad is the way, that leadeth to destruction, and many there be which go in there at:"* (Matthew 7:13 *KJV*). By simplifying the Gospel with the omission of the details, that man esteems superfluous or difficult to accept or understand we are taking the broad way. This is, *"the road through the Jordan Valley"*, of which I have been speaking.

In the same way, these believers, in their sincere desire to help souls to be saved have taken out the scissors of human reasoning and "simplified" the gospel to make it more pertinent and modern. It is no longer necessary to know about repentance from dead Works or other such bothersome "details". Let's talk about peace and love and success and other positive things. Make sure that man is the center of the world; people really like to hear about these things. "This is the 21st century and things change", some will say, "Everything is instant now; instant coffee, fast food, instant bank service, the Internet and of course, the way of salvation." But, I'm sorry to inform you that God does not live in the twenty-first century. He lives in eternity and His ways do not change.

- *And the watchman cried, and told the king. And the king said, if he be alone, there is tidings in his mouth. And he came apace, and drew near. And the watchman saw another man running; and the watchman called unto the porter, and said, Behold, another man running alone, and the king said, he also bringeth tidings. And the watchman said, I think the running of the foremost is like the running of Ahimaaz the son of Zadok. And the king said, He is a good man, and cometh with good tidings.* (II Samuel 18:25-27 *ASV*).

One of the dangers of those who carry a false message is that they also carry a false hope. It might be really good news that they bring, but these glad tidings don't contain the whole truth, or worse still they might carry bold face lies. News Flash! The Gospel does not *contain* the truth. *It is the truth!* There is a great difference between those two statements.

A Simple Glass of Milk

An awesome missionary friend of mine, Art Dappen[†], was drinking a cup of milk while driving down a narrow Mexican highway. He had placed the cup on his dashboard when a truck passed him going the opposite direction and tossed a large stone into his windshield right over where he had placed the cup still full of milk. The inside of his windscreen granulated into fine powder and fell right into his cup! Art immediately recognized a spiritual lesson from the incident.

He noticed that the milk still looked enticing – in fact, the milk, in itself, was still good. The problem consisted in that now it contained an element that was lethal rendering it all deadly. This cup of milk was far more deadly that a cup full of nothing but ground up glass because now the glass of milk with the fine glass crystals carried an aurora of deceit. It looked inviting, yet would bring death in the most excruciating way. This is the danger of a message that contains elements of the truth.

This milk is like a field that has been sown with two kinds of seed; an act prohibited by the Law of Moses.

- *You shall keep my statutes. You shall not let your cattle breed with a different kind. You shall not sow your field with two kinds of seed, nor shall you wear a garment of cloth made of two kinds of material* (Leviticus 19:19 *ESV*).

This kind of law is a message of spiritual application more than anything else. It's just like the law that Paul cited in I Corinthians 9:9-10 (GNB):

- *We read in the Law of Moses, "Do not muzzle an ox when you are using it to thresh grain." Now, is God concerned about oxen? Didn't he really mean us when he said that? Of course that was written for us. Anyone who plows and anyone who reaps should do their work in the hope of getting a share of the crop.*

The Bible compares its message to seeds. The teachings and values of men are also compared to seeds, but those seed are weeds and thorns that choke out the Word.

- *And Ahimaaz called, and said unto the king, all is well. And he fell down to the earth upon his face before the king, and said, Blessed be the LORD thy God, which hath delivered up the men that lifted up their hand against my lord the king. And the king said, Is the young man Absalom safe? And Ahimaaz answered, When Joab sent the king's servant, and me thy servant, I saw a great tumult, but I knew not what it was; and the king said unto him, Turn aside, and stand here. And he turned aside, and stood still* (II Samuel 18:28-30 *KJV*).

I've Got a Question

The king asked the messenger a question. People will also ask many questions to the heralds of the Gospel; but the questions are never the problem. On the other hand, the answer you give could either be the solution to the problem or a major contributing factor. One of the most important questions that can ever be asked is, "what must I do to be saved?" The danger for the lost soul today is in just how this twenty-first century church will answer this question.

When the king asked a direct inquiry as to the content of the good news that Ahimaaz carried, he had no answer. He's like a young man that came running into my office one day all excited and exclaiming, "Pastor, Pastor, I'm going to get married!" "Wow, Great! With whom will you get married?" I asked sharing his obvious enthusiasm. "Well", he replied, "I don't know, I haven't gotten that far yet. As a matter of fact, I don't even have a girlfriend!" The young man used to always tell me that he'd never get married. That day he decided that he was going to get married, but he still didn't know the other half of the story. I never could figure out why he was so excited. Anyway, in the same way, just as I am sure that the king was happy to hear that they had won the battle, he only knew half of the story; he didn't know the whole truth.

When we take the message of the Gospel and really don't know its content, in reality we are like those who Jude describes, *"clouds without water"*. We have the appearance of hope but are without the ability to bring alleviation. Another friend of mine always dressed as if he had a million dollars in his pocket, but in reality he was so poor that he couldn't even pay attention. One day he came up to me and said that he had that deep desire to buy a Mercedes Benz 500 again. Wow! I was surprised. So I asked him if he had ever been the proud owner of such a fine automobile. "Naw", he responded as he walked away, "I've only got that deep desire again". Poor dude, he was more shallow than a kiddie pool in the Sahara.

- *"And, behold, the Cushite came; and the Cushite said, Tidings for my lord the king; for Jehovah hath avenged thee this day of all them that rose up against thee. And the king said unto the Cushite, Is it well with the young man Absalom? And the Cushite answered, The enemies of my lord the king, and all that rise up against thee to do thee hurt, be as that young man is. And the king was much moved, and went up to the chamber over the gate, and wept: and as he went, thus he said, O my son Absalom, my son, my son Absalom! Would I had died for thee, O Absalom, my son, my son!"* (II Samuel 18:31-33 *ASV*).

When the messenger with the good news arrived, the one that had the truth, the heart of the King was completely broken. And this happened when he heard the message that brought him the good news. Just like that, the truth of the Gospel will break the heart of the hearer when the whole message is presented. When we hear the truth of the Gospel, it will happen as it did on the day of Pentecost, *"When the people heard this, they were deeply troubled and said to Peter and the other apostles, "What shall we do, brothers?"'* (Acts 2:37 *GNB*).

These words, *"deeply troubled"* are the Greek word, "katanusso" (κατανύσσω) and it means, "to pierce thoroughly – like being nailed to the wall with a spear, that is, (figuratively) to agitate violently". Now, my question to you is, whatever happened to this power of such crushing conviction of sin? Why is it not commonly found in a majority of our churches today?

CHAPTER 3
TRUTH AND TRADITIONS

⸺⸎⸺

What's Going On Here?

Evangelicals know that there exist problems in our churches and missions. Behind the front of ministerial reports and massive statistics, there is a profound apprehension behind the fact that the church actually has little power in its evangelism. While we valiantly try to produce an aurora of joy and victory in our congregations, leaders of the church are yet disconcerted and profoundly disturbed with the reality of our experience and the literal results of our efforts.

The church is full of questions about evangelism and the hope of revival. We have never had more missionaries, evangelistic campaigns, Christians studying personal evangelism, or huge conferences to seriously examine causes and solutions to our weaknesses and failures to produce true fruit in the evangelistic field. Since 1966, we have celebrated innumerable conventions on this subject. Ministries have gotten together with the principal goal of discovering the impeding barriers to our success in world evangelism.

Nonetheless, the confusion has deepened among the local churches as well as among sincere missionaries that earnestly seek solutions on this all-important matter. After analyzing, evaluating, praying and waiting, we have yet to see the urgently needed revival and the desperate, broken multitudes flock to Christ saying, "What must I do to be saved?", as witnessed in the ministries of Jonathan Edwards, Charles Wesley and Charles Finney. Rather what happens is that, if they do come en masse, they leave just as easily as if it were the ocean's tide. We never see a multitude come to Christ and remain through thick and thin, joy or martyrdom (or any other combination of good-bad situations) as seen with the three thousand on the day of Pentecost. Those three thousand and the five thousand that came to Christ shortly after them were truly *born again*; the evidence is that they remained faithfully rooted in the faith and their service to Christ notwithstanding the terrible persecution that they suffered right after they came to Christ.

It behooves us to ask probing questions like, "What's wrong with our evangelistic methods? What do we need to do to win the world for Christ? Where is that awesome power of the great evangelists of the past like Jonathan Edwards, Charles Finney, John Wesley and George Whitfield?"

We're Number One! We're Number One!

A while back, I was in Puerto Rico and I heard a radio announcer say that Puerto Rico was one of the most evangelized countries in the world and was among the countries that had more churches per capita than almost any other country in the world. This could be good news, or it could be an indictment! The announcer said it as if it were a thing about which one should brag. In one sense, this is quite an accomplishment and we praise God for this. However, I also see this as an accusing finger in witness to the ineffectiveness of the gospel that we preach. I'm going to repeat this, but it is not that the Gospel is inefficacious, but rather that the majority of that which is preached misses the mark or just plain is not the Gospel.

If the proclamation of this broadcaster was true, Puerto Rico should also have more missionaries sent into non-evangelized or less evangelized countries than any other. The crime and divorce rates should be almost nonexistent, night clubs, dance halls and businesses that deal in vice should close down because of lack of business because Jesus came to destroy the works of the devil[1].

Lamentably, this is not the case in Puerto Rico, for about the same time I read a chilling report entitled, "The Extinction of Marriage". This article explained that the divorce rate on that beautiful island is an astounding 42 percent[2]. Puerto Rico has the second-highest divorce rate in the world! Even though the Gospel was not the principal focus of this article found in a non-Christian periodical, the writer informed her readers that the number of people married by Evangelical ministers had gone up 21 percent in 1971 and up to 41 percent in 1994. But in my heart, while everybody seems to be shouting and exclaiming, "Revival, it's a revival!" I hear other voices that cry out saying,

- *Things are just fine", just as in the days of Jeremiah when he said, "They act as if my people's wounds were only scratches. "All is well", they say, when all is not well. Were they ashamed because they did these disgusting things? No, they were not at all ashamed; they don't even know how to blush. And so they will fall as others have fallen; when I punish them that will be the end of them. I, the LORD, have spoken." The LORD said to his people, "Stand at the crossroads and look. Ask for the ancient paths and where the best road is. Walk in it, and you will live in peace." But they said, "No, we will not!" (Jeremiah 6:14-16 GNB).*

Now then, I don't know where you live, but I do know that you cannot presume immunity to the moral decay that is found in the society of the country in which you live. Tell me, how are things there? Are they better, worse or getting worse? An honest inquiry will let you know that your country is also in perilous conditions.

Consequently, I must conclude one of two things: either the Gospel is ineffective or the gospel that we preach in its majority is not *the* gospel. Now, Brother, I wish to say with all confidence that, I believe in the Gospel! I also say as did Paul, *"I have complete confidence in the gospel; it is God's power to save all who believe, first the Jews and also the Gentiles"* (Romans 1:16 *GNB*). This is the message that Christ preached. Mark 1:14-15 (*ASV*) informs us, *"...Now after John was delivered up, Jesus came into Galilee, preaching the gospel of God, and saying, The time is fulfilled, and the kingdom of God is at hand: repent ye, and believe in the gospel"*. This is why I know with absolute confidence, that the Gospel is efficacious when preached as it should be.

Just Something to Consider

In an honest search for the return of the power of the conviction of sin in today's preaching, we Evangelicals have committed crucial errors. We who believe the Word of God have been utilizing the same superficial solutions that the world has adopted. Pertinence, respectability (be it intellectual or social), and unity have become the principal goals of the people of God with the hope that this would revitalize a weakened church.

It is true that unity is a noble goal and ideal. Can you imagine how beautiful it would be if all true believers would unite; perhaps then the world really would pay attention? If we could unite all of our ministries and have one healthy bank account for our funds and workers. If only we could be united in gigantic evangelistic projects. If we could do all of this and much more, could we really win the world for Christ or would we really be in the same situation because of the message that we have united to preach? The idea in itself is extremely praiseworthy and desirable, but also carries with it a gravely potential stumbling block. This would only bring about the desired effect if the gospel we preach were *the* Gospel.

Just like Walter Chantry said years ago[3], "*To accept the idea that unity is so indispensable for world evangelism ... we must find the lowest common denominator that all Christians have.*" This too, is not that bad of an idea and I am sure that there is a good balance to be found somewhere in here. But what we eventually come to is the fact that the church, as well as the individual must lower his calculated value of what he holds to be true. In a big evangelism convention, we could not insist on certain biblical truths that might offend another believer.

For example; if I believe (or don't believe, whatever the case might be) that God has given the Baptism in the Holy Spirit and the gifts of the Holy Spirit as essential tools for world evangelism today, I could not make mention of this. This would be divisive. The fact is that these very divisions are something that horribly grieves the Holy Spirit. Therefore, we have two undesirable things: division or unity at the cost of what we hold to be true.

Considering that which I said in chapter one, I want to be balanced in my assessment about doctrinal precision. The problem with this kind of unity is that the rest of the Bible is relegated to the realm of the nonessentials for ministry and world evangelism. This is a contradiction to what Jesus said when He confronted the devil saying, "*... It is written, Man shall not live by bread alone, but by every word that proceedeth out of the mouth of God.*" (Matthew 4:4

KJV). It would be relegated thus because unity, in this case, is more essential than doctrinal precision.

I think that this is why ministries and churches have not been willing to carefully examine the fundamental problem found in the lasting results of our preaching. Governing boards theologically vacillate when it comes to honestly answering the question, "Is what we preach the same thing as what Jesus and the apostles preached?" To give an exhaustive answer this question, we would have to discount summarily much of what is preached and what so many beloved believers espouse as not being the message of the gospel.

Evangelical Traditions in Evangelism

We Evangelicals hold our reformation heritage in high esteem. We are in line with such heroes of the faith such as Martin Luther and others that have broken the chains of papal superstitions. The Bible, the Holy Word of God, is our guide in all things. We do not kneel before human ideologies that would be so audacious as to contradict the Sacred Word.

Such a proclamation proceeds from a correct spirit of supreme allegiance to God. Even still, the cry of *"Sola Scriptura"*, is often an indication of good intentions rather that a fulfilled fact. How many times have we, as Evangelicals, found ourselves surrounded by practices and doctrines that are not biblically founded. Many habits and teachings that are associated with the Gospel are the product of tradition and human ideas just as were the indulgences of Tetzel. There are cases in which doctrines have been fomented in our midst that are as dangerous as those indulgences.

As far as the central theme of the way of salvation is concerned, a great sector of the church is involved in neo-traditionalism. What's even stranger or worse is that these are not ancient historical traditions. Many times our message and way of preaching the Gospel do not find their origins in the reformers and their creeds. Much to the contrary, they are innovatively recent. The biggest tragedy is that they are ideas that are foreign to the Scriptures. Generally, we have received a system of evangelistic preaching that is not biblical. This negligent handling and understanding of the Gospel have clearly been born of superficial exegetics resulting in the bankrupt reasoning of the last century or so. At times certain customs and traditions have come about as the result of a revival or spiritual movement that was truly of God, but we stayed with the relic of that custom while the great cloud of the Spirit moved on. We took something that God used as the absolute way God does things.

Take That! Spit in Your Eye!

To illustrate my point, imagine if the disciples would have reacted in the manner as today's church does. Christ comes along and heals a blind or mute man using His saliva. The disciples seeing this and knowing that this in truth was the sovereign work of the only true God Almighty, might have gone out and started to spit on the sick. It sounds repulsive (albeit very funny too), but that is exactly what we do in our churches today with our traditions. We have a fifth gospel: "We have the Evangel according to Evangelicals".

Brass Thing

It's evident that God anoints men and women that are completely yielded to His Spirit. He also anoints methods and tools that

we use: events and reunions, tracts, books, music, and so forth...
But these instruments must also be entirely given to Him so that it
doesn't happen to them as it did to the brass serpent. Hey, what *did*
happen to that brass serpent? Let's have a look at that story.

The children of Israel were acting up again and had begun
to complain about how long their journey was, when in reality
it was their fault that the journey was taking them so long. They
complained about the food- didn't God have anything else to give
them besides angel's food? Oh and how they really missed Egypt;
I just loved being a slave, working for no pay, having my children
snatched from my arms and thrown into the Nile. And I really
miss being beaten with whips and driven by the taskmasters. Wow!
Now those were the days! Well, God had just the solution for their
complaints: snakes!

- *"Then the LORD sent poisonous snakes among the people, and
  many Israelites were bitten and died"* (Numbers 21:6 GNB).

Now just look how God is. He presents them with a serious
problem, but He also has the solution right on hand if they cried
out to Him. The incident rather reminds me on the town drunkard
that was staggering along one day with a bag in each hand. Someone
asked him what he had in one of the bags. When he finally figured
out which one of the multiple figures he saw was the one that
spoke to him, he replied that he had a bottle of whiskey and that he
carried just in case a rattlesnake bit him. He heard that whiskey was
a good remedy. Well, asked the inquirer, then what's in the other
bag? The inebriate looked at him as if the answer was obvious, then
replied, "What … now what kind of question is that? Why I've got
my rattlesnakes!"

Well, let's get back to our story. God gave the snake solution to Moses. He said,

- *Make thee a fiery serpent, and set it upon a pole: and it shall come to pass, that every one that is bitten, when he looketh upon it, shall live. And Moses made a serpent of brass, and put it upon a pole, and it came to pass, that if a serpent had bitten any man, when he beheld the serpent of brass, he lived* (Numbers 21:8-9 *KJV*).

Up to this point, we're okay. God performed a wondrous work and He used the brass serpent that Moses had make for the occasion according the divine instructions. This marvel was completely the work of the hand of God! What's more, Jesus even compared Himself to this brass serpent in John 3:14-15 (GNB). "*As Moses lifted up the bronze snake on a pole in the desert, in the same way the Son of Man must be lifted up, so that everyone who believes in him may have eternal life*".

Even still, the Bible tells us that years after God told Moses to make the brass snake we can see the manifestation of man's traditionalistic and idolatrous tendencies. People had begun to worship the brass serpent! They had even given it a name; they called it Nehushtan! Nehushtan means "brass thing". Now that's just pathetic! Can you imagine yourself bowing down and prostrating yourself with uplifted hands saying, "Oh, Brass Thing, I worship you, please save me"? I say it's just plain madness. This is why God raised up Hezekiah and he had to rescue the people from their own foolishness and destroy the serpent. II Kings 18:4 (*GNB*) says:

- "*He destroyed the pagan places of worship, broke the stone pillars, and cut down the images of the goddess Asherah. He also broke in pieces the bronze snake that Moses had made, which was called Nehushtan. Up to that time the people of Israel had burned incense in its honor".*

Because of these tendencies, I know of groups that were followers of true ministers of the Gospel that were used by God in a great way in their day. These men and women preached and lived the truth in their lives. Yet after the death of these servants of God, their followers made demigods of them and they are now heretical cults destitute of the truth and (most probably) of the very glory of God.

Additives

I want to name three things that man has added to the Gospel that have nothing to do with the Bible. This is just a litmus test, so don't get freaked out. What I want to do is help us see how easily we can blur the lines and confuse our ideas with what God has really said in His Word.

Litmus Test 1. The "altar call" is not found in the Bible. There is *absolutely nothing wrong* with the idea of the altar call in and of itself. It's simple a call to set some time apart to seek the Lord – right now while someone can possibly minister to your needs. It's a good thing. Now repeat after me, "It's, ᶦᵗˢ a, ª GOOD, ᴳᴼᴼᴰ thing, ᵗʰⁱⁿᵍ". Nevertheless, admit it–it is simply not in the Bible and we must recognize this fact. If I share the Word in one of the many churches where I minister and don't happen to make an altar call, many times the people think that I missed the mark as to just how much God really could have done in the lives of those present. According to this criterion, God cannot work without the altar call. I have actually had people tell me, "Well, if it's not in the Bible, *is should be!*"

As of this date, the altar call is not even 200 years old in its practice in the church. Do you really think that God was not moving and working in tremendous ways in the lives of people throughout church history without this practice? What would God ever do without our inventions and us? (I think that He would probably do a whole lot more). This idea was first employed by Charles Finney (one of my favorite historical figures) around 1830. It was a way to separate those who wanted to talk more about this idea of their soul's salvation. He set apart the first row of seats and called it "the anxious seat". Finney never proposed that it would be an instrument, in itself, towards salvation nor did he insist on how those there should pray; and he *never* guided anyone in a "sinner's prayer". These things were never in his considerations nor in the manner that he understood salvation, I do believe that such a practice would have elicited thunderous rebukes from him. He'd probably have call it the "*alter* call", because today it certainly has the potential to mutate that which God really wants to do in people's lives.

When people began to get overly poignant in his meetings (because of their tremendous anguish over their conviction of sin that had begun to burden them), he would send them home so God could have time to deal with them. He gave them explicit instructions to return the next day to converse in a detailed manner about the question of the state of their souls. He was not an enemy of emotion in his meetings or in the life of the believer (he called it religious vigor). He know it would come *and he even expected it.* However when it came to salvation, he simply did not want it to interfere with such an imperatively more important matter; what the Holy Spirit was doing to bring about the salvation of an eternal soul. He knew that people had to come in through the "narrow gate" to be saved just as Jesus said:

- *Go in through the narrow gate, because the gate to hell is wide and the road that leads to it is easy, and there are many who travel it. But the gate to life is narrow and the way that leads to it is hard, and there are few people who find it* (Matthew 7:13-14 *GNB*).

Many people would leave his meetings groaning in anguish, weeping in deep brokenness and shouting. Many times, they wouldn't make it home but fall in the street utterly overcome by their need to cry out to God. They would return the next day as instructed by the evangelist and were then solidly converted and saved. Finney and his co-laborers prayed long hours with those people (sometimes they prayed for days). They shared, in detail, the way of salvation with them. He knew how to trust in the divine work of the Holy Spirit and the power of the Word of God.

Litmus Test 2. The act of leading someone in the confession of faith (known in most circles as "the Sinner's Prayer"). My simple question is this, where in the Bible do you see Christ or the Apostles leading someone in a prayer of repentance and having the people repeat, word for word, what they should say to God? We have to do this today because we have so little true conviction of sin in our churches. This is the same reason we have to convince people that they are saved when this is, in reality, the work of the Holy Spirit.

- *"The Spirit himself testifies with our spirit that we are God's children"* (Romans 8:16 *ISV*).

I do believe that though these things have been well intentioned, they have provoked countless spiritual abortions.

If a person truly recognizes that they are a sinner (an immutable prerequisite to being saved), nobody will have to tell them what to say to God. They will know that they are wretched before Him and they will understand what they must do to make things right with God. Our obligation is just to make sure that God's righteousness is declared and contrasted with man's sinfulness via the Word of God. We just have to point them in the right direction. When *the* Gospel is preached, man's sinfulness is manifested and made clear to him giving room for the Holy Spirit to elicit a response. The Scriptures in Acts 17:30 (*ISV*) tells man what his response should be to this Sovereign God: *"Though God has overlooked those times of ignorance, he now commands everyone everywhere to repent"*. I am not saying that we shouldn't pray for people or pray with people. What I am saying is that we should not take out a pair of scissors and help them out of their sinful cocoons. In the next chapters, we will see how Christ ministered to the sinner to bring them to repentance.

Litmus Test 3. Today's gospel tracts reduce the way to God to three or four simple steps that can easily be deceptive traps. In reality, they are just like the short cuts that the noncommissioned, half-message messenger took. These tracts have gone out all over the world by the hundreds of millions but they do not contain the same message that our Lord delivered to his disciples, making them potentially dangerous. Why is this so? If you will think about it, many of them never mention repentance from dead works and never explain what it means to believe in Jesus Christ. In this sense, the only thing that we could really distribute with absolute confidence, are Bible portions. Does this idea seem insufficient to you?

What if we just passed out copies of Romans 1:18-31, Acts 17:22-31, Psalms 1 or 2, or any number of tremendous passages of Scriptures that would really get people thinking and engaged in a true conversation and can lead them to the knowledge of God. God has anointed and promised to bless His Word, not our interpretation of it. He promised that His Word would always bring fruit. Do you have this kind of faith?

Taken By the Hand

Why do we embrace nonbiblical practices? Is it because we are evil and want to damage the work of God? For the vast majority of us, no, of course not. This is, without a doubt, not the case. In fact, I think that the opposite is true. We want to see the advance of the work of God! So I have thought deeply about the "why" of our need for human inventions and contraptions. Among the many conclusions that I have come to, it has occurred to me this is simply a part of our fallen nature. We really like to be in control of things. It makes us uncomfortable to think that we are not in control of the things that will eventually affect us, or that we feel that we should control. It's like we really are incapable of totally trusting in the power of God. Did He not tell us: *"so shall my word be that goeth forth out of my mouth: it shall not return unto me void, but it shall accomplish that which I please, and it shall prosper in the thing whereto I sent it"* (Isaiah 55:11 *ASV*). Let me try to illustrate it for you.

When I was a teenager I was invited to a series of retreats in the Catholic Church called "The Search" (later they were adopted for adults and called "Cursillos"). Even though I never came to know the Lord or even remotely understand the Gospel there, I did have some positive experiences. I remember that in one "Search" we did what they called "the walk of faith". This exercise consisted of closing your eyes (actually, we were blindfolded) and letting some else guide you about by the hand wherever they wanted to take you. We were out in the wilderness with mountain trails with holes and uneven terrain and forests and bushes everywhere. There was even a cliff with ocean waves crashing on a beach far below! It was actually a good thing that they didn't try to explain that these "steps of faith" could illustrate perfectly a life surrendered to the Lord. They just told us that we had to learn how to trust our neighbor. (What a joke! There was every type of clown up in those retreats– and this considering that we were the "good kids" of the barrio! There was no way in the world that we were going to trust with abandon the madhouse escapee sitting next to us! On the other hand, I can totally trust in the Lord.) Anyway, what the majority of us discovered that we did not like not being in control of that which directly affects us.

A Good Rest

Many times, I find myself in situations where I am extremely tired but have to drive great distances. Even still, it's rare that I can have someone else drive my car. I always end up trying to step on the brakes and wondering if the person has seen the curve or other vehicle up ahead and thinking that they're going too fast or too slow. I usually end up telling the person, "Give me that thing and let me drive! I sleep better when I'm driving."

Once again, I think about the kid who tried to help the butterfly. We feel like we just have to help God with our inventions and just love doing the work of the Holy Spirit for Him. Just like a three-year-old, who lovingly wants to help his dad paint the living room! Our duty is to present clearly and insistently the truth of the

Gospel to the people. God is in charge of dealing with, saving and transforming people.

A Predisposed Mind

"But, Brother Prince," you might say, "There is nothing wrong with these things," and, to a large degree, I agree. However, I find it very unsettling when we feel the need to add something to the Gospel, because every addition is superfluous. The danger consists in the facility in which we are prone to accept non-biblical things. It goes to prove a mentality that is ready to invent "things" and then preach them as if they were pure biblical truths and as if they were actually found in the Bible. There also exists the danger to take something that is of God and use it in a manner in which it was never intended to be used; like taking Scripture out of context. As an example we can take the verse, *"Behold, I stand at the door and knock: if any man hear my voice and open the door, I will come in to him, and will sup with him, and he with me"* (Revelation 3:20 *ASV*), being used as an invitation to sinners when it is actually a message to the church.

Great dangers often have small beginnings. A good example is the term, "Personal Savior". Where in the world does this title come from? It is not in the Bible. Still, we hear it so frequently in our preaching today as if in the Second Coming of our Lord, He will have written on His cape and thigh, as Keith Green also said, three names, not two, "KING OF KINGS AND LORD OF LORDS ... *AND PERSONAL SAVIOR*", (see Revelations 19:16). This creates a problem, because this added title foments the idea that man is the central focus of the gospel. This is a detour from the true presentation of the Lordship of Christ in the Gospel and is explained in detail in chapter 10.

The things that I have mentioned are things that are inoffensive and at times quite innocent in their intention and purpose. What I want to point out is that they are not biblical and we have accepted them with ease and eagerness as if they were. Some are even offended when I indicate that they are not biblical. Herein lies the danger: the fact that with said ease we are open to grafting human and cultural elements into the Gospel itself and then defending them as if they were the "Gospel truth".

This same mentality leaves us vulnerable to accept things that can be extremely dangerous. What I would like to show you are things that have entered into our teachings as well as vital elements that have actually been removed from our presentation of the Gospel. Nevertheless, there is a grave warning in the Bible that says,

- *I, John, solemnly warn everyone who hears the prophetic words of this book: if any add anything to them, God will add to their punishment the plagues described in this book. And if any take anything away from the prophetic words of this book, God will take away from them their share of the fruit of the tree of life and of the Holy City, which are described in this book* (Revelation 22:18-19 *GNB*)[4].

Now I understand that, exegetically, John is talking about the book of Revelation. But, I doubt that any true believer could not see this warning as extending to the entire Word of God! So to satisfy the desire for honest exegetics and to show that this application is in harmony with the entire biblical context, please note also that Deuteronomy 4:2; 12:32 and Proverbs 30:5-6 also sustain this exact interpretation and application. That is a major reason we have the Canon of Scripture – we rest in the Word of God knowing that it is, in fact God's immutable Word and no man can add to it or take away from it without incurring serious consequences from God. The Canon is complete and the autographs of Scripture are absolutely perfect! To this, we cannot add or subtract!

Just think about it, the oldest book in the Bible is Job. This is the beginning of Holy Writ. There was no other written, inspired Scripture during his day. Yet God dealt harshly with Job's friends saying,

- *I am angry with you and your two friends, because you did not speak the truth about me, the way my servant Job did... Job will pray for you, and I will answer his prayer and not disgrace you the way you deserve. You did not speak the truth about me as he did.* (Job 42:7-8 GNB).

Wow! Look how God dealt with them because they didn't speak the truth about Him and the cannon had not even begun to be written! What's he going to do with us if we don't speak the truth about Him having the complete written Word!

I have a very good friend here in Spain, who is a Catholic priest. He happens to hold doctorates in the same disciplines as do I, though from two very distinct schools of thought. He is also the rector of the Catholic seminary in Caceres, Extremadura, Spain (a city where I used to live). Anyway, he used to invite me to the seminary and other venues to share the Word. In one of these meetings, he read a Scripture about Mary, and instead of saying "virgin", his Spanish Catholic translation merely said, "young lady". I stopped him and said that he was reading an erroneous translation. He was stunned and thought that I was bringing on a Protestant argument. "No", I told him, "any girl is a 'young lady', but that doesn't mean that she is a virgin. The Greek word there is, *'parthenos'* (παρθένος), which by literal denotation and cultural implications means, *'virgin'*, and not merely a young lady." His shock turned to disgust and he almost dropped the translation he was holding and wiped his hands. He turned pale. "Why you're absolutely correct!" He exclaimed, "It definitely should say that she was a virgin! How in the world did a Catholic Bible let that one get by?"

So in considering the solemn words of Revelation 22:18-19, God informs us that what man considers a small thing, He holds in great importance. In Matthew 12:36-37, Jesus Himself gives more details about this when He said:

- *But I say unto you, that every idle word that men shall speak, they shall give account thereof in the day of judgment; for by thy words thou shalt be justified, and by thy words thou shalt be condemned* (Matthew 12:36-37 *KJV*).

When Jesus said, *"For verily I say unto you, Till heaven and earth pass, one jot or one tittle shall in no wise pass from the law, till all be fulfilled"* (Matthew 5:18 *KJV*), He was saying that EVERY WORD THAT COMES OUT OF THE MOUTH OF GOD HAS ITS PURPOSE AND SIGNIFICANCE. We do not have the luxury to take them lightly and to change them at our mere whims, and likes and dislikes. The Bible is perfect exactly as it is.

CHAPTER 4
WHAT HAPPENED TO MOSES?

⊶∞⊷

Details? What Details?

Man is a creature of habit. He is given to formulas and methods and is not very open to change. The problem consists in the fact that God isn't like that. Hmm, but wait a minute, Brother Prince, the Bible says that Jesus Christ is the same yesterday, today and forever. No it doesn't, it actually says, *"Jesus Christ the same yesterday, and today, and forever"* (Hebrews 13:8); the word, *"is"* is not in the Greek text. So that Scripture is actually talking about how our Christian behavior, or character, should be consistent. Well… yeah, but it also says, *"For I am the LORD, I change not; therefore ye sons of Jacob are not consumed"* (Malachi 3:6 *KJV*). Here God is talking about the steadfastness of His Word, promises and His nature – His consistency of character. He is not talking about how He works! He's always changing how He gets things done. This is why Moses had problems in the desert. God changed His methodology and Moses was still with yesterday's plan.

To clarify what I have been explaining a bit more, I would like to tell you another Bible story. It's a very interesting one of which we can learn much, but I want us to concentrate on the importance of <u>*paying attention*</u> to every *"jot"* and *"tittle"* of the Word of God. We also want to see, in this story, another example of man's tendency to form traditions and miss the mark concerning the will of God for their lives from things that were the work of God, just like they did with Nehushtan. The story begins like this:

- *And all the congregation of the children of Israel journeyed from the wilderness of Sin, after their journeys, according to the commandment of the LORD, and pitched in Rephidim: and there was no water for the people to drink. Wherefore the people did chide with Moses, and said, give us water that we may drink. And Moses said unto them, Why chide ye with me? wherefore do ye tempt the LORD? And the people thirsted there for water; and the people murmured against Moses, and said, Wherefore is this that thou hast brought us up out of Egypt, to kill us and our children and our cattle with thirst? And Moses cried unto the LORD, saying, What shall I do unto this people? they be almost ready to stone me. And the LORD said unto Moses, Go on before the people, and take with thee of the elders of Israel; and thy rod, wherewith thou smotest the river, take in thine hand, and go. Behold, I will stand before thee there upon the rock in Horeb; and thou shalt smite the rock, and there shall come water out of it, that the people may drink. And Moses did so in the sight of the elders of Israel* (Exodus 17:1-6 *KJV*).*

The children of Israel came to a part of the desert where there was no water. To resolve this problem God told Moses to strike a big rock that was there. Even though Moses had used his staff several times in the process of the liberation of the people, this is the third time he has been instructed to smite something with it.

Good News/Bad News

I like Good News/Bad News jokes.

Gallery Owner: I have some good news and some bad news.

Artist: What's the good news?

Gallery Owner: The good news is that a man came in here today asking if the price of your paintings would go up after you die. When I told him they would he bought every one of your paintings.

Artist: That's great! What's the bad news?

Gallery Owner: The bad news is that man was your doctor!

Okay, I'm on a roll, so here goes another one:

Lawyer: I have some good news and some bad news.

Client: Well, give me the bad news first.

Lawyer: The bad news is that the DNA tests showed that it was your blood they found all over the crime scene

Client: Oh no! I'm ruined! What's the good news?

Lawyer: The good news is your cholesterol is down to 130!

There are a lot of "Good News/Bad News" as well as "Bad News/Good News" stories in the Bible. This one about Moses is a good news/bad news (and ultimately good news again) story. It just seems to be one of the ways that God works. As far as our story about Moses is concerned, I think that even with all the works of God that he had seen at this point in his life that he was still as surprised as everybody else was by the tremendous quantity of water that burst forth from the rock. It was sufficient to satisfy the needs and quench the thirst of millions of people and animals. God truly worked an incredible miracle for His people that day.

That's the good news. The bad news is that the story doesn't end there; there's more.

- *There was no water where they camped, so the people gathered around Moses and Aaron and complained: "It would have been better if we had died in front of the LORD's Tent along with the other Israelites. Why have you brought us out into this wilderness, just so that we can die here with our animals? Why did you bring us out of Egypt into this miserable place where nothing will grow? There's no grain, no figs, no grapes, no pomegranates. There is not even any water to drink!" Moses and Aaron moved away from the people and stood at the entrance of the Tent. They bowed down with their faces to the ground, and the dazzling light of the LORD's presence appeared to them. The LORD said to Moses, "Take the stick that is in front of the Covenant Box, and then you and Aaron assemble the whole community. There in front of them all speak to that rock over there, and water will gush out of it. In this way you will bring water out of the rock for the people, for them and their animals to drink." Moses went and got the stick, as the LORD had commanded. He and Aaron assembled the whole community in front of the rock, and Moses said, "Listen, you rebels! Do we have to get water out of this rock for you?" Then Moses raised the stick and struck the rock twice with it, and a great stream of water gushed out, and all the people and animals drank* (Numbers 20:2-11 GNB).

So, the story continues telling us that time went by and years later similar situation arose: there was no water. Moses, tired of this terribly problematical people, received instruction as to what to do but he didn't pay attention to the details in what God told him. He did the same thing that he did the first time when they were in that situation: he struck the rock. Why? First, it was a reaction because he was really angry. The children of Israel had pushed him to his limit. Who wouldn't be ticked? The second reason is also important; he acted in unbelief and did not honor God before the people. The Bible exhorts us saying, *"… and whatsoever is not of faith is sin"* (Romans 14:23 *ASV*).

But, there is another reason that this happened to him that I want to bring out here, and that is that it was because *"he had always done it this way."* How many times had he used his staff? In times past, when he used his staff, he would lift it or strike something with it and when he did, God would work some kind of miracle. But this time, he just had to talk to a rock? God changed His way of doing things and it cost Moses everything because he didn't pay attention to the details of God's Word – he followed his traditions and habits.

Serious Implications

Moses didn't know that by way of these incidents God was illustrating great truths for the coming generations; that is to say, for us. The New Testament in 1ˢᵗ Corinthians 10:3-6, 11 speaks of this incident. It says,

- *All ate the same spiritual bread and drank the same spiritual drink. They drank from the spiritual rock that went with them; and that rock was Christ himself. But even then God was not pleased with most of them, and so their dead bodies were scattered over the desert. Now, all of this is an example for us, to warn us not to desire evil things, as they did, … All these things happened to them as examples for others, and they were written down as a warning for us. For we live at a time when the end is about to come.*

If Christ was the rock, as the Scriptures say He was, then that means that the first time that Moses smote the rock is was typological of the supreme sacrifice of our Lord. As a result of His death and resurrection we have access to the one who is the fountain of Living Water.

- *"It is done. I am Alpha and Omega, the beginning and the end. I will give unto him that is athirst of the fountain of the water of life freely"* (Revelation 21:6 *KJV*).

Being this the case, the second time that Moses struck the rock; it was as if he had crucified anew the Son of God. God would never permit such a thing. The sacrifice of Christ was a once-and-forever event. But the person who rejects Christ and despises the sacrifice has counted the shed blood as an unclean thing. Moses' action represented the blasphemy of the Holy Spirit. These verses explain this truth:

- *For it is impossible for those who were once enlightened, and have tasted of the heavenly gift, and were made partakers of the Holy Ghost. And have tasted the good word of God, and the powers of the world to come, if they shall fall away, to renew them again unto repentance; seeing they crucify to themselves the Son of God afresh, and put him to an open shame* (Hebrews 6:4-6 *KJV*).
- *For such an high priest became us, who is holy, harmless, undefiled, separate from sinners, and made higher than the heavens; Who needeth not daily, as those high priests, to offer up sacrifice, first for his own sins, and then for the people's: <u>for this he did once, when he offered up himself</u>* (Hebrews 7:26-27 *KJV*).

- *For Christ is not entered into the holy places made with hands, which are the figures of the true; but into heaven itself, now to appear in the presence of God for us: Nor yet that he should offer himself often, as the high priest entereth into the holy place every year with blood of others; For then must he often have suffered since the foundation of the world: but now once in the end of the world hath he appeared to put away sin by the sacrifice of himself. And as it is appointed unto men once to die, but after this the judgment: So Christ was once offered to bear the sins of many; and unto them that look for him shall he appear the second time without sin unto salvation* (Hebrews 9:24-28 *KJV*).

- *Then said he, Lo, I come to do thy will, O God. He taketh away the first, that he may establish the second. By the which will <u>we are sanctified through the offering of the body of Jesus Christ once for all</u>. And every priest standeth daily ministering and offering oftentimes the same sacrifices, which can never take away sins: But this man, after he had offered one sacrifice for sins forever, sat down on the right hand of God;* (Hebrews 10:9-12 *KJV*).

- *For if we sin willfully after that we have received the knowledge of the truth, there remaineth no more sacrifice for sins, but a certain fearful looking for of judgment and fiery indignation, which shall devour the adversaries. He that despised Moses' law died without mercy under two or three witnesses: Of how much sorer punishment, suppose ye, shall he be thought worthy, who hath trodden underfoot the Son of God, and hath counted the blood of the covenant, wherewith he was sanctified, an unholy thing, and hath done despite unto the Spirit of grace? For we know him that hath said, Vengeance belongeth unto me, I will recompense, saith the Lord. And again, The Lord shall judge his people. It is a fearful thing to fall into the hands of the living God* (Hebrews 10:26-31 *KJV*).

These are terribly strong verses! Let's pull it in for a moment to make it clear that we know that Moses was saved and is in heaven today. But we must understand that this is what happened to him symbolically or typologically that day. The typology that God had placed in motion for future generations had to follow its full course in order to illustrate the great message of the sacrifice for future generations. God was bringing to pass a prophetic work here. Moses interrupted the original direction of the message with his disobedience and in the process was utilized to illustrate the negative side of the same illustration. This is why he wasn't permitted, at that time, to enter the Promised Land (symbolic of heaven). I am sure that this incident broke the heart of God and that it was also not a part of God's original plan. But, in order to continue with the typology, He had to fulfill with the corresponding results of Moses' actions. The fact that centuries afterwards we see Moses in the Promised Land with Christ in the Transfiguration helps to clarify the truth that this incident was a typological message. To wrap this point up, I'll say that Moses had to go through that scare because he didn't pay attention to the little details and because he used his traditional tactics.

The Ways of Man

In the Bible, God always had problems with man and his traditions. Just look at the Jewish leaders of Jesus' day. Man, how they loved their temple, sacrifices and Sabbath days... too bad they didn't love God all that much. Christ always gave them problems because He did things terrible things like healed sick people on the

Sabbath, touched lepers, ate with sinners, beat up money changers and kicked them out of the temple and a few other bothersome things like that. For them, He was a killjoy! He was always messing up their religion and traditions. He was always bothering them with the little details... *He would bother them with the truth!*

That's the way man mixes and confuses the things of man with the things that God used at one time or another. The resulting product is a dangerous conglomeration; just the type that Satan would use to deceive last souls. What cult has not learned how to mix Bible verses with ideas that hold a shade of truth to establish their lies? This has been the devil's tactic since the beginning. *"For God doth know that in the day ye eat thereof, then your eyes shall be opened, and ye shall be as gods, knowing good and evil"* (Genesis 3:5).

Our Church Has Always Done It Like This

Many of you that are reading these pages have received practices and teachings that you take as the correct way to evangelize. You have never seen a church that is active and living evangelize any other way, this why you have never doubted it. I know that there are some that profess to have an exact theology of evangelism but are really doing very little to actually win sinners for Christ. Therefore, we have on one hand, the knowledge of truth with the absence of evangelistic zeal; and on the other, the danger of zeal without knowledge. Because another gospel has penetrated our generation, Satan has been using sincere men in the preaching of a disenthroned Christ. The glories of the Savior are hidden even from His servants because those preaching have not given the deserved attention to the gospel they are announcing. Many people are saved *in spite* of the gospel being preached and not *because* of the gospel being preached. "Decisions for Christ", sometimes have little significance for many have no true idea of exactly what they have decided. Only a small percentage of these people give evidence of a work of the grace of God by way of a transformed life.

All of this is directly related to the use of a message in our evangelism that is not biblical. The truth to impart life has been hidden behind the smoke screen of human inventions. Upon the quicksand of human logic, great multitudes have been guided to assume that they have entrance to eternal life and have been given a security that does not pertain to them. Evangelicals have swollen the files of the deluded by way of a deviant form of evangelism. Many of those who have "made decisions" in these modern churches and have been given assurance by their counselors that their sins have been forgiven will be as surprised as those who trusted in the indulgences of Tetzel when they hear, *"I don't know where you come from. Get away from me, all you evildoers!"* (Luke 13:27 ISV).

CHAPTER 5
ZEAL WITHOUT KNOWLEDGE

———— ∞ ————

For I bear them record that they have a zeal of God,
but not according to knowledge.
(Romans 10:2 KJV)

Have you ever thought about just how those "Jehovah's Witnesses" and Mormons can be in the streets day after day distributing their literature and doctrines? They really have an admirable amount of zeal. It seems like the devil never hinders them from going out and talking about their things. In reality, the devil doesn't want them hindered because they are busily going about building and reinforcing the kingdom of darkness. They have zeal, but it's not according to knowledge.

Oh, Brother!

Speaking of zeal without knowledge, in my ministerial experience, I have seen many foolish and unlearned believers cause all kinds of catastrophes in the church and the community at large. I'm sure that you've known somebody like this. The majority of these folks don't even have a good testimony within the local church to which they pertain and even less of one outside of the church. Nonetheless, it seems like these same believers are very effervescent in their religion and talk about God with such liberality with everybody the meet. They are always presented with marvelous opportunities to share their faith; opportunities that I would just love to have! Stranger yet is that I have even seen positive results come from their disastrous mannerisms. It just might be that they've got some kind of spiritual machine gun, and after having shot so many bullets and taken out so many good guys, that every once in a while they finally manage to hit the target.

Let me give you an example: there was this one brother that was always "*discombobulating*" things. He would say the things that were more "out of orbit" than a stray asteroid and just about as destructive as one. How many times we would just have to put our hands on our head and say, "Brother, please...!" Poor guy; at any rate, at least he was sincere and loved the Lord – despite his clumsiness.

Loose Tongues

One day he was out on the streets sharing the gospel with some other brothers when someone saw that he was busy in deep conversation with a highly respected Baptist pastor of the area. This pastor is a great man of God, but was hermetically entrenched against any form of charismas for today's church. When the other brothers approached to see just what they were discussing, they found out that "*Joe Idontknow*" (or whatever his name was) was speaking in unknown tongues so this pastor could hear what they sounded like! The other brothers just about fainted, but, to their surprise, this pastor was deeply impressed with what he heard and left expressing his deepest appreciation. From then on he adopted a very favorable and wonderfully tolerant attitude towards Christians of the Pentecostal persuasion and the move of the gifts of the Holy Spirit in today's church.

I don't pretend to understand it, but sometimes it happens like that. Unfortunately, these positive and apparently favorable occasions with this type of uncontrollable believers are few and far between and more often than not, the results are very negative. You've got the "prophet" that always goes about "profelying", the dreamer who always has these "spiritual dreams and visions", and those who you just have to give them the nickname, "Brother or Sister Hoofinmouth"; because the always end up sticking their foot in their mouths! Then the wiser or more mature believers have to come around and put out the fires they've started all over the place. In this sense, I have seen from A to Z!

Bad Witnesses

There are certain people that try to identify themselves as "brethren" and avow to be Christians. But the truth of the matter is that their fruit and testimonies are so poor that they really don't deserved to be called a cousin of the friend of our brother-in-law, much less a brother. I believe that the very devil sometimes sends these people to the church to work as stumbling blocks to the true believer, the new believers, and the unbeliever. Just like Jesus said in Matthew 23:13 (*GNV*), they to get in and they don't let anybody else enter.

- *… How terrible for you, teachers of the Law and Pharisees! You hypocrites! You lock the door to the Kingdom of heaven in people's faces, but you yourselves don't go in, nor do you allow in those who are trying to enter!*

It is very possible that these people have serious problems with demonic oppression. If this is the case, they are in great need for deliverance. In any case, they should not be permitted to speak or give testimony to try and glorify God. Many time Jesus stopped the mouths of the demons that proclaimed the truth the He was the Son of God. He didn't let them speak.

- *Suddenly there was a man in their synagogue who had an unclean spirit. He screamed, "What do you want with us, Jesus of Nazareth? Have you come to destroy us? I know who you are, the Holy One of God!" But Jesus rebuked him, saying, "Be quiet, and come out of him!"* (Mark 1:23-25 *ISV*).

In another occasion, Paul was grieved because a maiden with an evil spirit proclaimed the truth that he and Silas were servants of God and that they had the very Words of God.

- *"One day as we were going to the place of prayer, we were met by a young servant woman who had an evil spirit that enabled her to predict the future. She earned a lot of money for her owners by telling fortunes. She followed Paul and us, shouting, "These men are servants of the Most High God! They announce to you how you can be saved!" She did this for many days, until Paul became so upset that he turned around and said to the spirit, "In the name of Jesus Christ I order you to come out of her!" The spirit went out of her that very moment"* (Acts 16:16-18 *GNB*).

For a long time I didn't understand why they didn't let these evil spirits declare the <u>*truth*</u> about God and His servants. I would see movie stars and singers take a moment to talk or sing about God in a very positive way. I would think that this was a good thing. I remember a Brazilian Singer who would always talk about God or Christ in a very favorable way in his songs[3]. One way or another, it's kind of like free advertising, No? It's kind of like the times I've paid pagans to go around in their propaganda vehicles with the loud speakers to announce our evangelistic campaign or concert or something like that. Didn't Paul himself say,

- *Some are preaching Christ because of their envy and rivalry, while others do so because of their good will. The latter are motivated by love, because they know that I have been appointed for the defense of the gospel. The former proclaim Christ out of selfish ambition and without sincerity, thinking that they will stir up trouble for me during my imprisonment. But what does it matter? Just this, that in every way, whether in pretense or in truth, Christ is being proclaimed, and because of this I rejoice. Yes, I will continue to rejoice,* (Philippians 1:15-18 *ISV*).

What I couldn't understand was that the people in the book of Philippians were Christians who were ministering the gospel with evil intentions. These people we're talking about here are raw heathens! I mean like, wolves in *wolves* clothing. I think about this, and it takes me back to the vocabulary of my hippy days of the '60s and I just have to say, "I mean like…, wow…, what a bummer! Dude, what do you get out of doing something like that to somebody?" Well, I couldn't understand Paul's sentiment until I had my own experience with a person with an unclean spirit follow me around.

Many years ago when I was a church planter and pastor in Mexico, this dude started coming to our meetings. I could have dealt with the fact that he was an ill-smelling vagabond, extremely loud and effeminate and in-your-face insolent and lazy! I say that because even though he was in perfectly good health, he enjoyed begging on the streets and from house to house. What's worse was that he was mean spirited, proud and contentious! He was smoke in the eyes on the entire community. For the church he turned out to be worse that a migraine on a hot day. Well, what were we going to do with him? According to his own words, he really wanted to come to church and seek the Lord. Of course it didn't hurt that we had a food and housing program in the church. The entire congregation worked with him and put up with rubbish to try to win him to Christ and love him into the kingdom.

At times he would come to church (always late) while fighting with people on the streets and shouting horrid insults from the door of the church (while holding the door open) before entering. Now he's got the attention of the entire congregation and moments later he would be praying loudly with the most illustrious vocabulary. I was actually beginning to think that the local Catholic priest had sent him to infiltrate the church and make life impossible for us, (I still have my doubts.) Once someone said, "Brother, if we were more like Jesus, we would pray and cast those demons out of him." I never said anything but I wanted to be more like Jesus, and make a whip and *chase* him away. But, I employed self-control and opted not to do it.

Anyway, one day I was passing through the village plaza and guess who was there? He was now in the role of a stand-up comedian; he had a group of big macho men sitting there laughing at him as he "preached" to them. He was actually saying some really positive things about the gospel, the church and about me as the pastor. I made the mistake of passing too close to the incident because he saw me and went into sissified overdrive. He shouted, "Look, there's my pastor!", and began to proclaim my virtues real and imagined, and faun over me with exaggerated gesticulations. Now, with anybody else and under other circumstances, it might have been a humbling honor. In that moment I don't know what I felt by being identified with him; wrath or shame ("righteous indignation", of course… at least I'd like to think that it was). I did not want to be in his mouth for good or ill. I rebuked him in front of all and said that he had to repent of his sin and get right with God. Suddenly I heard applause; the men that had been listening to him were clapping for me. The Bible says it this way, "*But God says to the wicked, "Why should you recite my commandments? Why should you talk about my covenant? You refuse to let me correct you; you reject my commands*" (Psalms 50:16-17 *GNB*).

Now that's what God thinks about that kind of "*believer*". But the devil has no reason to hinder their paths, because they are sufficient stumbling-blocks all by themselves. As a matter of fact, these guys let demons take a day off because of the benefits they bring to the kingdom of darkness!

Good Witnesses

While these "*cousins*" (as opposed to "brothers") go around muddying the water so that the thirsty cannot drink, there are other believers who are prudent in their ways and manifest godly wisdom and are good witnesses; but it's always more difficult for them to share their faith in Christ. They always find more hindrances and adverse wind in their path because the enemy knows that they are a threat to their dominion. Doors to share their faith do not open as easily for them. It's not that they don't want to or don't know how to share their faith; quite the contrary. These are believers who are prepared and capable to give a good word in due season and honor His name. It's a question of spiritual warfare. The enemy attempts to keep people from crossing their paths.

Demons do not hinder from testifying yet another type of Believer. These are not the spiritually oppressed but rather sincere, humble and righteous believers. They walk in the purity and inno-cence of their faith. These are good people. They are not stumbling blocks because of poor testimonies and to know them is to love them. The problem is that they don't know the Word of God. They love the Lord, but are ignorant of His Word. They don't know how to do as the Scriptures command and, *"... sanctify the Lord God in your hearts: and be ready always to give an answer to every man that asketh you a reason of the hope that is in you with meekness and fear."* (1 Peter 3:15 *KJV*). The Scriptures also say, *"Let your speech be always with grace, seasoned with salt, that ye may know how ye ought to answer every man"* (Colossians 4:6 *KJV*).

These beloved brethren are always coming to me asking for help and counsel on how to talk to, or answer, a person whom they have been conversing with about Jesus. They come with tremendous testimonies of fantastic opportunities for marvelous conversations that they have had with people. But, unfortunately the majority of the time they have not known how to answer the very good and honest questions that the people have presented to them. The enemy does not fear to allow their subjects to have conversations with them, because they do not know what to say to them.

A Student of the Word

When I was a new believer, this happened to me three times. The last time it happened was when I was about a month old in the Lord and was in my sociology class. The professor asked me a question that presented an opportunity to share my faith. She knew that I had become a believer and was trying to set up a trap for me. I answered the question concisely, but my answer inspired another question, and another, and another. Before I knew it, all of the other students were also riddling me with questions, which for me at that time, were difficult to answer. It became a shark's feeding frenzy!

I finally said, "Enough! I cannot answer your questions." They all started to laugh and to mock my faith and me. However, I sat back, observed how inane the situation was, and said that their laughter and mockery was the result of an atrophied way of thinking for three reasons:

1. I was a new believer and the only thing that they had proven was that *I* could not answer their questions.

2. My deficiency did not prove that their questions did not have a conclusive answer in the Bible.

3. My deficiency did not prove that there was no one who could answer their questions; it only showed, as I had said, that right now, *I* could not answer them.

I ended the session by promising them that this would never happen to me again. I would never again be taken aback to the point of not having an answer to someone's honest question about the things of God. Afterwards I read in II Timothy 2:15 (KJV), "*Study to show thyself approved unto God, a workman that needeth not to be ashamed, rightly dividing the word of truth.*" I lifted up a complaint before the Lord saying that my brain did function like that. So He also showed me James 1:5, "*Now if any of you lacks wisdom, he should ask God, who gives to everyone generously without a rebuke, and it will be given to him.*"

He then told me, "*I will help you and I will give you that which you lack.*" I immediately began to dedicate myself everyday to the deep study of the Bible and wholly gave myself to prayer asking the Lord for wisdom, understanding and intelligence so that I might be able to give succinct answers to the any sincere biblical question people might ask me. In effect, since that day many years ago, I have never been stumped by a sincere question someone has randomly asked me without giving an answer with intelligence and spiritual wisdom. There have been times I have been asked questions by people that naturally expected for me to take time to investigate and find an academically plausible response. God has always been faithful (of course He has) to give a response that left the inquirer satisfied.

Brothers and Sisters, lets dedicate ourselves to the sincere study of the Word of God so that we might, *"Be ready at all times to answer anyone who asks you to explain the hope you have in you,"* (1 Peter 3:15 *GNB*). Colossians 4:6 also says, *"Your speech should always be pleasant and interesting, and you should know how to give the right answer to everyone"* (*GNB*).

Who the Heck is Malchus?

Speaking of Malchus, you know that they say that Vincent Van Gogh got into painting because he didn't have an ear for music. He reminds me of how Malchus was for a little while. I'll get back to him. Anyway, these dear brethren that we've been discussing, remind me of Peter. He was a sincere man, but just a tad bit impetuous, and every once in a while missed the will of God even though he wanted to fulfill it (sounds a bit like me). In some measure, the problem consisted in the fact that at times he just didn't pay attention to the things that Jesus said to him.

Case in point, in Matthew 26:41-45, Christ told His disciples, *"Watch and pray, that ye enter not into temptation: the spirit indeed is willing, but the flesh is weak."* But what did they end up doing? They got comfortable and started snoring. Then Jesus lovingly exhorted them about their lack of diligence in prayer. He told Peter, "*What, could ye not watch with me one hour?*" (Matthew 26:40 *KJV*). Then what happened?

- *Again, for the second time, he went away and prayed, "My Father, if this cannot pass unless I drink it, your will be done." And again he came and found them sleeping, for their eyes were heavy. So, leaving them again, he went away and prayed for the third time, saying the same words again. Then he came to the disciples and said to them, "Sleep and take your rest later on. See, the hour is at hand, and the Son of Man is betrayed into the hands of sinners* (Matthew 26:42-45 *ESV*).

The hour of trial had come and the disciples thought that they could handle it and overcome in their own strength; but it was not to be so. More than Peter's denial, I have been impressed with what he did with the sword.

- *And one of them smote the servant of the high priest, and cut off his right ear. And Jesus answered and said, Suffer ye thus far; and he touched his ear, and healed him* (Luke 22:50-51 *KJV*).

In John 18:10 the Scriptures tell us that the servant's name was Malchus.

Then Simon Peter having a sword drew it, and smote the high priest's servant, and cut off his right ear. The servant's name was Malchus.

Do You Know How To Use The Sword?

We all know that the sword is symbolic of the Word of God.

- *For the word of God is living and active, sharper than any double-edged sword, piercing until it divides soul and spirit, joints and marrow, as it judges the thoughts and purposes of the heart* (Hebrews 4:12 *ISV*).

- *... also take the helmet of salvation and the sword of the Spirit, which is the word of God* (Ephesians 6:17 *ISV*).

In his disobedience and lack of good judgment and knowledge of the will of God, Peter cut off the ear of a non-Christian with the Word of God! The ear fell into the filth of the earth and Jesus had to come along and undo the damage that Peter caused. He healed Malchus and put his ear back where it belonged. Now, I'm completely sure that Peter did not intend to cut Malchus' ear off; he was out to completely and permanently change the way that man combed his hair! But, being that he didn't know how to utilize the sword well, he just ended up cutting his ear off.

Show Me Where!

This man Malchus represents the sinners that, in their ignorance, oppose the gospel. Without a doubt they are servants of the enemy just like Malchus was the servant of the high priest. Perhaps they are following the multitudes trying to be a part of the latest fad without clearly understanding what this attack was all about.

Many times, I've spoken to people who say, "The Bible contradicts itself!" I don't have a problem with this comment, I simply pass them my Bible and say, "Show me where". They are almost always shocked into silence mumbling something about, "Well, uh, I, uh, he, uh, they, uh, I don't know..., I don´t read the Bible". It's almost always the case that they've never read the Bible themselves; they are simply repeating a popular refrain and have not really come to this conclusion of their own accord. They are just following the crowd as Malchus probably was. A wise procedure and a good presentation of the gospel will win those who oppose; but if we knock them upside the head with the Bible and a bad witness and don't correctly and wisely answer their questions, we end up cutting their ear off with the Word. All of this happens because we were asleep at the wheel when we should have been praying and because we haven't learned how to skillfully and correctly use the sword.

How many times, because of the lack of prayer and knowledge of the Word of God, believers go out to "evangelize", and end up chopping off a bunch of ears because they don't know how to handle the Word? When somebody gets their ear cut off by someone using the Word of God, they can't stand to hear about the things of God. Just like Malchus, whose ear fell into the dust of the earth, the ear that has been cut off with the Word falls into the filth of this world. These people then become far more open to hear things that go against the Word of God and get involved in unclean activities.

Can you imagine Malchus' confusion on the Day of Pentecost when he heard Peter preach that powerful sermon? Perhaps he was saved that day; we don't know (but somebody in the church knew this guy). Anyway, if he was ever saved, it was surely not because of Peter's testimony, but rather because of Jesus' miraculous healing touch. Even still, as a member of the church, I can see Malchus counseling a rebellious brother while rubbing his ear, "Dude, watch your step. I know the pastor and you'd better pay attention and do what he says."

Just like Malchus after having his ear cut off, only God's miraculous touch can undo the damage cause by what was probably a well-intentioned believer. I don't know how many times I have had to minister to somebody that had received damage caused by the ignorance of some of these believers.

CHAPTER 6
SEVEN THOUSAND PROPHETS

———— ✺ ————

E lijah thought that no one else was proclaiming the Word of God until God said to him, "*Yet I will leave seven thousand people alive in Israel—-all those who are loyal to me and have not bowed to Baal or kissed his idol.*" (1 Kings 19:18 *GNB*)

I know that many believers that have concise teachings and knowledge as to what the Gospel really is, and how it should be shared. The problem is in that they are not the ones who bring to pass the major portion of world evangelism. Those who transmit the incomplete message are those who are carrying out the larger portion of this task. Brothers and Sisters, do we really have the luxury to lead souls astray or de misguide the fine results of the toils of the believers who have gone before us just because we have not paid rapt and zealous attention to the details of the message that we are announcing? Have you scrupulously examined your message and methods in the light of the Word of God?

Pastors, this is not a question without practical purpose. Have you never wondered about the "converts" that remain just as carnal as they were before they made their "decision"? Please forgive the redundancy when I ask about those who have "made decisions" for Christ when, in reality, they don't even know or understand precisely what they have decided. There is no conviction of sin or zeal for God. There is no hunger for His Word and it doesn't matter to them if they are absent when His Word is ministered. Often their families are in sorrier conditions than those who do not confess Christ as their Lord. There is no evidence of a true conversion to Christ. Is it perhaps because they have never really been evangelized? Could it be possible that because of our teaching and preaching that we have misled them into a consolation without Christ? Is it possible that we ran without the complete message? Though the answers might painful, you should ask if your church, its missionaries and evangelists, its Sunday school teachers and perhaps even you yourself are truly preaching the Gospel of our Lord Jesus Christ. If we do not have a total disposition to insist that the message we carry and proclaim to the nations be the very story of Christ, why then do we continue with world evangelism?

A Delicious Photograph

You know, there is a great difference between being big and being fat. A bodybuilder is someone who is dedicated to muscle sculpturing exercises and has developed an impressive (though many times exaggerated) physique. They are usually heavyweights because muscle weighs more than fat. The large numbers on the scale that make up their total weight are not, for them, a negative factor because they are the results of their concerted efforts to obtain excellent physical condition. On the other hand, there are those who lift only the weight found at the end of a spoon or fork. They might weigh the same as a bodybuilder, but it's all fat and nothing of substance. Those many pounds are counted against them. Those pounds also come at the price of their health. The contrast is that one is a picture of health and strength and the other is sickly and out of shape… unless you count round as a shape.

Isaiah 29:8 gives us a rather humorous and graphic example of those who fight against the Lord. This is what it says:

- *And it shall be as when a hungry man dreams, and, behold, he eats; but he awakes, and his soul is empty. Or as when a thirsty man dreams, and, behold, he drinks; but he awakes, and, behold, he is faint, and his soul hath appetite: so shall the multitude of all the nations be that fight against mount Zion.*

Many years ago in Latin America, I was an associate pastor in a church that I helped to found that grew to be over 1,000 strong. This was back in the day when churches of such size were rarely, if ever, seen in that part of the world. We were all hype and very encouraged by the tremendous "move of God", we thought that we were seeing. This work attracted all kinds of attention and brought people in from all over the world to minister in the pulpit. Overall, this was a blessing and very good news. God *did* do some awesome things in the lives of many. There are several who were part of the youth and university ministry in that church that are now pastors and servants of God in various parts of the world. Nonetheless, when it came time to work, pray extra or at long and odd hours and go the second mile, only about 30 or 40 people would show up (those aforementioned young people were among them). After a while, I concluded that we really only had a church of 30 or 40 people. The rest was just fat.

In similar fashion, I have seen close up, various "big" churches in various countries and have heard their sermons. I have been in their counseling rooms where, supposedly, they guide people to "receive Christ" and sometimes the Baptism of the Holy Spirit. I have also been horrified to hear how they were counseling these thirsty souls. It is as if a hungry person comes up to you asking for a morsel of bread and you give them a photograph of a delicious meal. It doesn't matter how delicious the meal in the photograph looks, it is totally insipid and incapable of satisfying their hunger or provide the nourishment their body needs. Many times seeing a photo of a scrumptious meal is worse, because it only aggravates the problem. Moreover, even if you do eat the photo of seemingly delicious food, you will still die of malnutrition.

I have come to the conclusion that many (not all) of our big churches are not actually big in the sense that they are strong and healthy; they're just fat. The people have not been fed with the sustenance of the Bread of Life but with religion and social culture, the colorful, yet insipid plastic bag in which the Bread is often carried. We think that this colorful plastic bag has made it very convenient to deliver the Bread to the hungry. At best, many times those seemingly delightful meals are actually a constant diet of fast food *"happy meals"*. The people are coming to us as the starving dead begging bread. We have at our disposal freshly baked Bread that we toss aside, proudly serving them the bag in which we have conveniently placed it. Sadder still, there are people in our ranks who don't even know that we are supposed to eat the Bread and not the bag! We tell the people that they cannot digest the Bread now. We must wait until they are much stronger and more mature. Pray tell, how can they grow on a diet of the photos of Bread so that we might then feed them the True Bread?

Spiritual Somalia

I once saw a documentary about famine that showed a person who was at death's gates because of famine in the country of Somalia and I learned something very significant. Some workers from World Vision had found this dying young Muslim woman. Her sister tenderly held her in her arms and attempted to feed her a vitamin-enriched liquid in order to begin the slow process of recovery. They soon learned that, sadly, they were too late. The muscles in her trachea were paralyzed and had ceased to function properly. From this point, any substance introduced buccally could kill her. Her body had moved into the aggressive stage of self-cannibalization. Their next step was to move to intravenous alimentation, but her veins were deeply degenerated and weakened to the point that they would immediately rupture with the slightest perforation.

In this field situation, there was no other recourse of intervention. Her body had reached the point that it could not tolerate any form of alimentation. It was locked in, like a Kamikaze on a mission of self-immolation. The body no longer recognized any substance that could save it and had reprogrammed itself for self-destruction though salvation was near at hand. As a matter of fact, the very substance that was there to save her would have provoked a gruelingly painful death for her. Her family, seeing her helpless plight, resorted to euthanasia and suffocated her with a wet towel.

There are many churches and believers that do not know how to recognize the Bread of Life when it is presented to them as solid food. Perhaps they have never been fed a healthy diet and do not know how to distinguish the difference between true sustenance and junk food. Now their spiritual man cannot tolerate real food; it proves to be harmful to them. They complain that the study of the Bible is boring and reject the meat of biblical truth because they are not capable of receiving it but can watch reality TV programs for hours. They are like children who can't stand vegetables, but can eat candy all day long! This is spiritual inanition and I have seen its deadly symptoms in many churches in the United States.

Now hold on, before you go off (or think I'm going off) on some anti-American rant. It is not that I have anything in particular against the United States, quite the contrary. As a matter of fact, try to name a perfect country with a perfect history – this is why Jesus had to come to Earth! Say what you want, but the United States is a country that, even in its clumsiness, has done a tremendous amount in favor of the extension of the Gospel worldwide. There are many tremendous churches that are on fire and revived. However, what concerns me many times is that whatever happens there, be it good or bad eventually spreads to the whole world. In addition, as I have already asked, why is it that so often the bad news spreads quicker than the good?

I have ministered in many countries of the world. Some time back I was ministering in the north of Nigeria near the border of Niger. This was a place totally immersed in a third-world situation and condition. It was like being in some forlorn city of an Indiana Jones movie or something. It was comical and sad at the same time to see the pastors imitate the churches, methods, and customs that pastors employ in the prosperous churches of the United States. It reminded me of the time that I was ministering somewhere in some dirt village on the other side of the planet. It was so far removed from the twenty-first century that the people had never seen electricity or paved roads. I met there a wonderful but weathered woman close to 80 years old who had never owned a pair of shoes yet donned a shabby "Metallica" concert tour tee shirt.

At times, I have seen the national pastors and ministers in those countries imitate what they have seen and heard in the churches in the United States in an effort to obtain the *"results"* that have been interpreted as success there. On one occasion I saw something that looked absolutely clownish, but the humor in my smile quickly disappeared when I saw some pastors driving luxury cars (Mercedes Benz) into those villages among their congregants who had no shoes, clothing or electricity and living in dilapidated mud huts. They were preaching prosperity and taking three and four offerings from those who clearly had nothing. God bless the people, for they gave and in heaven they shall receive the reward of their faith. But, those who "… *devour widows' houses and say long prayers to cover it up. They will receive greater condemnation!*" (Mark 12:40 *ISV*).

Is Our Gospel THE Gospel?
Part Two

───※───

Resolving the Problem

B rothers and Sisters, we have many examples of the way Jesus evangelized as well as many apostolic sermons that are defining instances of evangelism. The story of the interview that Christ had with the rich ruler in Mark 10:17-27 is a vivid case that presents the primary elements that are essential to the preaching of the Gospel found in the New Testament. This is a classic example of how Christ evangelized.

The contrast between that which is announced today as the Gospel and that which Christ preached is so alarming that if Jesus used these same methods today in our churches, He would be classified as a cult leader or at best and sent to one of their classes to "learn" how to evangelize. The difference between today's gospel and Jesus' Gospel is not found in minor peripheral details, but in the very heart of the matter. These modern changes are so dangerous that they can eternally misdirect hungry souls. I used to think it impossible to keep a thirsty soul from finding the truth, but apparently, it can be done. Just look at Matthew23:13.

No sincere Christian desires to deceive people. In their love for people, true believers inevitably present some profound truths when they testify. Nonetheless, because of an unconscious omission of indispensable ingredients of the Gospel, many are not able to communicate the impact of the Word of God that they fully intend to impart. When a half-truth is presented as the truth, it ceases to be true.

In the following chapters, you will observe the manner in which Christ "evangelized" a tycoon that, according to outward appearances, would have been a convert that any modern pastor would love to have as a member of their congregation. In fact, perhaps the congregations are already full of "converts" who are just like this wealthy socialite.

Let us observe how the Master Evangelist of all ages evangelized. Listen to His message, contemplate His motives, and take note of His message. We will see the faces of the people we encounter reflected in this young man. Then let us consider our own ministry.

CHAPTER 7
CHRIST IS THE EXAMPLE

—— ❧ ——

The Law

God knows that when people are in the midst of emotional fervor, many times they don't reason clearly and often make uncontemplated decisions not taking into account the consequences of their actions. He always demands that people reason and consider deeply each step that they take towards their decisions for Him.

Remember, Jesus several times told the great multitudes following Him:

- *Those who come to me cannot be my disciples unless they love me more than they love father and mother, wife and children, brothers and sisters, and themselves as well. Those who do not carry their own cross and come after me cannot be my disciples. If one of you is planning to build a tower, you sit down first and figure out what it will cost, to see if you have enough money to finish the job. If you don't, you will not be able to finish the tower after laying the foundation; and all who see what happened will make fun of you. 'You began to build but can't finish the job!' they will say. If a king goes out with ten thousand men to fight another king who comes against him with twenty thousand men, he will sit down first and decide if he is strong enough to face that other king. If he isn't, he will send messengers to meet the other king to ask for terms of peace while he is still a long way off.* (Luke 14:25-32 *GNB*).

When Christ saw the multitudes that were following Him, He knew that the great majority were there because of the euphoria of the moment. He held no interested in retaining such followers. This is why he sifted the multitudes in order to separate the sincere from the emotionally deceived. It's not that there is anything wrong with emotion; that's not my point. What I want to indicate is this; a decision based purely on emotion is not a mature choice and will eventually prove to be short lived. Our natural reaction is to try to take advantage of every opportunity that presents itself before us and sort out what we really want later. If there is emotion involved, so much the better. People almost always respond this way, but Christ *never* appealed to this tendency.

In the Gospel of John 6:66-69, Jesus thinned the multitude that had come together for the free food and the spectacular miracles that He produced. When Jesus saw that, you might say that He ran everybody off who could be shooed away and then showed His disciples the door if they wanted to leave too.

- *"Because of this,* (The word *"this"* is in reference to His teachings that had offended the people) *many of Jesus' followers turned back and would not go with him anymore. So he asked the twelve disciples, "And you—-would you also like to leave?" Simon Peter answered him, "Lord, to whom would we go? You have the words that give eternal life. And now we believe and know that you are the Holy One who has come from God."* (John 6:66-69 *GNB*).

This is exactly what Jesus saw in the rich ruler, and by doing this, He was manifesting the character of God. In Psalms 51, the psalm of repentance, the psalmist recognizes that God is only interested in the sincere heart.

- *Indeed, you are pleased with truth in the inner person, and you will teach me wisdom in my innermost parts* (Psalms 51:6 *ISV*).

The Advantages of the Rich Ruler

- *And when he was gone forth into the way, there came one running, and kneeled to him, and asked him, Good Master, what shall I do that I may inherit eternal life?* (Mark 10:17 *KJV*).

We're going to talk quite a bit about this individual. As a matter of fact, from here on out he continues to come up. So, before we go any further on this rich ruler guy, though the Bible leaves him nameless, to me, it only seems right to give him a name. I feel that it would be just plain rude not to do so. So, how about Richie Rich? … No, that one's taken… How about Richard Ruhl? No, I went to school with a guy with that name... Got it! I have the perfect name: Richard Ruler! We'll call him Richie or Rich for short. Oh my, it seems that we've come full circle, haven't we? We still end up calling Rich Ruler.

Moving right along, the first thing that we can observe in this case is that Richard is very demonstrative in his of expression of reverence and submission. His effervescence reminds me of another case of a man that expressed his desire in a similar animated fashion found in Luke 9:57-58. Christ answered him in a very frank way and for as much as we know, we never hear any more from him. Here's how that went down:

- *As they went on their way, a man said to Jesus, "I will follow you wherever you go." Jesus said to him, "Foxes have holes, and birds have nests, but the Son of Man has no place to lie down and rest."*

It was as if Jesus was saying to him, *"Are you sure about that following me 'wherever I go' part?"*

One look at Mr. Ruler would indicate that he was a person worthy of our esteem and confidence. He was a man of culture and fine mannerisms. When he approached our Lord, he greeted Him with all courtesy on bended knee and called Him *"Good Master"*. His interest in religion might also inspire our respect. He came running to Christ in his apparent enthusiastic search for spiritual help. Richard had never had to run for anything. Why? Richard was of the Ruler family and they never arrived late. Nothing really got started until the Rulers arrived anyway. So why should he rush for anything? Nevertheless, he seemed so agitated over this issue of eternal life that he could not wait for a private interview. He pushed his way through the crowd and rushed into Jesus' presence. However, Jesus just looked at him with his head slightly turned to the side and asked, *"Why do you call me good? No one is good except God alone."*

Richard had caused quite a spectacle by making his desire known in such a public manner. It could very well be that he was quite accustomed to being the center of public attention and knew that his actions would find him favor with the people who knew him because of his flattering confession of faith and recognition of Jesus. Nevertheless, Christ wanted to put his words to the test by inquiring about his motives.

Briefly, I want to re-enforce this comment concerning Jesus inquiring about Richie's motives by pointing out that the word "good" here is the Greek word, *"agathos"* (ἀγαθός) and can actually refer to anything. It is used approximately 102 times in the New Testament and is employed liberally in reference to people and things. In the Septuagint, the word is used about 398 times and is even more varied in its application and its use as an adjective or parts of speech. Nothing particularly distinguishes or limits it to being solely an adjective referring to divinity. Jesus investigating motive, He was not trying to employ a semantical finagle.

I want to get into more detail of this part of the conversation in chapters 10 and 18, but in essence, Jesus said, *"If you are calling me 'Good' then I am sure that you also understand that no one is "good" but God. In other words, are you admitting that I am God? Are your words a declaration of faith in my deity? Let's see if this is really what you believe. I'm going to perform a little test on your sincerity. Are you ready? I'm going to display a list of requirements and then I am going to ask you something. Is that okay with you? What I am going to ask of you will be easy if you truly believe that I am God."*

- *You know the commandments: 'Do not commit murder; do not commit adultery; do not steal; do not accuse anyone falsely; do not cheat; respect your father and your mother.'* (Mark 10:19 *GNB*).

Wait a minute, what an outrageous presentation of the Gospel! What in the world is Jesus thinking by presenting the law when this sincere man is asking about eternal life! Here is this earnest seeker of truth who comes to Jesus, no less, and Jesus tells him about keeping the law! Jesus, don't you know anything about evangelism? This is totally against almost everything that is taught in our churches today. It's true that there are many churches that are very legalistic today. But, this has absolutely nothing to do with that which Christ is teaching here.

Good and Bad Use of the Law

- *What should we say, then? Is the Law sinful? Of course not! In fact, I wouldn't have become aware of sin if it had not been for the Law. I wouldn't have known what it means to covet if the Law had not said, "You must not covet"* (Romans 7:7 *ISV*).

I think that legalistic believers are a stand-up comedy act, a genuine roar-out-loud laugh! One time a friend of mine from Brazil was in a ministers meeting in which laws and rules about women's dress were being deliberated. The question in particular that they were debating was whether a woman should wear trousers or not. Some were saying it was an abomination before God that a woman should wear trousers because they were men's clothing. My friend, a bit frustrated with the leader of the legalist tribe, suddenly asked him, "Brother, would you ever wear a pair of women's slacks?" The other brother, a tad bit insulted by the question, answered antagonistically, "Why of course not! That's absurd!" My friend then sat down comfortably and said, "Well then, I rest my case." Slowly but surely, others caught on to the irrefutability of his argument.

Legalists do not and cannot keep the law that they attempt to utilize for their justification. If a person wanted to use the law as their righteousness, they would have to keep the whole law, not just a part of it. To transgress just a part of the law would make you guilty of violating all of it. For example, in this case where they were disputing women's of trousers, the law says, "*The woman shall not wear that which pertaineth unto a man, neither shall a man put on a woman's garment: for all that do so are abomination unto the LORD thy God.*" (Deuteronomy 22:5 *KJV*). Yet, the very same law says a few verses ahead, "*Don't wear material made from wool and linen mixed together.*" (Deuteronomy 22:11 *ISV*). I can pretty well assure you that all of those who argue the point of verse five would be violating verse 11. This only goes to prove that we are all guilty of breaking God's law and this, my dear friend, is one of the main objectives of the law. It is there to make us aware of just how impossible it is for us to justify ourselves by way of our works or the law.

On one occasion when I was sharing the Gospel with some Muslim friends in Spain, I explained to them the danger found in trying to justify one's self by way of our own works. This is how I explained it: "Let's say that Mustafa wants to disarm a certain bomb and it is exigent that you follow precisely ten steps (the Ten Commandments). It is of no avail to carry out the first nine steps correctly and blow it on the last one. The results would be absolutely the same as if you would have erred on the first step. Boom! Now you have a forty-foot crater right where Mustafa was working to disarm the explosive! Poor Mustafa, he just lost and arm. Look at the size of that explosion! What do you mean he only lost an arm? Yeah, we found everything else …

This is why Paul said,

- *Those who depend on obeying the Law live under a curse. For the scripture says, "Whoever does not always obey everything that is written in the book of the Law is under God's curse!* (Galatians 3:10 *GNB*).

- *Once more I warn any man who allows himself to be circumcised that he is obliged to obey the whole Law.* (Galatians 5:3 *GNB*)

- *I refuse to reject the grace of God. But if a person is put right with God through the Law, it means that Christ died for nothing!* (Galatians 2:21 *GNB*)

It is impossible to keep the entire law for life. At some point, you are going to fail. If the way of salvation could have been found in the law, then why did Christ have to come and die for us? Paul spoke clearly about this subject in the majority of his letters. To try to justify yourself by way of the law is as ludicrous as the example of a man who looks in a mirror and sees that his face is dirty. In his effort to clean his soiled face, he takes the mirror down and begins to rub his face with the mirror. The mirror is not a cleansing agent! Its purpose is to show us good or bad depending on what is reflected there. Our uncleanness is made known to us there. This man must seek another source to resolve the dilemma of his uncleanness; in this case, the sink where there is soap and water. (Now if ugly is your problem, soap and water might not help. That goes all the way to the bone and doesn't even scrape off with a spatula!)

- *For no one is put right in God's sight by doing what the Law requires; what the Law does is to make us know that we have sinned.* (Romans 3:20 *GNB*)

The Purpose of the Divine Fiat

What the Bible explains to us in Romans 4 and Hebrews 11 is that faith has *always* been the way in which God has employed to justify people. There are tomes of excellent books that have been written in exceptional fashion on this subject. I do not propose to do the same here. What I do want to help you clearly understand in the simplest way are three things:

1. The difference between the law and grace.

2. The function that both serve,

3. How they cooperate today?

The law is of God. God established His divine law to serve as a sign that would indicate the way of salvation. In no way has the law been rejected by God in any part of the Bible. Quite the contrary, how many times in the Old Testament as well as in the New Testament does it tell us that the law is good? Let me mention a few:

- *How I love your law! I think about it all day long.* (Psalms 119:97 *GNB*).
- *The law of the LORD is perfect; it gives new strength. The commands of the LORD are trustworthy, giving wisdom to those who lack it.* (Psalms 19:7 *GNB*).
- *Open my eyes, so that I may see the wonderful truths in your law.* (Psalms 119:18 *GNB*).
- *Those who love your law have perfect security, and there is nothing that can make them fall.* (Psalms 119:165 *GNB*).
- *Does this mean that by this faith we do away with the Law? No, not at all; instead, we uphold the Law.* (Romans 3:31 *GNB*).
- *So then, the Law itself is holy, and the commandment is holy, right, and good.* (Romans 7:12 *GNB*).
- *We know that the Law is spiritual;* (the problem is not with the law) *but I am a mortal, sold as **a slave to** sin.* (Romans 7:14 *GNB*).

Paul also said, *"My inner being delights in the law of God."* (Romans 7:22 *GNB*). So, having understood this, we learn that the Bible does not expel the law from the New Testament. The problem is then reduced to our ignorance of exactly what the law and grace really are. The law is a vital part of the Word of God and for this reason is also eternal and irrevocable. The law continues to hold its divine purpose – even in this era of grace.

Different Kinds of Laws

I want to reiterate that this is not an exhaustive academic and theological effort to study this subject, but rather a light clarification of these great biblical truths.

First, it is indispensable to understand that there are basically three kinds of laws:

1. *Ceremonial Laws:*

    a.) These laws are commandments over the order of the religious services of the Tabernacle and the Temple. They hold deep and powerful messages in typological and symbolical fashion that show us with all clarity the ministry of our Lord Jesus Christ today.

    b.) The ceremonial laws are not to be physically practiced today. They have been fulfilled and are yet being fulfilled both physically and spiritually by way of the person and ministry, past and present of our Lord Jesus Christ.

2. *Health Laws:*

    a.) These are laws that cover personal hygiene and public health that have saved millions of lives from plagues and sicknesses that are easily avoided when these laws are observed.

    b.) These laws include instructions on subjects as:

      1.) Dietetic Laws.

        a.) They speak of which plants, animals and even insects we should eat as well as how to cultivate and prepare them.

      2.) There are laws on how to avoid and handle sicknesses and physiological contaminations. These laws are extremely practical. They were never given as a source of salvation and if you obey them to the letter and trust in them as your salvation, you will go to Hell. But, look at the bright side; you'll be in really good shape when you go! Well, … that's not true either. If you go to Hell that means you're *dead!*

As I was saying, my own criteria of the health laws is that, they are a manifestation of the great love of God for His people. He has taken the, time in the most explicit way, to explain how we can enjoy a healthy lifestyle. Being that our bodies are the temple of the Holy Spirit and have been bought with the precious blood of Christ, we belong to Him. Didn't you give your life to Him? Then threefold so, you are not your own: He made you, He bought you and you voluntarily gave your life to Him. He has every right to tell us show we should take care of ourselves.

- *Or do you not know that your body is a temple of the Holy Spirit within you, whom you have from God? You are not your own, for you were bought with a price. So glorify God in your body* (1 Corinthians 6:19-20 *ESV*).

Of course, if someone wants to ignore these laws and eat pig, dog, aardvark, and frog, you are at liberty to do so. This has absolutely no effect over your relationship with God. Knock yourself out, because you can do all of that and go to heaven too. No problem… you just might get there a bit quicker than you wanted. However, as I see it, it is only logical to pay attention to how God said that we should take care of ourselves. For this same reason, most Christians normally do not smoke or engage in other such activities. But we're used to hypocrisy. We tell people not to smoke yet say nothing about unhealthy diets that can kill just as easily.

Here it's convenient to quote the psalmist when he said,

- *The law of the LORD is perfect; it gives new strength. The commands of the LORD are trustworthy, giving wisdom to those who lack it. The laws of the LORD are right, and those who obey them are happy. The commands of the LORD are just and give understanding to the mind. Reverence for the LORD is good; it will continue forever. The judgments of the LORD are just; they are always fair. They are more desirable than the finest gold; they are sweeter than the purest honey. They give knowledge to me, your servant; I am rewarded for obeying them* (Psalms 19:7-11 *GNB*).

3. *The Moral Laws:* "He that saith, I know him, and keepeth not his commandments, is a liar, and the truth is not in him." (1 John 2:4 *KJV*).

    a. These laws are completely current and in vigor concerning your very soul's well-being. Everything that dictates the believer's moral conduct today is primarily based on the moral laws of the Old Testament.

    b. The foundation of all moral laws is the Ten Commandments.

    1. Throughout every book of The Law, the instructions that God has given concerning moral questions are concepts that we Christians embrace faithfully because they are eternal and godly.

    2. Galatians 5:19-21 is simply a list of things that are condemned by the moral laws of God.

        a. A great part of Jesus' teachings are things already written in the law. Jesus said:

- *Think not that I am come to destroy the law, or the prophets: I am not come to destroy, but to fulfil. For verily I say unto you,*

> *Till heaven and earth pass, one jot or one tittle shall in no wise pass from the law, till all be fulfilled.* (Matthew 5:17-18 *KJV*).

3. The sincere Christian knows that to follow and obey every one of these moral laws is a natural part of their daily convictions. These things are just logical. Nobody in their sound judgment would say that the believer is not under the law, and therefore we need not heed these moral laws.

A "Normal" Guy

It's difficult to evangelize on the streets of Europe. In Spain and in France the people are aggressively apathetic towards God (that's almost an oxymoron – but it's the perfect way to describe the general attitude). Just so you have an idea, I have had more success having excellent conversations about Jesus and the eternal state of their souls on the streets of Spain with Muslims than with your average European. For many God has no place or context with any pertinent part of their lives. I do not believe in atheists, but others confess to be and want nothing to do with God. Interestingly enough, in Spain, atheism is more directed at the Catholic Church than at God Himself. They have an indoctrinated confusion and have great difficulty discerning the difference between the two. It is also very interesting to notice that when I speak of the absolutes of that which is right and that which is wrong according to the righteous moral laws of God, I can almost always get the people involved in a conversation.

On one occasion in the plaza of a small Spanish city, I was able to engage in a conversation with two Young men. One was a drug addict and the other, his friend, defined himself as just a guy with "normal" problems. The "normal" guy didn't want to get involved in the conversation. He said, "My friend really needed help and talking to him about God could be a good thing ... but for him – not me". He then promptly dismissed himself from the conversation. He held that position until I read Galatians 5:19-21.

- *Now the works of the flesh are manifest, which are these; Adultery, fornication, uncleanness, lasciviousness, Idolatry, witchcraft, hatred, variance, emulations, wrath, strife, seditions, heresies, envyings, murders, drunkenness, revellings, and such like: of the which I tell you before, as I have also told you in time past, that they which do such things shall not inherit the kingdom of God.*

When the "normal" guy heard this he snatched the Bible out of my hands and read the verse for himself while shouting, "Dude! The Bible says all that!" After reading the verses again, genuinely terrified, he shouted out in common Spanish Street slang, "Man! That's me all up in every one of these things!" Up until this point, I didn't even know that he was listening to our conversation. Now, I really had his attention.

Do I Need A Tutor?

At this point in our study, we can rightfully ask the question, "If God never had it in mind to make The Law a way of salvation, why does the law exist?" I'm so glad that you asked because I wanted to talk to you about this very thought. First of all, if we had no laws, the universe would be more chaotic than a fire in a madhouse. The entire universe in ruled by immutable laws, and thank God for them. By way of these laws, we can enjoy all of the benefits of life as we know it.

The Bible says that the law was our tutor or schoolmaster.

- *Wherefore the law was our schoolmaster to bring us unto Christ, that we might be justified by faith. But after that faith is come, we are no longer under a schoolmaster.* (Galatians 3:24-25 *KJV*).

The Word *"schoolmaster"* is the Greek Word *"paidagogos*[1]*"* (παιδαγωγός) which means, tutor, guardian, a servant that raises the children of his master in his absence and assures that they are finely instructed and guided. They are constant counselors and protectors. Their lives and wellbeing depended on these results.

In the same way, the biblical laws serve us. They also establish the norms and guidelines of righteousness and unrighteousness that man would be completely incapable to conceive by way of his own notions. When man is alienated from God, his darkened understanding twists and disorients his ideas of righteousness.

- *This I say therefore, and testify in the Lord, that ye henceforth walk not as other Gentiles walk, in the vanity of their mind. Having the understanding darkened, being alienated from the life of God through the ignorance that is in them, because of the blindness of their heart: Who being past feeling have given themselves over unto lasciviousness, to work all uncleanness with greediness. But ye have not so learned Christ;* (Ephesians 4:17-20 *KJV*).

We must study the law because people enslaved to sin do the strangest things. A lot of these things are mentioned and condemned in the Moral Law. All of these things are practices that cause disasters in the personal humanity of the individual. Life, as God has purposed for us becomes corrupted beyond recognition and loses all sense of value. For this reason, when a society leaves these convictions as guideposts of moral conduct, graphic violence and immorality increase in intensity.

When we read the strange commandments prohibiting totally perverted customs and practices, God was speaking of things that the nations that surrounded Israel practiced as a normal way of life. This is why He warned the children of Israel (and us too) with the words in Leviticus 20:23 (*ASV*), "*And ye shall not walk in the customs of the nation, which I cast out before you: for they did all these things, and therefore I abhorred them.*"

In this way, the law of God has established itself in our concepts of righteousness, because those are the concepts that God has of moral uprightness. Thank God for this, because He is the only one worthy to establish any concept of righteousness being the only Righteous One. In no uncertain terms, the law also shows us that man is completely incapable of obtaining righteousness by way of his own merits.

A "Righteous" Architect

Once, while ministering in Mexico, I was sharing the Gospel with a distinguished gentleman; he was an architect. He was a genuine modern day Richard Ruler. He considered himself an educated and culturally refined fellow with a highly respected social position and a trophy, eye-candy wife. Of course, we should understand that being financially accommodated or any of these other things have absolutely nothing to do with righteousness. (As a-matter-of-fact, if you look at it, quite literally, in the middle of bu*sin*ess is "*sin*" ... I'm just saying ...)

Anyway, according to this world's standards, He was a righteous man. As we sat in his beautiful house on the outskirts of Acapulco, he told me assertively, "I don't kill, I don't steal, I'm faithful to my wife, I don't do anybody wrong. As a-matter-of-fact," he continued,

"I'm not a sinner; I go directly from my house to my job and from my job back home. How can you in<u>sinu</u>ate that I am a sinner?" I knew this guy wasn't the least bit convinced of his own bragging and neither was I. So I replied, "Wow! Now that is impressive. You mean to tell me that you have never sinned? Are you then perfect?"

"No, of course not, I didn't say that! Nobody is perfect. Sure, I've sinned. But it's no big deal. God wouldn't hold a few sins against me. I do a lot of good things too," he answered.

"Oh, I see." I said. "So, you think that your good works outweigh your bad ones?"

"Why, yes. It's only right to do so."

"So what would happen if you were drinking a nice full liter bottle of refreshment and suddenly found a nasty green fly in your mouth; it was in the bottle? It's just a one green fly. Would you continue enjoying the soda?"

"Ugh! How repulsive! Of course not! I would probably regurgitate first, then I would most surely throw the rest out!"

"You mean just one little filthy cockroach has contaminated the entire drink? What do you think that your sin does to all of your good works? And that's just one sin. Would you say that you might sin three times a day? The Bible says that a righteous man might fall seven times[2], but I'm going to give you much more credit and ask if you might sin only three times a day. That might classify you as a righteous man, right?

He was beaming with contentment at my assessment of his virtues and assented saying, "Yeah, I think that might sum it up. Maybe an errant thought, word or deed every throughout the day. Three sins a day, yeah, that's me."

"Well, the only problem with this scenario is that there are seven days in a week. On your best behavior, that's an average of 21 sins a week. It gets worse when you consider that there are 52 weeks in a year. That's 1,050 sins–not counting your bad days. Oh, and I forgot to ask, just how old are you? What! 42? Do the math! You are a walking catastrophe of fetid sins! We easily talking far more than 40,000 sins! That's giving you far more merit than you deserve! Would any judge in a court of law be a righteous judge if he allowed a criminal who had committed 40,000 crimes to walk free just because every once in a while he gave some money to the judge's favorite charity?" He turned pale with shock and responded, "I've never looked at it that way."

"I know. You have never seen your sin as God sees it, from the perspective of His own nature and His Word." I continued, "So I want to give you another chance. You already know what God says in His Word about what He thinks righteousness is and you have rejected it saying that you are so righteous that you really have no need of God's mercy and forgiveness. You have rejected the message of the Gospel by establishing your own righteousness as the standard that opens the way for you to get into Heaven. So, I am going to give you another scenario. Let's say that *you* were God and you get to establish *your own* standard of righteousness. Now you get to decide that which is right and wrong. Do you measure up to a completely righteous man with no sin?" He blurted out, "Look, I've already told you that nobody is perfect!"

"You do not understand me," I said, "you can now decide and define exactly what perfect is. You can tell me what is just and what is unjust, what is sin and what is not sin, what acceptable behavior is and what behavior is not acceptable. Remember, you are now God. Do you measure up or not?"

He remained quiet and contemplative. After a few minutes, he mumbled under his breath, "No."

"I'm sorry. What did you say?" I asked (I know, I was being mean).

"I said, *no!*" he shouted, "If I were God, I could not even live up completely to my own standards of right and wrong! My life would not be acceptable – even in my own eyes!"

"What? You mean that even if *you* were God, your life wouldn't even be acceptable to *you*? You would even have to condemn you own behavior? Why, then, do you think that God, the One True God, should accept you just as you are on your own merits or concepts of righteousness? God Himself is the very definition of holiness, purity, and righteousness. You, yourself know full well that your fledgling standards of righteousness fall far short of the holiness and righteousness of God!"

His righteousness was proven to be, before his own eyes, as filthy rags. Just as the Prophet Isaiah said, *"But we are all as an unclean thing, and all our righteousnesses are as filthy rags; and we all do fade as a leaf; and our iniquities, like the wind, have taken us away."* (Isaiah 64:6 *KJV*). He was nailed to wall under his profound conviction of sins because the holy law of God brought the consciousness of sin into his life and before his eyes.

CHAPTER 8
HOW CHRIST USED THE LAW

———— ❧ ————

The Commandments of Men

Not giving heed to Jewish fables,
and commandments of men, that turn from the truth
(Titus 1:14 KJV).

The law that Christ used in His message to Richard Ruler was not based on the traditions of men or the Jewish culture. Christ ardently rejected such "laws and rules". Though useless for the saving of the soul, some of those things were good; like the custom of washing your hands before eating. However, others were direct violations of the Word of God (the law). Worse still, their importance had been exaggerated to the point of giving them spiritual significance.

- *And when they saw some of his disciples eat bread with defiled, that is to say, with unwashen, hands, they found fault. For the Pharisees, and all the Jews, except they wash their hands oft, eat not, holding the tradition of the elders. And when they come from the market, except they wash, they eat not. And many other things there be, which they have received to hold, as the washing of cups, and pots, brasen vessels, and of tables. Then the Pharisees and scribes asked him, Why walk not thy disciples according to the tradition of the elders, but eat bread with unwashen hands?*

He answered and said unto them, Well hath Esaias prophesied of you hypocrites, as it is written, This people honoureth me with their lips, but their heart is far from me. Howbeit in vain do they worship me, teaching for doctrines the commandments of men. For laying aside the commandment of God, ye hold the tradition of men, as the washing of pots and cups: and many other such like things ye do. And he said unto them, Full well ye reject the commandment of God, that ye may keep your own tradition. For Moses said, Honour thy father and thy mother; and, Whoso curseth father or mother, let him die the death: But ye say, If a man shall say to his father or mother, It is Corban, that is to say, a gift, by whatsoever thou mightest be profited by me; he shall be free. And ye suffer him no more to do ought for his father or his mother; Making the word of God (the law) *of none effect through your tradition, which ye have delivered: and many such like things do ye.* (Mark 7:2-13 *KJV*).

Manmade Rules

In my ministerial travels around the world I have seen churches that have laws and rules that are so removed from the biblical commandments that they seem as if they are from another world altogether, they're certainly from another kingdom. These are things like, men must be clean-shaven – no beards, (We all know it's not biblical to wear a beard! Beards and facial hair are of the world and of the devil. The devil wears a beard, you know) or, women shouldn't wear make-up or cut their hair. When I find people that are adamant on the "women should have long hair" thing, I promptly let them know that they serve a racist god. People of a pure Sub-Saharan Black African bloodline and their descendants worldwide cannot naturally grow their hair long unless there is a racial mixture involved in their genetic makeup. So apparently, the god of those who hold to this "women must have long hair to be godly" doctrine has not counted the Black races of the world as a part of His church. This is not the God of the Bible. A major difference between the law of God and manmade laws is that the law of God convicts and liberates and the rules of man frustrate and enslave. The "ridicu-list" goes on.

By the way, if you want to find these things in the Bible they are from the book of Hesitations chapter 13. Look it up, they're right there. To help you find it, it's found right before the book of 1ˢᵗ Heresies.

A Big Difference

The more we closely analyze Jesus' message to Rich Ruler, the more that the contrast with today's gospel stands out. After having inquired about Richard's intentions, Jesus devoted the major part of the interview talking about the law, as it is found in the Ten Commandments. Jesus' first comment to Rich was also related to the perfect law; the moral law reveals the character of God. A partial knowledge of God had impeded this seeker from worshiping in truth according to the first four commandments. Richard was inclined to seek praise from man and to praise man over the praise of God Himself. Jesus' rebuke should have convinced him that he was in violation of the first part of the Holy Law. This is why Jesus continued His conversation with the following five commandments in a casual manner by not quoting them in their exact order.

Once again I say, to our understanding of things today, who would answer the question of, *"What must I do to inherit eternal life?"* in this way? Surely, Christ did not think that Mr. Ruler could actually obtain eternal life by keeping the law.

- *Knowing that a man is not justified by the works of the law, but by the faith of Jesus Christ, even we have believed in Jesus Christ, that we might be justified by the faith of Christ, and not by the works of the law: for by the works of the law shall no flesh be justified.* (Galatians 2:16 *KJV*).

You Think That You Have A Better Idea?

Why didn't Jesus talk to him of the gift of God offered to all? What a brilliant idea, why not offer Himself as his "Personal Savior"? Why did He have to go and give all the attention to the law? Once again, we have to keep in mind that Jesus Christ is the master evangelist and knows exactly what He is doing! We must keep in mind that our messages and methods must be judged in the light of what He has done and not in the light of what we do. The law was essential in the presentation of His message, *"…for by the law is the knowledge of sin."* (Romans 3:20 *KJV*). The absence of the preaching of the law of God is probably as responsible as any other factor for the evangelistic impotency in our churches today.

We must simply ask ourselves, if the apostles did not preach the Old Testament Scriptures, what, then did they preach? The New Testament had not yet been written. James, the leader of the early church, said, *"For from ancient generations Moses has had in every city those who proclaim him, for he is read every Sabbath in the synagogues"* (Acts 15:21 *ESV*). Christ expounded the plan of God from the Old Testament to His disciples on the road to Emmaus, *"And beginning at Moses* (the law) *and all the prophets, he expounded unto them in all the scriptures the things concerning himself."* (Luke 24:27 *KJV*).

Abraham told the rich man in hell (hopefully not our Richard Ruler or a member of his family) that his brothers had "Moses and the prophets".

- *Abraham saith unto him, They have Moses* (the law) *and the prophets; let them hear them. And he said, Nay, father Abraham: but if one went unto them from the dead, they will repent. And he said unto him, If they hear not Moses* (the law) *and the prophets, neither will they be persuaded, though one rose from the dead.* (Luke 16:29-31 *KJV*).

Perhaps you might say to me, "this is just a parable". I would answer you that I am of the school that affirms that this is not a parable, but that Christ was relating an actual event. Jesus was saying that the brothers of this rich man must see and understand the truth of the Christ found in the law and the prophets. If they did not believe the law and the prophets, neither would they believe in the resurrection of Christ as we see in clearly presented in the New Testament today. I'll say again, that a major factor of our problem consists in that, in our majority, we do not know how to preach Christ using the entire Bible.

Could You Do It?

Here in Spain, at the theological seminary, I challenge my students to think seriously about just how complete their understanding of Christ would be or how effective would their ability to communicate the power of the Gospel as the Early Church did if they could use only the Old Testament for one year. Even today, the ministries that are dedicated to the evangelization of the Jews cannot utilize the New Testament. They would be able to teach us some tremendous lessons of how we should preach Christ as did the first Christians. Now because I've expressed this point don't go around with some exaggerated gossip saying that Dr. Parker doesn't believe in the New Testament. Calm down! What I am saying is that the majority of believers do not know how to share the whole counsel of God in which we confess to believe.

Why Didn't I Think of That?

During the sever-year war between Iraq and Iran, the Iranian army was able to build a bridge that was several hundred meters long for the transportation of troops, tanks and supplies. The bridge was clearly visible from the ground and air. The Iraqi military never thought to use their air force to bomb the bridge. Instead, they constantly sent in troops to fight, face to face, with their enemy costing them a great many lives. When I heard this, I was tempted to say, "What a bunch of idio- ... I mean ... How silly of them". Nevertheless, we do the same thing when we don't make proper use of the law for it is a tremendous weapon against our enemy in our war with the kingdom of darkness.

A Dead Conscience

Our conscience is like a noisy little dog that barks at everything that moves. Some dog owners cannot stand that much racquet and every time the dog barks, they throw a shoe or yell at it. Eventually they might succeed in teaching the creature not to bark so much. Then it happens that late one night, a thief breaks in and carries off all the furniture and leave the owners sleeping on the floor. As for the dog? Oh, he was just fine, thank you. Why the heck was he going to bark? Just so they could throw another shoe at him? This is exactly what many have done to their consciences.

Have you ever had somebody walk by you, step on your foot and not even notice it? The pain shot up your leg and made you see stars and stripes, but they never noticed a thing. The vast majority of sinners are like that. They live in sin and ignore the roaring of their consciences warnings. They never understand that they have crippled and callused the sensitivity of their conscience and expose themselves to the eminent danger of eternal perdition. This is why Richie Ruler was perplexed. He had not the slightest idea of what he needed to receive eternal life. Whom had he offended? What had he ever done to offend God? While Jesus began to count off the commandments, Mr. Ruler sincerely exculpated himself of all guilt before God. That is until Jesus demanded that he fulfill the first commandment. In the face of this law he was completely disarmed.

Only by way of the illumination of the law could the blindfold of deception be removed from over the eyes of his heart. After all, what is sin if not a violation of the law? The Bible says, *"Whoever sins is guilty of breaking God's law, because sin is a breaking of the law" (1 John 3:4 GNB).* The word *sin* loses significance without the law of God. How could Mr. Rich understand his sinfulness if he didn't understand where he stood with the law of God? This is even more distressing being that he was not ignorant of the law, he was just ignorant of it's application to his life!

Now for us, how can sinners, totally ignorant of the holy law of God and its demands and authority over our lives, see themselves as guilty and condemned? The idea of sin is a foreign concept to them because the law of God has no place in their understanding of life.

Feeling Sorry for Jesus

Many of the people that followed Jesus on the way to Calvary wept for Him. Though He was appreciative for their love and compassion, He said something rather strange to them.

- *Jesus turned to them and said, "Women of Jerusalem! Don't cry for me, but for yourselves and your children. For the days are coming when people will say, 'How lucky are the women who never had children, who never bore babies, who never nursed them!' That will be the time when people will say to the mountains, 'Fall on us!' and to the hills, 'Hide us!' For if such things as these are done when the wood is green, what will happen when it is dry?"* (Luke 23:28-31 *GNB*).

The people were crying for Him because of His physical sufferings, yet they had absolutely no idea of what was happening in the spiritual realm. If they would have understood that He was suffering for all of the sins that they had committed that deserved the very death that they were witnessing, their weeping would have been turned into anguished shouts of lamentation and true repentance. The miserable suffering of our Lord seems a senseless tragedy in the eyes of those who those who had (and have) no reverential understanding of these perfect commandments. "Oh, poor Jesus," they say, "Look what <u>they</u> have done to Him." (As if we had no part in His sufferings). This happens for two reasons:

1. God has no use for our carnal sympathy.
2. The cross was satisfying the righteous demands of the law against <u>our</u> sins.

If sinners are not aware of the requirements of the Decalogue (the Ten Commandments) for them and its authority over them, they will not see the personal significance of our Lord's broken body and shed blood. Without a knowledge of the condemnation of the law, the cross can only draw carnal and useless sympathy; it will never produce the intended godly sorrow and saving faith in sinners. Christ was placed as the propitiation, or substitutional objective that received the outpouring of the judgment of God against the violator of the holy law.

We must ask the question; what sense is there in the offer of salvation from eternal condemnation when the sinner is only nebulously aware of certain danger? Even though Richard Ruler held certain doubts as to if he would inherit eternal life, he never really considered himself as a lost sinner and violator of the law of God. Remember, that *sin is a breaking of the law* and he did not believe that he was a sinner. But Christ did not come to call the righteous, but sinners to repentance (Luke 5:32).

True Recognition

Much of modern preaching only grants lip service to the concept that man must recognize himself as a sinner before he can genuinely embrace the Savior. The bait that is commonly used to extract this vague admission is something like, "Do you think that all men are sinners?" If there is some vacillation in their response, you can establish your point with the verse, *"For all have sinned, and come short of the glory of God;"* (Romans 3:23 *KJV*). However, no definition of sin is ever given. I believe that there are very few people alive that would not concede to the truth of such a cushioned admission for anybody would answer, "Of course, nobody is perfect". This is the result of a darkened understanding that believes that there are some sins that are really bad and others that really aren't so bad.

Seeking an Application

I should first say that I believe that a great majority of contemporary Christians are innocently ignorant of the fact of how we should use the law or even that we should use the law. Others fear the use of the law as if it were a prohibited hex from the "Dark Side". They believe that the use of the law would be an impediment to sinners. The truth is that the lack of the use of the law impedes sinners from reaching the grace of God. Our Savior used the law as a principal tool of evangelism. He knew that the preaching of the commandments was the only way to teach the sinner of his guiltiness and awaken his sense of need and inner desire for the grace of God.

Christ applied the seventh commandment to the conscience of the Samaritan woman to open the understanding of her need for the Messiah. Paul applied the tenth commandment as an example when he attributed his own conversion to the ministry of the law.

- *Shall we say, then, that the Law itself is sinful? Of course not! But it was the Law that made me know what sin is. If the Law had not said, "Do not desire what belongs to someone else," I would not have known such a desire* (Romans 7:7 *GNB*).

The truth of the matter is that to the measure that a man understands God's moral law, he can also be made to understand his total moral degradation and that only the grace of God can save him. When he understands this, his spontaneous reaction will be to call out to God for mercy.

Our generation is more ignorant of God's moral law than many previous generations. The pulpit skips over Exodus 20 and many Christians are unaware of its practical applications that should be evident in their daily lives. How can the world feel any guilt for its negligence of worshipping the One True God?

The Law or Love

Satan has effectively used a very ingenious instrument to silence the law necessary to lead people to Christ. He has spread the idea that the law and love are irreconcilably antithetical. The people are convinced that if they are conflictive, then we must clearly choose between love while holding the law in disdain. In this way, "the Evil One" has declared that love is independent from and contrary to the law. The truth is that the law and love hold a mutual affinity.

Jesus plainly taught that the express purpose of the law provoked people towards love. Christ said that the righteous commandment could be summed up like this: "*... "Love the Lord your God with all your heart, with all your soul, and with all your mind.' This is the greatest and the most important commandment. The second most important commandment is like it: 'Love your neighbor as you love yourself.' The whole Law of Moses and the teachings of the prophets depend on these two commandments.*'" (Matthew 22:37-40 *GNB*).

In other words, the law is a precise elucidation to the demands of love. Did not Christ say, "*If ye love me, keep my commandments.*" (John 14:15 *KJV*).

- *He that hath my commandments, and keepeth them, he it is that loveth me: and he that loveth me shall be loved of my Father, and I will love him, and will manifest myself to him.* (John 14:21 *KJV*).

Love cannot be expressed without the guidance of the law, and the law cannot be spiritually kept without love as a primary motivation. John added this, "*For this is the love of God, that we keep his commandments: and his commandments are not grievous."* (1 John 5:3 *KJV*). Love makes the law delightful. Whoever loves God delights in keeping His precepts. The man that loves God will cry out as did David, *"Make me to go in the path of thy commandments; for therein do I delight."* (Psalms 119:35 *KJV*).

To the natural man the laws of God are chains; the imposition of the strong-armed will of an intolerant governor. The Word of God says this is evidence that the law has revealed just how destitute that man is of love for God and his neighbor. If, in truth, I love my spouse, why would I consider it a sacrifice to offer form of service or to concede any petition they might ask of me?

Practical Love

Love that does not have an outlet of expression will die. IN the same way, love makes the law a delight. Love makes the law practical. How can I manifest my love for God? The Bible repeats the answer and tells us how:

- *And this is love, that we walk after his commandments. This is the commandment, That, as ye have heard from the beginning, ye should walk in it.* (II John 1:6 *KJV*).

The commandments are also a guide to show the love for others. Romans 13:8-10 presents this truth: *"Owe no man any thing, but to love one another: for he that loveth another hath fulfilled the law."*

So Where Is the Conflict?

There is no disaccord between the law and love. The conflict arises between the law and grace when the works of the law are presented as a way of salvation. The law provides no path to life for the sinner. For the lost soul, the law only offers death and allows him to see his need for the grace of God as the only hope for his justification. Salvation comes only by way of grace through faith in Jesus Christ.

- *For sin, seizing an opportunity through the commandment, deceived me and through it killed me.* (Romans 7:11 *ESV*).
- *For by grace are ye saved through faith; and that not of your-selves: it is the gift of God: Not of works, lest any man should boast.* (Ephesians 2:8-9 *KJV*).

So then, as believers, why do we need the law? I'll give four principle reasons:

- First, as I have said, the law gives an expression of our love for God.
- Next, there is the fact of the need for the moral guidance of the law, not just for the Believer, but also for the entire world.
- In third place is the fact that the law brings to light the reality of sin by giving us the knowledge of what God says is right and wrong.
- Finally, the law helps us to understand the purpose that God has for our lives. Ephesians 2:10 tells us: *"For we are his work-manship, created in Christ Jesus unto good works, which God hath before ordained that we should walk in them."*

The Tenth Commandment

Jesus knew that the knowledge that Mr. Ruler had of the commandments was merely superficial but had some external exigencies over his external visible behavior. However, Richard had to learn *"… that the law is spiritual"* (Romans 7:14). As a practicing Jew, he recognized the strict external dominion of the law, but he could not grasp the fact that the law called for Lordship over his thoughts and intentions of the heart. This is why the Lord had to be even more thorough in the demonstration of the law and use it as a probe to provoke a profound pang in his conscience and pain the midst of his very soul.

The Lord could have added a spiritual application such as He did in the Sermon on the Mount. With *"Thou shalt not commit adultery"*, He could have explained, *"That whosoever looketh on a woman to lust after her hath committed adultery with her already in his heart"* (Matthew 5:28). He could have explained, *"Thou shalt not kill"* to include, *"whosoever is angry with his brother without a cause shall be in danger of the judgment"* (Matthew 5:22). But, the "Master Evangelist" wanted to put His finger in the festering sore of the most cherished sin in the heart of the proud Mr. Richard Ruler. When Jesus said, *"Go and sell all you have and give the money to the poor"*, He was revealing the true meaning of the tenth commandment, *"Thou shalt not covet"*, and the first commandment, *"Thou shalt have no other gods before me"*, in an applicatory manner. Jesus was using the law as a scalpel to open the putrid wound of avarice in Richard's soul. Paul understood this when he wrote, *"You must put to death, then, the earthly desires at work in you, such as sexual immorality, indecency, lust, evil passions, and greed (for greed is a form of idolatry)"* (Colossians 3:5 *GNB*). As a result, for the first time, the two edged sword of the commandment penetrated Richie's conscience.

If Christ had merely cited these two commandments as He did the others, old "Shifty Rich" would have dodged his guilt of them like he tried to do with the others. But Jesus applied the Word directly to his spiritual and moral problem. Richie loved his riches more that he loved God showing him that he was guilty of violating all ten of the commandments! He was shown to be capable of committing any crime for the Bible says, *"For the love of money is the root of all evil: which while some coveted after, they have erred from the faith, and pierced themselves through with many sorrows"* (1 Timothy 6:10 *KJV*).

When Mr. Richard Ruler left Jesus' presence, he knew that he was an avaricious sinner and had fallen far short of his professed desire to truly seek eternal life and love God. He knew that he was guilty of having other gods and idols. If money beckoned him to violate the Sabbath, so be it. How would that honor the name of the Lord? From there on down, any of the other commandments that concern love for our neighbor, would be easy to cast aside. How many unthinkable horrible crimes have been committed against countless multitudes for the love of money and greed?

Today most would say that Jesus failed in His effort to evangelize the distinguished Mr. Ruler, because he did not make a decision for God. Nevertheless, the truth be told, he most certainly did make a decision – he decided that he loved sin more than God and he was clearly conscious of this fact. I believe that God loves the sinner so much that if they are lost, at least He lets them know why.

Jesus and the Holiness of God

Jesus spoke to people about the holiness of God to show them the danger in which the found themselves. He is the immutably pure God who is also our judge. The touch of holiness that Christ applied to His conversation with Richard was particularly pertinent to bring the fear of God into him. Before this, he probably knew that God was the judge of humanity. But now, he was fully aware that God was His judge! (For those of you that like that modern touch you can say that God was now, "his Personal Judge".) Jesus impressed him with the holiness of said judge. It's a holiness "... *that will by no means clear the guilty; visiting the iniquity of the fathers upon the children, and upon the children's children, unto the third and to the fourth generation."* (Exodus 34:7 *KJV*).

We are now told that we should begin haring Christ by saying, "God loves you and has a marvelous plan for your life." That might be a nice suggestion for an icebreaker, but Christ didn't start like that. Countless of sinners think that the only attribute of God is love. The love of God is indispensable, but a sinner cannot have any appreciation for the love of God until he sees the value of this love. For him, everything is just fine. They think, "Why wouldn't God love me?" The sinner doesn't understand that his life is in mortal danger. When you say, "God loves you", at the beginning of your message, the darkened understanding of the mind of the sinner registers something like "of course it's true. God would never do anything harmful to me." This is why so many sinners ask the rhetorical question, "If God is a God of love, why does He send 'His children' to Hell?" They are those who hold the holiness of God and the dreadfulness of sin in little esteem.

They are like children playing with plastic guns running around shouting, "Bang, Bang! You're dead!" without understanding the true horror that results when real guns are actually discharged. For the man in darkness today there is no idea of the holiness of God, only an ephemeral and perverted concept of some kind of effusive benevolence that permits everything. Modern evangelism is helping to enforce and foment this misconception by way of silence and vagueness. The Bible says, *"Behold therefore the goodness and severity of God: on them which fell, severity; but toward thee, goodness, if thou* continue in his goodness: otherwise thou also shalt be cut off." (Romans 11:22 *KJV*). The love of God is present to save the repentant sinner. Yet, in their present state, *"God is a righteous judge, a God who is angry with sinners every day"* (Psalms 7:11 *ISV*). The sword of the wrath of God has been suspended over the heads of the guilty. This sword will most surely be a bane to them if they do not repent and turn, in trust, to Christ. This is not such a "marvelous" plan. The redeeming love of God for sinners is found only in Jesus and the sinner is at present outside of His favor. Christ did not console the ignorance of Mr. Rich; rather he woke up his conscience with dread for the holiness and the righteous of God.

You've Got the Wrong Guy

Many people simple do not understand that holding a false concept of God is sin. I know that we are all continually growing in our relationship with the Lord, but I'm talking about something else. I am talking about an abjectly erroneous concept of who God is! I'll talk about this in more detail in chapter 11.

Case in point; People today use the name of God as frivolously as did Richie Ruler, but it's a mistake to assume that they are talking about the same God as we are. When we say "God", we mean, "The Creator, He With Whom We Have To Do". When our contemporaries say "god", they are talking about some higher power in some distant (or not so distant) part of the universe that in reality has little to do with our daily lives. When a believer says "God", they are saying, "He Who Is Ineffable In Holiness, He Who Is Terrible In Power, the Sovereign of the Universe to Whom We Must Submit and Bow our Knees and Will". When sinner say "god", they are generally referring to a god that had submitted himself to the all-powerful will of man. Concretely, when we say "God", we are speaking of the One that cannot vacillate in His holiness and *"that will by no means clear the guilty"*. Sinners frequently think that God is so flexible that He would permit man's vain caprices. Remember, your concept of God will dictate your lifestyle!

If you rush to explain the four steps to get to heaven to a disorientated sinner who has a totally distorted concept of who God is, you will be speaking two different languages. You will guide him into a prayer of a confession of faith, but he will be praying to another god. It is more probable that he believes that he is actually doing God a favor for turning his life over to Him.

- *How then shall they call on him in whom they have not believed?* (Romans 10:14).

Paul was a missionary evangelist par excellence. He could say to the elders of Ephesus, *"Wherefore I testify unto you this day that I am pure from the blood of all men."* (Acts 20:26). How could he make such an affirmation? Most certainly it was not because he had given every the four spiritual laws. His answer is found in his words, *"For I have not shunned to declare unto you all the counsel of God"* (vs. **27**). In his itinerate ministry, Paul preached a complete theology, not an anemic four-step version of eternal life.

CHAPTER 9
GRACE

———— ∞∞∞ ————

I f we want to understand the law, it is absolutely exigent that we also learn about grace. There are many fine books and expository studies on this subject. Therefore, once again, I do not propose to present a profoundly academic and theologically exhaustive investigation. What I do want to do is to expound on the aspect of the manifold grace of God. Very few times have I heard accurate teachings over this particular aspect of the grace of God, which I believe to be one of the most important.

What Is Grace?

- (II Timothy 2:1 *KJV*) *Thou therefore, my son, be <u>strong in</u> the grace that is in Christ Jesus.*

You will have to excuse me, but exegetics is one of my specific areas of study as a professor of theology. This is one of those verses that I think the Good News Bible actually has a better translation. The use of the preposition *"through"* is far more consistent with the definition than is the word *"in"*. The GNB says, *"As for you, my son, be <u>strong through</u> the grace that is ours in union with Christ Jesus"* (II Timothy 2:1 *GNB*). I pray that with this short treatise you will be able to comprehend in a much broader way a vital aspect of the grace of God.

First, it is absolutely indispensable to understand what the grace of God is not. So teachings are openly and dangerously erroneous and other, are at best, just plain worthless. So let's take a look at some of the false teachings on the grace of God.

A. What the grace of God is *not*:

1. The grace of God <u>is not</u> "the indulgence of God" that permits us to do whatever we want. I have honestly been astounded when I have heard supposed believers justify their libertinistic activities and lifestyles with horribly mistaken ideas about grace. They say things like, "But, Brother, we're not under the law, but under grace." They are ignorant of the fact that the Scriptures have warned us that people would come with dangerously erroneous attitudes. Jude, the half-brother of Jesus, saw those in his day who had this perverted caricature of God's grace.

   - *For some godless people have slipped in unnoticed among us, persons who distort the message about the grace of our God in order to excuse their immoral ways, and who reject Jesus Christ, our only Master and Lord. Long ago the Scriptures predicted the condemnation they have received.* (Jude 1:4 *GNB*).

Paul also warned us about this lie from the devil saying, *"What shall we say then? Shall we continue in sin, that grace may abound? God forbid. How shall we, that are dead to sin, live any longer therein?"* (Romans 6:1-2 *RVG*). The apostle showed us that to follow our own carnal desires was to go directly against the will of the Holy Spirit.

   - *This I say then, Walk in the Spirit, and ye shall not fulfil the lust of the flesh. For the flesh lusteth against the Spirit, and the Spirit against the flesh: and these are contrary the one to the other: so that ye cannot do the things that ye would* (Galatians 5:16-17 *KJV*).

Galatians 5:18 teaches us that the Holy Spirit will never violate God's law. This explains why if we live in grace we do not have to worry about the law. *"But if ye be led of the Spirit, ye are not under the law."*

2.) The grace of God is not the removal of the temporary consequences of transgressing God's law.

The law contained curses for those who transgressed it. Being that Christ made the freedom from these curses possible (Galatians 3:13), many believe that there are, therefore, no negative consequences for sinful acts or lifestyles. They think that when you confess your sin everything is erased and you're all ready to go again. Spiritually speaking, this is one of the greatest blessings of the sacrifice of Christ! Nonetheless, every sin carries a physical result that produces the fruit of the sin committed.

- *Christ hath redeemed us from the curse of the law, being made a curse for us: for it is written, Cursed is every one that hangeth on a tree:* (Galatians 3:13 *KJV*).

A Tremendous Move of God in Spain

During the last part of the decade of the '80s and just about all of the '90s, God began to work in a miraculous way among the drug addicts and other marginalized sectors of Spanish society. Spaniards who had been addicted to heroin and other deadly addictive vices for years began to come to Christ by the hundreds. Praise God for powerful ministries such as REMAR, Reto, Betel, and others have been incredible instruments en the hands of God to reach these precious souls. In fact, for a long time, the only churches that had obtained numerical and spiritual growth in their congregations were those who had centers of rehabilitation incorporated into their infrastructure.

The first ones to come to Christ son manifested strong leadership abilities and as they matured son became great leaders in these works. These brothers and sisters grew to be beloved and respected servants of God in Spain. They have sent many missionaries to dozens of other countries of Europe, Africa, the Middle East and the Americas from those who have been saved via these ministries.

Never the less, after about ten years of ardent and faithful service our Lord, the first converts, now leaders, began to get sick and die. It turns out that many of them had contracted AIDS as a result of their nefandous activities before they knew Christ. God could have healed them, but He didn't. We loved them and we miss them, but God gave us a message through their lives and deaths. They were clearly forgiven of all of their past sins and activities; that's not the issue. These brethren were saved, their sins were forgiven. Spiritually, they were fully justified. Nonetheless, physically they had to pay the price for the deviant ways of their past.

Once and For All

I knew a young believer from a church in the north of Spain. She was the only believer in her family and was a virgin. She was thirty years old and thought that she would never find a husband because, at that time, there were very few Evangelical Christians in the entire country and, of course, even far fewer in her region. Her family constantly mocked her faith and constantly criticized her saying that she was going to die a religious old maid. One night, in a gesture of protest against the dealings of God in this aspect of her life, she took off to another city, found a handsome young stranger and went to bed with him. She doesn't even remember his name. From this, once-in-a-lifetime experience, this one night stand – the only sexual act she ever engaged in, turned out to be her last.

A short while later she manifested signs of a venereal disease. She went to her doctor and found out that she not only had contracted that venereal disease, but that handsome young stranger also contaminated her with HIV. Now, she knows that she will never marry. She ruined the plan of God for her life- that precious life of which there now remains little. She personally urged me to tell others of her plight. It pains me to use these precious and beloved brethren as examples here, but they illustrate a hard biblical truth.

- *Do not deceive yourselves; no one makes a fool of God. You will reap exactly what you plant. If you plant in the field of your natural desires, from it you will gather the harvest of death; if you plant in the field of the Spirit, from the Spirit you will gather the harvest of eternal life* (Galatians 6:7-8 *GNB*).

3.) The grace of God is not the liberty to reject God's moral laws.

- *For by such grace you have been saved through faith. This does not come from you; it is the gift of God and not the result of actions, to put a stop to all boasting. For we are God's masterpiece, created in the Messiah Jesus to perform good actions that God prepared long ago to be our way of life* (Ephesians 2:8-10 *ISV*).

That word *masterpiece* is an interesting Word. In Greek, it's the word *poie⁻ma* (ποίημα) and can be translated "work of art or poem". What a beautiful thought! Wow! In God's eyes, that is what He has made us! However, this verse, (verse 10) is the one that follows the famous words of *"by grace we have been saved"*. Yet He has not saved us to walk in our own ways, rather that we would live a completely new life. We now honor Him not with our own works, but with the works that are of God. Though Isaiah is talking about the Sabbath day, this very thought reminds me of what He said in Isaiah 58:13, "*... and shalt honour him, not doing thine own ways, nor finding thine own pleasure, nor speaking thine own words:*" (Isaiah 58:13b *KJV*). When we begin to follow the works of the Holy Spirit en our lives, God begins to write a poetic love letter to everyone that knows us. The Bible says: "*Ye are our epistle written in our hearts, known and read of all men:*" (II Corinthians 3:2 *KJV*).

No, My Friend, the grace of God *is not* the freedom to reject God's moral laws. As a matter of fact, it is quite the opposite. I would like to offer this definition to summarize a major aspect of the grace of God: The grace of God is the desire and the power to do the will of God.

An Elephant Is Like...

We've all heard the folksy parable about four men that were born blind that were taken to discover what an elephant was like. Of course it's hyperbole, but we will take it for what it can offer us in the way of an illustration. The first man grabbed the tail and stated that the elephant was similar to a rope. The second man touched his ear and concluded that the elephant was like the leaf of a banana plant. The third man touched the abdomen and was sure that the elephant was much closer to a huge barrel. The fourth man embraced one of the legs and affirmed that the elephant was far more similar to a tree trunk. Which one was right? From their point of view, or lack thereof, all were correct. Is this not so?

This is how it is with the grace of God. There are many ways to see the love of God in it. The grace of God is as vast as is

God Himself because it is one of His principle attributes. Grace is as is God and no single explanation is sufficient to adequately encapsulate it. The Bible says that grace is *"manifold"*. This means that grace has multiple aspects and ways to see it correctly. It is exigent to understand this, for if you don't, you will not have a correct concept of this ineludible truth.

- *As every man hath received the gift, even so minister the same one to another, as good stewards of the manifold grace of God.* (I Peter 4:10 *KJV*).

Clarifying the Definition

The grace of God is the desire and the power to do the will of God.

In my ministry, I have seen many people addicted to substances such as alcohol or drugs cry saying they want to be free from their vices. What they lack is not will power; they lack the grace of God to obtain a new life. The grace of God is not just the desire, because many have the desire to do that, which is good, but are found unable to do so. They have no power. There are others who *"say"* that the can, but just don't want to. However, it is the desire, *"to will"*, and the power, *"to do"*, (they must both be present) to bring to pass that which is good. It is God that work in us to do this! This, in no way proceeds from our human strength or efforts.

- *For it is God who is producing in you both the desire and the ability to do what pleases him.* (Philippians 2:13 *ISV*).

This is a key verse in our understanding of this particular aspect of the grace of God. Now then, having given my definition I will simply say that it is *a* definition. I'll not say that it is the only characterization, nor will I say that it is the most (or least) important explanation. Nonetheless, it is a definition that has been forgotten (to our harm) in the teachings of the modern church.

I repeat, the grace of God is the desire and the power to do keep God's moral laws – not the liberty to reject them. Titus 2:11–12 (ISV) clearly says, *"For the grace of God has appeared, bringing salvation to all people. It trains us to renounce ungodly living and worldly passions so that we might live sensible, honest, and godly lives in the present age"*. This verse explains that the grace of God is an active force in our lives. The grace of God teaches us. All of the attributes of God are active. For example, love is also an attribute of God and throughout the Bible we can see the activity of the love of God. God is love and the love of God had an active manifestation in the life, death and resurrection of Christ.

- *For God so loved the world, that he gave his only begotten Son, that whosoever believeth in him should not perish, but have everlasting life* (John 3:16 *KJV*).

Therefore seeing the law and grace together John 1:17 sums it up perfectly with the words, *"For the law was given by Moses, but grace and truth came by Jesus Christ."* Allow me to help you to understand what John said here.

"For the law was given by Moses…"–Moses gave us the law that demands the righteousness that God requires of us, but there is no way that we can possibly fulfill this legal mandate. The same law conclusively proves this in Romans 3:10 (citing Ecclesiastes 7:20), *"As it is written, There is none righteous, no, not one"*. In the same chapter Paul says, *"For all have sinned, and come short of the glory of God"* (Romans 3:23).

"... **grace and truth came through Jesus Christ**." – When Christ came and shed His blood on the cross, He forgave us and put His Holy Spirit in us. Now, because of the power of His Spirit in us, He has given us His grace by which we can now actually fulfill the righteousness that has been demanded us by the law and bring the will of God to pass in our lives.

Hebrews 10:29 calls the Holy Spirit the Spirit of grace. Grace came through Jesus Christ and not through the Holy Spirit, because if Jesus had not shed His precious blood, it would not be possible to receive the Holy Spirit. This is the very reason that God put such a high price for the blasphemy of the Holy Spirit.

- *Anyone who disobeys the Law of Moses is put to death without any mercy when judged guilty from the evidence of two or more witnesses. What, then, of those who despise the Son of God? Who treat as a cheap thing the blood of God's covenant which purified them from sin? Who insult <u>the Spirit of grace</u>? Just think how much worse is the punishment they will deserve!* (Hebrews 10:28-29 *GNB*).

The grace of God also has an active manifestation in us. <u>I Corinthians 15:10</u> (*GNB*) says, *"But by God's grace I am what I am, and the grace that he gave me was not without effect. On the contrary, I have worked harder than any of the other apostles, although it was not really my own doing, but God's grace working with me"*. This verse evidently demonstrates that Paul understood this virtue. He recognized that he himself had no power to do that which he did. He naturally did not have any desire to do this, because when he did what he wanted to do, he was persecuting the church. Paul unmistakably recognized the miracle that took place in his soul by the grace of God.

In another occasion, Paul was exhorted by the Lord Himself to trust in the power of grace, for through that power he could withstand any fiery trial that he had to endure.

- *And lest I should be exalted above measure through the abundance of the revelations, there was given to me a thorn in the flesh, the messenger of Satan to buffet me, lest I should be exalted above measure. For this thing I besought the Lord thrice, that it might depart from me. And he said unto me, My grace is sufficient for thee: for my strength is made perfect in weakness. Most gladly therefore will I rather glory in my infirmities, that the power of Christ may rest upon me* (II Corinthians 12:7-9 *KJV*).

Power in the Ministerial Gifts

There is one thing that is absolutely indispensable to understand before we can proceed any further, and that is that nothing good, virtuous, and spiritual that is found in us is of us – it does not emanate from our own nature or character!

I know so many brothers and sisters that are faithful and diligent in the work of the Lord. They are gifted and used of God. Nevertheless, some are proud to almost to the point of arrogance because they actually believe that they themselves are the fount from which their virtues and qualities stem. They do not recognize that everything that they do that is praiseworthy, musical gifts and abilities, their hours in prayer, profound study and understanding of the Scriptures, diligence in evangelism or other ministerial gifts, do not proceed from them. It is the grace of God operating in them for God's own reasons. Many times (all the time if they don't understand) they come to the conclusion that if others are not doing or accomplishing everything that they do, it's because they are not as spiritual or as gifted as they are.

Jimmy Swaggart

When as specific direction of grace is in operation in a person, many times there is an anointing to function in specific ministerial gifts. If a believer is deceived and carried away by the arrogance that I have mentioned, the enemy can easily convince them that everything they do is approved of God; And why not? Can't you see all that God is doing through my ministry and me?

This reminds me of a notorious incident that happened many years ago. I want to handle the following very delicately, but I am going to use our Brother Jimmy Swaggart as an example. I want to use him, not because I do not respect him; the truth is quite to the contrary. I deeply respect him. His has been a brother whose ministry I followed since his humble beginnings when he had just a few radio programs. The brother's ministry was one that had a tremendous impact on the twentieth century and was, truly, a very good work.

He joyfully gave millions of dollars to the work of the Lord yet drove a ten-year-old car. His tithes were over $14,000,000.00 (US) a year, and this does not include the offerings that he freely and generously gave to works for the Lord in Latin America, Spain and countless other places. When he was in his ministerial zenith, Latin America was greatly touched and unnumbered thousands we benefitted through his ministry. Nobody remembers these things now and it is a painful shame that they don't.

My wife and I were invited to a ministerial retreat in Baton Rouge hosted by Brother Swaggart's ministry. Brother Jimmy paid all the expenses; all we had to do was go. There was an impressive list of pastors and missionaries that were present as guests and a tremendous team of ministers that were there to minister to us for those three days. Everything was magnificent, but the apex of the entire retreat was the service in which Brother Swaggart himself participated. The sermon was incredibly profound and anointed. It was true solid food for the mature believers that were there to receive the Word. Permit me to tell you that there were at least 3,000 invited ministers present. Most of us were from the same denomination as Brother Swaggart himself. Of those 3,000, you probably had more than 60,000 combined years of ministerial experience. This means that the crowd was particularly practiced in the discernment of good and evil (this wasn't just any old crowd that was gathered for this retreat).

In my opinion, he had gifts given by the grace of God that are seldom seen at that level of anointing. Every minister present left there invigorated, revitalized and edified. Since then, I have met ministers in different parts of the globe who were also at that retreat, and all of us have the very same testimony. I can tell you that, that meeting defined and set a standard for what the anointing is to me. I had never before nor since, experienced anything similar.

Yet, what was our surprise one month later? We discovered that for quite some time, Brother Swaggart had been living in a practiced sin! I was completely astonished and left deeply pensive. Had we not just experienced the power of God in our lives – in the lives of over 3,000 servants of God? Had we *ALL* been deceived? I thought this highly improbable and not to be the case, but this was still a great mystery for me. I have always been fairly apt at discerning spirits, and my wife usually picks up and warns me about those who managed to slip by me.

The Reason

I began to pray concerning this incognita and the Lord revealed a simple truth about His gift of grace that works within us. This truth also put the fear of God in me in a new way. Perhaps this is nothing new to you, but to me, it was a revelation that cleared up many mysteries.

When God bequests us His grace for some ministerial gift, He never takes back the gift or its empowering abilities or virtues that He has given us with said gift. Of course we know that the Scriptures say, *"For the gifts and calling of God are without repentance"* (Romans 11:29 *KJV*). The Greek word for "repentance" is *"ametameletos"* (ἀμεταμέλητος), which means, in short, irrevocable. In other words, once He gives you a gift, He is not going to take it away. That's the scary part!

You see, God has His own purposes, this means He also has a purpose for us. If we want to be obedient and live an upright life in a correct relationship with Him, fine. We will then also be beneficiaries of our service. If not, too bad, that that's also no problem. He will continue to use us and even use us greatly. The blood-chilling danger with this continued use is that we so often think that God approves of our nefarious works and actions because He continues to anoint and use us. He will not take back the gift that He has given us, but we are responsible of the stewardship, both of the gift and of our personal lives!

Remember, even though Moses disobeyed God, the river of water still gushed from the rock. Even though Balaam was in grave and deadly error and had dangerously deviated from the will of God, his prophecies were still right on point. In I Kings 13, a lying prophet prophesied precisely over a disobedient prophet. Did not Christ admonish us with these sobering words?

- *When the Judgment Day comes, many will say to me, 'Lord, Lord! In your name we spoke God's message, by your name we drove out many demons and performed many miracles!'* (Matthew 7:22 *GNB*).

They did prophecy and they really cast out demons, but it was to no avail for them. They received absolutely no benefits from all of their labors for in the end, they were disqualified.

We should not believe that because of the manifestations of the Holy Spirit in our lives and ministries that God is in approval of our lives. *All of that is simply the grace of god in operation in us.* Paul understood this and explained that it was necessary to crucify continually his carnal nature. He said this because it is possible that he could continue to carry out his ministry and afterwards personally receive no reward or benefit. He said, "*... but I buffet my body, and bring it into bondage: lest by any means, after that I have preached to others, I myself should be rejected*" (1 Corinthians 9:27 *ASV*). We can continue to operate in the gift that God has given us with the same power because *it is not of us, nor does it depend on us, it is the grace of God.* Many servants of God have fallen into great error and catastrophe because that failed to understand this great truth. This is why we have seen so many powerful servants fall into ruin.[1]

Understanding What We're Talking About

The Greek word *charis* (χάρις) or grace appears 103 times in the Pauline epistles and 13 times in the general epistles. It is commonly accepted to be academically understood as *"the divine influence upon the heart, and its reflection in the life"*. I think that is an extremely fitting understanding of the original Greek word, for with this concept we can safely conclude that just about all of the verses that speak of grace imply the active power at work in the believer.

A closer look at the word the word *charis* shows us that it is aptly translated into English in five different ways according to the syntax and context of its use. It is translated as: Joy (Philemon 1:7), Liberality (I Corinthians 16:3), Benefit (I Corinthians 1:15), Thanks or thankworthy (II Corinthians 2:14, 8:16, 9:15) (I Timothy 1:12) (II Timothy 1:3).

The word *euprepeia* (εὐπρέπεια), also translated as grace in most English translations. It is used once in James 1:11. Its meaning is similar but also puts forth the inference of something that is good or has suitableness. Almost all of the verses that speak of grace indicate that it is an active power in the believer. The work of the ministry is brought to pass by the grace of God. I just want to mention a few verses.

Faithful Service Is the Fruit of Grace

Paul exhorted the believers who were conscious of the work of grace in operation in them to discover their particular spiritual gift.

- *We have different gifts based on the grace that was given to us. So if your gift is prophecy, use your gift in proportion to your faith* (Romans 12:6 *ISV*).

- *And God is able to make all grace abound toward you; that ye, always having all sufficiency in all things, may abound to every good work* (II Corinthians 9:8 *KJV*).
- *As every man hath received the gift, even so minister the same one to another, as good stewards of the manifold grace of God* (1 Peter 4:10 *KJV*).

Paul also recognized that the great work that he was able to bring to pass was not because of his own strength or virtue.

- *Nevertheless, brethren, I have written the more boldly unto you in some sort, as putting you in mind, <u>because of the grace that is given to me of God</u>. That I should be the minister of Jesus Christ to the Gentiles, ministering the gospel of God, that the offering up of the Gentiles might be acceptable, being sanctified by the Holy Ghost"* (Romans 15:15-16 *KJV*).
- *"<u>According to the grace of God which is given unto me</u>, as a wise masterbuilder, I have laid the foundation, and another buildeth thereon. But let every man take heed how he buildeth thereupon* (I Corinthians 3:10 *KJV*).

The other apostles also recognized the works that were of God and those who proceeded from man, for they saw this grace in Paul.

- *And when James, Cephas, and John, who seemed to be pillars, <u>perceived the grace that was given unto me</u>, they gave to me and Barnabas the right hands of fellowship; that we should go unto the heathen, and they unto the circumcision* (Galatians 2:9 *KJV*).

Paul understood that any good witness that he could give was because of the grace of God.

- *For our rejoicing is this, the testimony of our conscience, that in simplicity and godly sincerity, not with fleshly wisdom, <u>but by</u>*

the grace of God, we have had our conversation in the world, and more abundantly to you-ward (II Corinthians 1:12 *KJV*).

How Can You Grow In Grace?

God gives His grace to believers to grow in grace. I have already quoted II Timothy 2:1 (GNB) *"As for you, my son, be strong through the grace that is ours in union with Christ Jesus"*. How was it that Paul expected Timothy to be strong in the grace of God that is ours in Christ Jesus if grace was only the unmerited favor of God? How can you demand something of me that is not under my control or is not in my hands to decide?

Several verses in the Bible exhort us to "grow in grace". How, pray tell, am I to grow in "unmerited love"? God loves me and that's it! He cannot change this and He cannot love me more (or less). Think about it. His love is the maximum expression of love in the universe and there is no greater love. He has loved us to the max. You face this conundrum if grace is only "the unmerited love of God". Everything we have of God is unmerited. So, should we conclude that everything is grace? That's rather vague and very nonspecific. Yet the Scriptures tell us:

- *But continue to grow in the grace and knowledge of our Lord and Savior Jesus Christ. To him be the glory, now and forever! Amen* (II Peter 3:18 *GNB*).

Now it's worth it to ask the question: "Just how can I grow in the grace of God?"

That is an excellent question and I'm going to answer it this way. Being that grace is an active attribute, the Holy Spirit begins to work in your heart to obey Him more attentively in every detail of your life. You now have to choose between obedience, that is to say, following Him or continuing in your own ways. If you show meekness, you will humble yourself and submit to the will of God. God will give you more grace, that is to say, the desire and ability to continue to follow and obey His will.

- *But he gives all the more grace. And so he says, "God opposes the arrogant but gives grace to the humble."* (James 4:6 *ISV*).

- *In a similar way, you young people must submit to the elders. All of you must clothe yourselves with humility for the sake of each other, because: "God opposes the arrogant, but gives grace to the humble."* (I Peter 5:5 *ISV*).

Have you never noticed in your own testimony that the more that you obey God, the easier it is and the more you want to obey Him? You are now growing in grace. In the same measure, if you are arrogant and resist the grace of God, God will also resist you and it becomes much more difficult to obey Him the next time. The Christian life is not hard. Living a loving, joyful monogamous marital relationship with your spouse is really easy if your love your spouse more that all others! In the same way, the Christian life is only hard for those who love themselves more than they love God.

Yes, you heard me correctly; when I said that you could resist the grace of God. The grace of God is not irresistible, as some would affirm. Remember that the Scriptures say, *"For the grace of God that bringeth salvation hath appeared to all men, Teaching us that, denying ungodliness and worldly lusts, we should live soberly, righteously, and godly, in this present world"* (Titus 2:11-12 *KJV*). If this is true … and it is, then why aren't all men saved? It is because some continue to resist the grace of God that *"hath appeared to all men"*.

Galatians 2:21 says, *"I do not frustrate the grace of God: for if righteousness come by the law, then Christ is dead in vain"* (Galatians 2:21 *KJV*). In this verse, the word *frustrate* is the Greek word *atheteo* (ἀθετέω) which means, "reject, frustrate, cast away, reduce to worthlessness or nothing, annul, make void". Hebrews 12:15 (*ISV*) adds this thought saying, *"See to it that no one fails to obtain the grace of God and that no bitter root grows up and causes you trouble, or many of you will become defiled"*. This phrase, *"fail(s) to obtain"* is just one word in Greek, *"hustereo"*. This word means: (1) to fall behind – as in a race. (II) To arrive late. (3) Not reaching the goal. (4) To lack and be without, to fail.

Salvation Was Not Your Idea

God called us by His grace so that we could be saved. It was 100 percent the work of God. It is not as if one day we woke up and said, "Duhhh, I got it! I think I'm going to give my life to Christ". No, it was not your idea! *"For it is God which worketh in you both to will and to do of his good pleasure."* This includes the entire work of our salvation. The Bible says that we were called by His grace. God has given His grace to Non-believers to believe in Him. These famous Scriptures declare this precious truth:

- *For by grace are ye saved through faith; and that not of yourselves: it is the gift of God ...* (Ephesians 2:8-9).
- *I marvel that ye are so soon removed from him that called you into the grace of Christ unto another gospel* (Galatians 1:6 *KJV*).
- *But when it pleased God, who separated me from my mother's womb, and called me by his grace, To reveal his Son in me, that I might preach him among the heathen; immediately I conferred not with flesh and blood:* (Galatians 1:15-16 *KJV*).

The Grace of God in Power over Sin

Paul recognized that without the grace of God his efforts to obtain righteousness were always frustrated.

- *For I know that in me (that is, in my flesh,) dwelleth no good thing: for to will is present with me; but how to perform that which is good I find not* (Romans 7:18 *KJV*).

Once again, in this verse we find the words, *"to will"* and *"to perform"* (to do).

Now, this thought that I'm going to share might be a tad bit shocking for some of you, and I well understand why. It's even shocking to me! But I don't believe that Paul was describing the Christian life in Romans 7. I believe that Paul was describing to perfection what life was like for him as a Non-Believer. Why do I think this? Because He concludes this part of his discourse by saying, *"O wretched man that I am! Who shall deliver me from the body of this death? I thank God through Jesus Christ our Lord. So then with the mind I myself serve the law of God; but with the flesh the law of sin"* (Romans 7:24-25 *KJV*).

Wait, wait… what do you mean, Dr. Parker? Hasn't Christ already delivered us? Well, if you are saved, the answer is a resounding, *yes!* This is why Paul continues his discourse in chapter 8 with the prime objective of the direction of chapter 7 by saying:

- *There is therefore now no condemnation to them which are in Christ Jesus, who walk not after the flesh, but after the Spirit. For the law of the Spirit of life in Christ Jesus hath made me free from the law of sin and death* (Romans 8:1-2 *KJV*).

Chapter 8 is simply a sub-conclusion of the idea of his dissertation in Chapter 7. Chapter 7 – speaks of being a slave to sin; chapter 8 – speaks of being free in Christ by the grace of God!

The reason that this interpretation is difficult for me is not exegetical, but because of my personal feelings and frustrations with my own particular weaknesses. I feel as if I have lived and mirrored what Paul describes in this passage innumerable times throughout my personal Christian journey. The hermeneutical observation that I have put forth here is on point; I am just uncomfortable with what the Word of God tells me here. I can honestly say that this is one passage of Scriptures that really nails. Nevertheless, I must believe the entire Word of God, not just the "pretty" parts that make me feel good about myself. Doesn't the Word say:

- *There hath no temptation taken you but such as is common to man: but God is faithful, who will not suffer you to be tempted above that ye are able; but will with the temptation also make a way to escape, that ye may be able to bear it* (1 Corinthians 10:13 *KJV*).

It also says, "*Submit yourselves therefore to God. Resist the devil, and he will flee from you*" (James 4:7 *KJV*). Jesus Himself told us to pray, "*And lead us not into temptation, but deliver us from evil: For thine is the kingdom, and the power, and the glory, forever. Amen*" (Matthew 6:13 *KJV*).

Now we have to answer the question, Does God answer prayer or not? Unquestionably and without a doubt, God answers prayers! Therefore, that being the case, I have to understand that God has delivered me from, not just from sin, but also from the power of sin! So now, the problem actually consists in if I really understand or not the fact that God has delivered me from the power of sin. But, how has He delivered me from this power? Well, the answer is simple—by way of His grace. What we are seeing here is the power of grace that overcomes the power of sin. This is why the Bible also says:

- *Moreover, the law entered, that the offence might abound. But where sin abounded, grace did much more abound* (Romans 5:20 *KJV*).

I have to ask myself if I really believe that God can give me the power to overcome sin. You see, the law was weak because we had to depend on the power of the flesh to fulfill it.

- *For what the law could not do, in that it was weak through the flesh, God sending his own Son in the likeness of sinful flesh, and for sin, condemned sin in the flesh: That the righteousness of the law might be fulfilled in us, who walk not after the flesh, but after the Spirit* (Romans 8:3-4 *KJV*).

This was the plan of God, because the law convinces of that we are sinners when we see how far we are from fulfilling God's standard of righteousness. But now, we have power over sin through grace.

- **"For sin shall not have dominion over you: for ye are not under the law, but under grace"** (**Romans 6:14** *KJV*).

I Need My Brain Washed!

As a university student, I studied psychology. I discovered that in the scientific world nobody knows what a thought is or what feelings are. Our ability to love and have compassion and the ability to create and to admire the beauty of the creativity of art and music are things that basically set us apart from the rudimentary animal kingdom. We know about neurotransmitters, hippocampal synapses, hormones, and their relationship to our physiological responses. Nevertheless, man's developed neocortex, prefrontal cortex and temporal lobes are biological contributors, but they are not for what we experience as true sentient beings. Even snails, flys and plants experience sentience to some degree. An octopus can resolve fairly complex problems and elephants, dolphins and other animals also display a high degree of intelligence. However, man's inner desire to seek transcendent meaning makes us unique and cannot be explained by the mere possession of a developed brain. None of that even remotely explains reasoning, thinking, perception and love.

So I thought, surely the Word of God has the answer to this scientific mystery. After some study of the Word, I discovered that the word *psuche̅* (ψυχή), the root Greek word from which we derive words such as psyche, psychologist and psychology is also the word that the New Testament uses for soul, life, mind, and heart. The word also means breath, spirit, the foundation for base or carnal emotions, reasoning and eternal existence. It is that which is commonly known as the mind.

This is very distinct from *pneuma* which also means breath and spirit, but without emotions. When I understood the reason the Bible says, *"Behold, all souls are mine; as the soul of the father, so also the soul of the son is mine: the soul that sinneth, it shall die"* (Ezekiel 18:4 *KJV*). Or as it is stated in the Good News Bible, *"The life of every person belongs to me, the life of the parent as well as that of the child. The person who sins is the one who will die."*

You might say, *"Well, Brother Prince, if this is the case with what you have been telling us, why do I suffer so many temptations and struggles with my flesh?"* My brother, I can't answer for you, but I will be honest with you and explain what happens in my life. Satan cannot tempt me with that which my sinful nature does not like. I have never smoked cigarettes, so the only thing they produce in me is nausea. But if, in some corner of my mind, I keep a little place of refuge for the entertainment of sinful thoughts, the enemy can afflict me horribly, because these thoughts leave a stronghold or fortress in my head where the enemy can lodge. That's why Paul said, *"It is true that we live in the world, but we do not fight from worldly motives. The weapons we use in our fight are not the world's weapons but God's powerful weapons, which we use to destroy strongholds. We destroy false arguments; we pull down every proud obstacle that is raised against the knowledge of God; we take every thought captive and make it obey Christ"* (II Corinthians 10:3-5 *GNB*).

I have to be honest and admit that if I am going through something like that; my flesh still wants to enjoy, in some way, certain sins (Wow! Now doesn't *that* really sounds disgusting?) I have to decide every day if I am going to walk under the grace of God or in my flesh. The New Testament says that we must crucify (put to death) our carnal desires every day.

Before I was born again, I had no choice in the matter. As Christ said in John 8:34 *(ISV)* *"Truly, I tell all of you with certainty that everyone who commits sin is a slave of sin"*. I was a slave to sin. I could not change my life though I desperately attempted to do so. I was living according to the flesh and we know that the Scriptures say, *"Because the carnal mind is enmity against God: for it is not subject to the law of God, neither indeed can be"* (Romans 8:7 *KJV*). Worse still, Paul goes on to tell us, *"So then they that are in the flesh cannot please God."* (Romans 8:8 *KJV*). Even if I would have wanted to, I couldn't. But, Brothers and Sisters, this *is not* our case now that we are in Christ Jesus! Doesn't the Bible say, *"...Nay, in all these things* we are more than conquerors through him that loved us" (Romans 8:37 *KJV*).

When I surrendered to Christ, some old *friends* tried to mock me saying, "Prince, you have gone and gotten mixed up with those Christians and they've brainwashed you!" I answered them, "Yep, mind was so contaminated and dirtied by the world that it really needed to be washed." One of the first things that I understood when I became a new creature was that my mind needed to be renewed. The Bible says, *"And be not conformed to this world: but be ye transformed by the renewing of your mind, that ye may prove what is that good, and acceptable, and perfect, will of God"* (Romans 12:2 *KJV*). In another place it reiterates, *"And be renewed in the spirit of your mind"* (Ephesians 4:23 *KJV*).

This is why a great part of the new birth is the renewal of our mind. The New Testament mentions the mind 18 times and every time it mentions it in reference to be in a right or wrong relation with God. The mind can be an instrument of life or death for us. The grace of God, by way of the Holy Spirit operates in you according to the measure that you concede to Him in your mind. The grace of God helps us to obtain "the mind of Christ".

- *For they that are after the flesh do mind the things of the flesh; but they that are after the Spirit the things of the Spirit. For to be carnally minded is death; but to be spiritually minded is life and peace* (Romans 8:5-6 *KJV*).

For who hath known the mind of the Lord, that he may instruct him? But we have the mind of Christ (I Corinthians 2:16 *KJV*).

CHAPTER 10
SUCH A NICE YOUNG MAN

———✦———

N ow then, let's get back to see how Richie Ruler, the other "normal" kid is getting along with the test that Jesus put before him. Let's go back to Mark 10:17-22:

- *And when he was gone forth into the way, there came one running, and kneeled to him, and asked him, Good Master, what shall I do that I may inherit eternal life? And Jesus said unto him, Why callest thou me good? there is none good but one, that is, God. Thou knowest the commandments, Do not commit adultery, Do not kill, Do not steal, Do not bear false witness, Defraud not, Honour thy father and mother. And he answered and said unto him, Master, all these have I observed from my youth. Then Jesus beholding him loved him, and said unto him, One thing thou lackest: go thy way, sell whatsoever thou hast, and give to the poor, and thou shalt have treasure in heaven: and come, take up the cross, and follow me. And he was sad at that saying, and went away grieved: for he had great possessions (KJV).*

I have discovered that everybody has a better estimation of themselves than reality dictates. Five minutes with one of those reality TV shows, "talent" shows included, is more than enough time to convince unbelievers of this truth. With this, I have learned that every time a person comes to me with a grudging complaint against another I discover that the majority of the fault lies with the person that lodged the initial complaint. A majority of times that a man or woman comes to me with a tale of some crime or injustice committed by their spouse, I find that they usually hold the key to the problem or and its solution in their very own hands. The Bible says, "*The first to put forth his case seems right, until someone else steps forward and cross-examines him*" (Proverbs 18:17 *ISV*). Again it states, "*You may think everything you do is right, but the LORD judges your motives*" (Proverbs 16:2 *GNB*).

In this way, the Lord was observing the assertions of Mr. Ruler, because the Lord Himself said, "*... I do not judge as people judge. They look at the outward appearance, but I look at the heart.*" (1 Samuel 16:7 *GNB*). Concerning what we can see, Mr. Rich was a man of moral action. When Christ began to recite the commandments, he responded, "*all these have I observed from my youth*". As far as anything the people could see, his life was clean. In our churches today, Richard Ruler would have "a tremendous testimony". When Jesus said, "*Do not commit adultery*", he sincerely reported that he was chaste. This is notable, for today's statistics inform us that the youth in our churches are as sexually active as those who do not embrace the faith. To the Lord's commandment, "*Do not steal*", he could say that he was honest in his business dealings. He had not gained his wealth by way of fraud. He has always respected his parents, he didn't bear false witness. Wow! A genuine feat today! The truly admirable thing is that all of this integrity wasn't occasional or a recent practice. According to his confession, his morality had been woven into his character and habits since his youth.

The Filthy Rich and the Dirt Poor – They're All Unclean

It is often more difficult for a wealthy person to surrender to Christ than a person that is, let's say, "financially challenged". The same holds true for a person that is socially considered a good person than one who knows that he is a scamp and a scoundrel. This is why Jesus had an easier time ministering to tax collectors and prostitutes that with the religious group. For me, the most horrid nightmare that could possible occur would be to believe that you're going to heaven, trusting in your own righteousness and end up in hell! Jesus, in His infinite love, wanted to wake up Mr. Rich from his lethargic dream and the delusional concept of his self-righteousness. He was going to use the law to do this, because he lived in constant violation of the very law that he claimed to keep so zealously.

Verse 22 says that he had "great possessions". He was prosperous in worldly goods. It is also clear that he was a man of nobility, influence, and authority (be that by birthright or personal accomplishments is unclear). Matthew 19:20 says that he was a young man, which by the Greek word implies that he was under forty, which, when you consider his achievements, is quite impressive. In our society he would a probably be a candidate for the "Citizen of the Year" award. I can hear many whispering, "Richard Ruler is a member of our congregation". To the carnal mind, this cause for bragging rights.

Personally, I have never had this kind of temptation to brag in the churches that I've pastored. As a matter-of-fact, the bragging rights I've had are that, according to the promise of Christ, everybody in my congregations were well on their way to heaven. Why, didn't Jesus say, *"Blessed be ye poor: for yours is the kingdom of God."*

(Luke 6:20 *KJV*)? Nobody ever has money in the churches where I've been pastor! (*It's a joke, Folks...*)

Moving right along ... Today, with the "normal" (or should I say, "carnal") way that we think, how would you react if you found yourself with the illustrious young Mr. Rich begging you to tell him how he could get to heaven? Wow! Now I admit that's a heavy question! Personally, with my "natural" reaction, I most probably would not have answered as did Christ. Yet this is the dream of every believer who desires to win souls for Christ. Would you open your Bible to ask him some essential questions? Questions such as: "Did you know that you are a sinner? Did you know that Christ died for sinners? Do you accept Jesus as your Personal Savior? Please repeat this prayer..." He would answer in the affirmative to each one of these questions and a tad bit of instructions. It's a simple matter of showing him the practiced verses.

Richie was ripe for our style of evangelism. Our counselors would have taken full advantage of his "decision" and open attitude. In fact, they would have even given him full assurance that he was not the proud possessor of eternal life. He would be promptly added to a list of statistics and his conversion would be reported worldwide. Such a celebrity would deserve an interview and special report on an Evangelical TV program – one of the big ones! What a testimony!

By our commonly used tactics of evangelism, we place in dire scrutiny that which Christ did here. We are saying that we are disillusioned to see how Jesus turn away this tender soul. How could our Lord use such tactics so clearly deficient in reaching this poor sinner? He starts with a reprimand and ends with the Ten

Commandments. He demanded an immense sacrifice as a condition to obtain eternal life and allow the big fish get away. What's going on here? Didn't He know how to lead a soul unto Himself? Remember, that the first thing that Christ did was to ask him a question. He immediately put Mr. Ruler to the test. His question was, *"Why callest thou me good? There is none good but one, that is, God:"*[1] When I was a new believer, this question disturbed me. I would think, *"What in the world are you saying, Jesus? Are you saying that you're not God?"* Afterwards I understood that He had two reasons for asking this question. I will explain one of the reasons here, and the other I will elucidate in chapter 18.

The first reason was that Christ was saying to Richie, "If you are calling me 'good', then you are recognizing my deity and me as Messiah. Is this not so? If things are truly as you have stated, nothing I request of you could be too much to ask. Why would it be difficult if, as you have said, I am the God of heaven and earth and I hold eternal life in the palm of my hand?" The Lord wanted to show the truth of his faith, or lack thereof, by the use of the law. From the beginning, Christ was putting Richard's faithfulness to the first commandment to the test.

"Good Master"

Jesus did not direct His first comment in answer to the indignation of this young celebrity; rather to the formal greeting Mr. Ruler used. Remember, he called Him, "Good Master (Teacher)" (*agathos didaskalos*) There are at least three Greek words for "Master". Greek word used here, *"didaskalos"*, means, "an instructor (generally or specifically):–doctor, master, teacher". Under ordinary circumstances, it would be deemed as odd that our Lord would refuse this acclaim. The problem here consists in that the inquirer only recognizes Him as a great teacher and not the Christ, the Son of the Living God. The Savior took advantage of this opportunity to inform him of this truth: "A person's goodness (and you see me only as another person) does not deserve to be named such or considered in this way. God is the only one that is originally and essentially good." As far as the word, "Master" is concerned, it is the Greek word *rhabbi* (ῥαββί), or "rabbi" (Strong's defines this word like this: Of Hebrew origin with pronominal suffix; my master, that is, Rabbi, as an official title of honor:–Master, Rabbi.)

In Matthew 23:7-8 (*KJV*) Jesus reaffirmed the same declaration that He makes here to Mr. Rich, "... *and greetings in the markets, and to be called of men, Rabbi, Rabbi. But be not ye called Rabbi: for one is your Master, even Christ; and all ye are brethren.*" The interesting thing is that He continues in His discourse in Matthew 23:9-10 by reaffirming His proclamation with the use of another Greek word that is also translated Master.

- *And call no man your father upon the earth: for one is your Father, which is in heaven. Neither be ye called masters: for one is your Master, even Christ (KJV).*

Here the Greek word for "Master" is, *kathēgētēs* (καθηγητής) and, though Strong says the same thing, I will defer to Thayer's definition: "a guide, a master and teacher."

Now, we should understand that the Gospel of Matthew was written to the Jews, so for Jesus to teach such strong exactness over the use of lexicon, it was something that rang true and convicting the mind and soul of Jewish consciousness of His day. Mr. Richard Ruler claimed to be fully abreast of the convictions that governed moral Jewish behavior since his youth. Such a comment as Jesus made was a perfectly fitting exhortation for him. It is also true for us that we should not predicate our most illustrious adjectives upon men, because if we do, what then should we reserve for God alone? When men began to praise Herod, he believed their adulation and was eaten by worms in the sight of all those who praised him. (Eeeuuuu!) Yet it was not for this reason that Jesus interpreted the Young Mr. Richie so literally. May we not use the term "good" in courteous reference to individuals? Does the Lord want us to literally interrupt people in every conversation to correct the admiration expressed to others or us? What was Christ's purpose in marking such an emphasis on this apparently minor point?

Wrong Interpretation

The Great Evangelist is not a nitpicker nor does He want us to go out on a campaign against the word *good* in description of other men. I can just see certain churches prohibiting the use of the word *good* because of this verse. This would only go to show a total lack of exegetics.

Sometime back in Ethiopia, there was a group of missionaries working with an unevangelized people group. A war broke out and the situation worsened to the point that the government ordered all foreigners to leave the country. The church, still in its infancy stage, was left to fend for itself. The new converts began to work so diligently that a great revival was birthed. Thousands came to Christ and churches were established in hundreds of villages. Years later, the missionaries were permitted to return and what was their surprise? They found a church a thousand time bigger, stronger and healthier than when they had left. All of this happened without trained pastors or Bible teachers, for there was no one equipped to train them.

On one occasion, a missionary settled into their new house in a village that had one of the churches that that been planted after they were expelled. They rejoiced when a group of new believers came to visit them one day. But the family pet, a dog, came trotting into the room and the new believers left immediately appalled by what they had seen in the house of the missionaries that had come to help them grow in their knowledge of the Word of God. When the missionaries inquired as to how they had offended them, they answered, "Have you not read in the Bible where it says, *'Beware of dogs...*'" (Philippians 3:2 *KJV*). In the same way, many times, people misinterpret the words of our Lord. Added to the intrigue of our Lord's commentary, He Himself called men good in Matthew 5:45, *"...for he maketh his sun to rise on the evil and on the good, and sendeth rain on the just and on the unjust."*

Probing the Heart

Nonetheless, this was no ordinary conversation, it was rather intense. Jesus was censuring the man for having a ready disposition to flatter people while holding little reverence towards God. Christ wanted to start the interview correctly and wake up a reverence for the Holy character of God. So He began to use the first thing the Richie gave Him as an instrument of instruction; his salutation. Jesus began His evangelistic message by focusing His attention on the attributes of God's infinite holiness and goodness.

Jesus' Motives

Verse 21 says explicitly that Jesus loved him and had compassion for him while He talked to him. When Richard departed from Jesus' presence, hc left because he couldn't save his soul and love his possessions too. He must have also left an unmeasurably deep and pulsating pain in Jesus' heart. Jesus cried when He saw that Jerusalem had rejected His mercy. It is certain that a similar grievance filled His heart when our friend Mr. Richard (Richie) Ruler turned his back on Him. For Jesus, this man was not a statistic or a trophy that would embellish our crusade reports. Jesus profoundly loved this man.

Considering all of this, the concern for our noble young friend's soul was not the primary motive that moved Christ to testify to him. Jesus' goal was to do the Father's will and to make known His glory among men. After He humbled Himself to enter this world, Christ said, *"Then I said, 'Here I am, to do your will, O God, just as it is written of me in the book of the Law.'"* (Hebrews 10:7 *GNB*). During His earthly ministry He said, *"And he who sent me is with me; he has not left me alone, because I always do what pleases him."* (John 8:29 *GNB*). One His way to the cross, Jesus gave a summary of His earthly ministry like this, *"I have shown your glory on earth; I have finished the work you gave me to do"* (John 17:4 *GNB*). This passion consumed Him His entire earthly life.

If someone desires to share the Gospel today, they must know what it means to be wholly given to glorify God over all other motives that he or she might have. Some show passion for correct doctrine, in doing so, they place a question mark over their love for God by the lack of evidence of an active love for lost sinners. This absence of missionary passion is frightening. Nonetheless, it is essential to be moved to compassion for the lost, it is even more essential to be deeply moved because of our love for God.

What a Jackonkey!

I heard a little story about a burro that came into the barn bragging about all of the attention that humans had given to him that afternoon. They sent people to look just for him, they put a beautiful new blanket on his back, they didn't even let his hoofs get soiled by the dust of the path in which they travelled but people tended their personal clothing before him. Everyone had palm branches that they were waving and shouting words and phrases that he couldn't quite understand, but they were looking at him what they were doing all of those things. Oh, and by the way, they also put some guy on my back – it was odd, for at first I thought that I was going to kick him into next week. But then, a sensation entered into me that I had never felt before and I could have carried him anywhere he wanted to go. I felt like I was created to be this man's servant. Anyway, the whole thing was absolutely marvelous!

For me, this explains the concept that people have of the Gospel. One of the greatest perversions of the Gospel that is preached today is the disoriented focus towards man as the center of the message. It is a homocentric, and not a Christocentric message. This is where the very idea of the invention of phrase, "Personal Savior". Instead of honoring God, this gospel puts man as the spoiled child in the center of the focus of God's plan. It's a gospel that appeals to man's egocentrism. On the other hand, the Bible has Christ as the center of the love and plan of God. Jesus Christ is the center of the Bible. It's all about Jesus and not about us!

One of our favorite phrases today's evangelism is, "God loves you and has a marvelous plan for your life". But the raw biblical reality for the sinner is,

- *Or despisest thou the riches of his goodness and forbearance and longsuffering; not knowing that the goodness of God leadeth thee to repentance? But after thy hardness and impenitent heart treasurest up unto thyself wrath against the day of wrath and revelation of the righteous judgment of God; who will render to every man according to his deeds* (Romans 2:4-6 *KJV*).

The sinner has made himself an enemy of God and in the present rebellious state in which they live; there is absolutely no hope for their life. In fact, the only plan that God has for the sinner at this point in their life is an eternal separation from Him in Hell. Didn't He say, "*I tell you, Nay: but, except ye repent, ye shall all likewise perish*" (Luke 13:3 *KJV*).This doesn't sound very charming, but it is the truth. Christ spoke more about hell in His teachings than He did about heaven.

A good example of this detour of man's gospel is the common use of Revelations 3:20. Normally, people talk about Jesus as if He were a beggar outside in the cold rain pleading at the door of your heart to be let in and given lodging. Once again, the truth is a far cry from this concept. The sinner is actually the one that is outside of the Kingdom of God, and if they do not repent, they can call at the door all they want, but God will not open it until He sees fit to do so. Jesus placed all focus and attention of the seeker towards God and His glory. His entire message was constructed to honor His Father. Richie Ruler wanted a quick and easy solution for resolve his fear of death and judgment. Jesus eventually directed his attention to this subject, but first, it was necessary to lay a foundation and give a conclusion to a far more important matter. The answer Jesus gave indicated that He had come to exalt God, to declare His name and His incomparable goodness. His coming to save the lost was totally rooted in this.

Evangelism always requires the preaching of the attributes of God. When Jesus met the Samaritan woman at the Jacob's Well (John 4), He taught that God was Spirit. When Paul spoke to the pagans at the Areopagus (Acts 17), he had to dedicate even more of his evangelistic message to the character of God, who was unknown to them. He began to speak of God as the Creator. Then he explained how He was also the Sustainer of all life and for this reason, He raised Jesus Christ from the dead. This element of the exaltation of the character of God is essential to give honor to God in our preaching. Much of today's preaching is anemic; the blood of the life of the nature of God is absent. Evangelists concentrate their messages on man. *Man* has sinned and lost a great blessing. If *man* wants to recuperate his immense loss, he must live such and such a way. However, the Gospel of Christ is very distinct. It begins with God and His glory. Then it explains that men have transgressed a holy God, who, in no wise, will ignore their sin. It reminds the sinner that the only hope of salvation is found in the grace and power of the same God that they have betrayed. The Gospel of Christ sends sinners to their knees to beg for the forgiveness of the Most Holy God.

Do you see that the difference between the two is abysmal? One seeks to open a way into heaven with the Lord of Glory as an incidental step, just one of the necessary steps to obtain the result you desire. The other struggles to magnify the God of all grace in the salvation of eternal souls. The first one gives and answer to the question, *"what must I do to inherit eternal life?"* without laying down the proper foundation. This would be worse that a surgeon

entering into the operating room without the demanded preliminary preparations. It does not matter how urgent the intervention
is, the preliminary preparations are indispensable. The second one
says, *"Wait, The God with whom we have to do is three times holy, the
only one that is good, inaccessible in shining holiness! Let's get back to
your question after we have placed it in its correct setting. But now, take
your eyes off yourself and look unto the Holy God of the Scriptures. Only
then will you see yourself as you are in truth, an unclean and undone
creature, filthy in your rebellion against a holy and infinitely pure God.
You are not yet ready to speak of yourself and eternity."*

The Case of the Adulterer

Numerous times, I have had conversations with people that
want to change their lives, not because they have seen the holiness
of God and their own uncleanness, but because their sin has caused
countless problems in their lives and the want to be free from their
problems. Jails are full of people who are sorry- not because they
did wrong and possibly ruined other people's lives, but because
they got caught. That is not repentance!

Once a wealthy man approached me during a service and asked
to speak with me. He was not a believer, but his wife was a member
of the church. We went outside and sat in his luxury car to talk
about something that was clearly disturbing him. It turns out that
he was involved in an adulterous relationship and wanted to be free
from it because a demon had begun to torment him. He knew that
it was a malignant spirit that would overcome him and keep him
involved in this relationship. He was requesting prayer for deliverance. I asked him if he was conscious of the sin that dominated his
life because of his spiritual rebellion while I spoke to him about the

repentance of his sins, the righteousness of God, temperance and the coming judgment.

Then I asked him if he sought me out because he wanted to surrender his life to Christ. He told me no, that he just wanted me to pray for him to get free from the demon that tormented him. In that moment, I understood exactly how Joab felt when he said, *"I'm not going to waste any more time with you,"* (II Samuel 18:14a *GNV*). I promptly said goodbye and got out of his vehicle. He was totally taken aback, and with terror in his eyes asked me where I was going, why was I leaving? Wasn't I going to pray for him? "No," I responded, "you have every plan to continue with your love affair with Satan and his minions; you just don't like the situation in which you now find yourself! You don't like the demons, you don't love the concubine, you are betraying your wife and don't like that either, but you really love living in sin as long as you feel that it 'benefits' you."

This kind of person will continue joyfully in their sin and will never approach the church if it were not for the multitude of calamities in their lives that come because of their sins. They have never considered the holiness of God and we are propagating this crime if we admit this attitude as a legal recourse to obtain eternal life.

The True Consciousness of Sin

The preaching of the attributes of God is essential for the conversion of sinners. Without a knowledge of God, a sinner will not know just whom he has offended or who can save him. His faith will be so vague like the faith of one that believes in a god that for them is simply a "higher power". Apart from a clear understanding of God, there cannot be a personal approach to God.

Jesus directed the egocentric eyes of Richie Ruler to One whose holiness caused Isaiah to cry out, and say, *"There is no hope for me! I am doomed because every word that passes my lips is sinful, and I live among a people whose every word is sinful. And yet, with my own eyes I have seen the King, the LORD Almighty."* (Isaiah 6:5 *GNB*). Do you think that this is a secondary part of the Gospel? If you think that it is, it is because your own understanding of the faith is based on an erroneous foundation.

Mr. Rich had come running because he suspected that he did not have eternal life. The problem was that he didn't know why! Whom had he offended? Even his own words are in contradiction to the Old Testament[3], he had never offended God. *"... all these have I observed from my youth."* There was not the least bit of evidence of lamentation for having sinned against God. He was prepared to speak of religion; yet was ignorant of God. He was anxious to ask for the joy of salvation yet did not see himself as one in need to cry out as did David, *"Against you, you only, have I sinned, and done what was evil in your sight. As a result, you are just in your pronouncement and clear in your judgment"* (Psalms 51:4 *ISV*). He that came running to Jesus was ignorant of the ineffable worthiness of God and the immensity of his own criminality against Him. He claimed to have kept the all of the commandments, but he did not love the Lord with all of his heart and saw it not as criminal negligence. Yet, how could he? He had never truly contemplated the glory of God. In no way was he ready to hear about the way of salvation.

CHAPTER 11
PREACHING THE UNKNOWN GOD

- *For as I passed by, and beheld your devotions, I found an altar with this inscription, TO THE UNKNOWN GOD. Whom therefore ye ignorantly worship, him declare I unto you (Acts 17:23 KJV).*

M any times, we take things lightly that which God takes very seriously. The Bible says that *to have a false concept of God is sin.* If you don't believe me, look at Exodus 20:3-5 (*KJV*). This is the whole purpose of the first two commandments!

- *Thou shalt have no other gods before me. Thou shalt not make unto thee any graven image, or any likeness of any thing that is in heaven above, or that is in the earth beneath, or that is in the water under the earth. Thou shalt not bow down thyself to them, nor serve them: for I the LORD thy God am a jealous God, visiting the iniquity of the fathers upon the children unto the third and fourth generation of them that hate me.*

Even though the inquirer was Jewish, and most probably a devout Jew, Jesus did not assume that he knew who God was. He needed to be taught about the attributes of God. Today's evangelists calculate with egregious error then they automatically conclude that sinners know who God is. The sad truth is that in our day, people know even less about God that the Jews of the first century.

Even still, Evangelicals run to take shortcuts with those "five things that God wants you to know". Everybody concentrates on the eternal riches of man and completely overlook the question of, "Who is God?" The sinner that is automatically treated after this fashion concludes that his own concept of God is correct. If his concept were correct, he would not be living in sin far from the presence of God. Here we find a practical application of the truth that your concept of God will determine your lifestyle. Such a sinner will never understand the gravity of his situation and the tragedy is that instead of helping them escape the morass of sin, we sink them more.

Someone might say, "This guy does understand the things of God, he just doesn't want to serve Him right now." I would respond to that, "If in truth, he understood, he would serve God. Even if he doesn't and claims to know who God really is, this would only seal the righteousness of his condemnation. In the day of judgment, nobody will just be hanging around casually waiting for their name to be called. When the see they reality of their plight, they will be overcome with the greatest, most indescribable horror know to any living being!"

Paul's Sermons to Pagans

The first incident:

- *And saying, Sirs, why do ye these things? We also are men of like passions with you, and preach unto you that ye should turn from these vanities unto the living God, which made heaven, and earth, and the sea, and all things that are therein: Who in times past suffered all nations to walk in their own ways. Nevertheless he left not himself without witness, in that he did good and gave us rain from heaven, and fruitful seasons, filling our hearts with food and gladness* (Acts 14:15-17 *KJV*).

In the Book of Acts, we have two examples of sermons in which Paul preaches to people completely ignorant of the One True God of the Bible. The first case is found in chapter 14:15-17 where Paul and Barnabas were mistakenly identified as Mercury (Hermes) and Jupiter (Zeus). Paul tore his clothes and ran in the middle of the crowd to rectify the flawed concept that they had of God. The crowd barely was open to hear everything that they said, but they could not leave the people with a false idea of One True God. The apostles simply announced some basic attributes of the only True God of all creation. It's important to notice that they did not even present an invitation to "receive Christ" although they had the audience in the palm of their hand. Why? *Because the people were not yet prepared for this great truth!* If they would have done it our way, the people would have been cemented into a false concept of who God really is. We have no record that anybody was converted in that incident. even still, God was glorified.

The second incident:

- *So Paul stood up in front of the Areopagus and said, "Men of Athens, I see that you are very religious in every way. For as I was walking around and looking closely at the objects you worship, I even found an altar with this written on it: 'To an unknown god.' So I am telling you about the unknown object you worship. The God who made the world and everything in it is the Lord of heaven and earth. He doesn't live in shrines made by human hands, and he isn't served by people as if he needed anything. He himself gives everyone life, breath, and everything else. From one man he made every nation of humanity to live all over the earth, fixing the seasons of the year and the national boundaries within which they live, so that they might look for God, somehow reach for him, and find him. Of course, he is never far from any one of us. For we live, move, and exist because of him, as some of your own poets have said: 'For we are his children, too.' So if we are God's children, we shouldn't think that the divine being is like gold, silver, or stone, or is an image carved by humans using their own imagination and skill. Though God has overlooked those times of ignorance, he now commands everyone everywhere to repent, because he has set a day when he is going to judge the world with justice through a man whom he has appointed. He has given proof of this to everyone by raising him from the dead." When they heard about a resurrection of the dead, some began joking about it, while others said, "We will hear you again about this* (Acts 17:22-32 *ISV*).

Here we find Paul preaching in the Areopagus to a group of humanist philosophers. A group whose' entire purpose was to develop false concepts of God. Paul expounded his discourse taking the hearer from the known and then progressed to the unknown. We don't see Paul performing with his prolific exegetic mastery of the Scriptures, rather with informed quotes of the philosopher Epimenides of Crete and from the poem "Phainomena" by the Greek poet Aratus. He did not degenerate his argument by presenting the "first principles" as would have done the Greek philosophers. His argument was firm and based on the biblical revelation of the person of God giving echo to the thoughts and in occasions the language of the Old Testament. Just as the biblical revelation, he began with God the Creator and ended with God the Righteous Judge of all flesh.

His sermon proved to be repugnant and offensive to some and they cut him off when he began to speak of the resurrection of the dead and eternal judgment. As in the first registered occasion, we also do not have an account of large quantities of conversions because of this tremendous message. Nonetheless, God was glorified. I believe that with this I see that God cares more that people have a correct knowledge of Him in than to have ignorant masses vagrantly meandering blindly and saying that are following a God whom they don't really know.

How Did Paul Plant So Many Churches?

Have you every contemplated the marvel of just how Paul planted so many churches in such a relatively short period? His usual modus operandi was: he entered a town or city, was there two or three weeks, ministered in a few Sabbath day services in the synagogues, then usually got beaten up or thrown in jail or something like that, then a church was born. How was that possible? For example, in Paul's first missionary journey (Acts 13:3-14:28), he was in Antioch for two weeks before they ran him out of town. (There were two cities named Antioch; one was Syrian Antioch or Antioch on the Orontes and the other, Antioch of Pisidia located in the Isparta province in modern day southern Turkey).

He was in Iconium for an undetermined amount of time, but even then, it is difficult to conceive that it was for more than a year. He was also in Lystra and Derbe for unknown lengths of time, yet still we are talking scarcely a few months. In all of these places and many more Paul left strong churches with mature believers in the congregations. He could establish elders in very little time after planting these new churches. This is something that we cannot do today in non-evangelized lands. Considering what we have talked about with establishing a true foundation of who God really is, it is profoundly worth our consideration to first ask the question, to whom did Paul minister?

To Whom Did Paul Minister?

Paul made it clear that he evangelized the Jew first then the Gentile.

- *For I am not ashamed of the gospel, because it is God's power for the salvation of everyone who believes, of the Jew first and of the Greek as well* (Romans 1:16 *ISV*).

But to evangelize the Jews, it's necessary for us to understand that there were basically three kinds of Jews:

A.) *The Natural Hebrew Jew*; Hebrew of Hebrews. These Jews could prove their genealogy from Abraham to their fathers. Paul of one such Jew. Most of them lived a large part of their lives in or around the Palestine of that day.

- *Are they Hebrews? So am I. Are they Israelis? So am I. Are they among Abraham's descendants? So am I* (II Corinthians 11:22 *ISV*).

- *circumcised on the eighth day, of the people of Israel, of the tribe of Benjamin, a Hebrew of Hebrews; as to the law, a Pharisee* (Philippians 3:5 *ESV*).

B.) *Greek or Hellenistic Jews*: These Jews were born in foreign countries. They carried a mixture of their adopted countries with the Hebrew Jewish culture. Many times they had Greek names as did the deacons chosen in Acts 6:1, 5, "*In those days, as the number of the disciples was growing larger and larger, a complaint was made by the Hellenistic Jews against the Hebraic Jews that their widows were being neglected in the daily distribution of food... This suggestion pleased the whole group. So they chose Stephen, a man full of faith and the Holy Spirit, Philip, Prochorus, Nicanor, Timon, Parmenas, and Nicolaus, a gentile convert to Judaism from Antioch".*

C.) *The Proselytes:* Gentiles converted to Judaism by way of circumcision.

- *Now when the congregation was broken up, many of the Jews and religious proselytes followed Paul and Barnabas: who, speaking to them, persuaded them to continue in the grace of God.*

Where Did Paul Minister?

You might notice that in every city that Paul entered to establish a new church, he went first, to the synagogues and there announced the Gospel. Paul was not talking to people that were ignorant of the Word of God. I would like to give you a few examples from his first missionary journey:

- *And when they were at Salamis, they preached the word of God in the synagogues of the Jews: and they had also John to their minister* (Acts 13:5 *KJV*).
- But when they departed from Perga, they came to Antioch in Pisidia, and went into the synagogue on the sabbath day, and sat down (Acts 13:14 *KJV*).
- *And it came to pass in Iconium, that they went both together into the synagogue of the Jews, and so spake, that a great multitude both of the Jews and also of the Greeks believed* (Acts 14:1 *KJV*).

In the cities where the Jewish population was too small to establish a synagogue, the local Jews that were there gathered every Sabbath day at the nearest riverbank. This is what they did in Psalms 137:1 while yet in Babylon. They gathered and remembered that they were still in exile and that Jerusalem was their true home.

- *By the rivers of Babylon, there we sat down, yea, we wept, when we remembered Zion.*

It was in Babylon that the concept of the synagogue was birthed. The very reason that they were found in Babylon was because the people had forgotten the Word of God. With the institution of the synagogues, the people now had centers of learning and a constant reminder of the principles of the Word of God. In this way they were instructed so they would not fall, once again, into idolatry and the paths that lead the people away from the truth of the Scriptures; this is why Paul knew exactly where to go to find any Jews on the Sabbath that might abide in Philippi.

- *And on the sabbath we went out of the city by a river side, where prayer was wont to be made; and we sat down, and spake unto the women which resorted thither* (Acts 16:13 *KJV*).

Three Kinds of Congregants

Seeing this, we now find it necessary to understand that there were basically three kinds of people were found in the synagogues: Jews... of course, the Proselytes and the God Fearers.

Wait a minute, Brother Prince. I've got that about the Jews and the proselytes being in the synagogues. But, what's up with this about *God Fearers?* What is a *God Fearer?* Good question, I'm glad that you asked.

To begin with, the God Fearers we Gentiles that had heard the Word of God, and were plainly convinced that it was the truth and the God of the Jews was the One and Only True God. The only problem that stood in their way was this question about circumcision. This is why there were far more female proselytes than male.

- *... Which was with the deputy of the country, Sergius Paulus, a prudent man; who called for Barnabas and Saul, and desired to hear the word of God* (Acts 13:7 *KJV*).

(This man feared God).

- *My brothers, descendants of Abraham's family, <u>and those among you who fear God</u>, it is to us that the message of this salvation has been sent* (Acts 13:26 ISV).

The Good News Version is historically correct here and states it a bit clearer:

- *My fellow Israelites, descendants of Abraham, and all Gentiles here who worship God: it is to us that this message of salvation has been sent!* (Acts 13:26 GNB).

This fact was a major feature in the majority of Paul's problems with the Jews. He came preaching salvation through faith in Jesus Christ without the need for circumcision. These Gentiles God Fearers heard this Word and rejoiced, and they converted in great numbers. In just about every synagogue, there were God Fearers.

I would like to mention a few famous God Fearers. Matthew 8:5-13 tells us of a centurion whose servant was sick. Luke 7:1-10 (*GNB*) tells us that this same centurion loved the Jews and even went as far as to built a synagogue to minister the Word of God:

- *When Jesus had finished saying all these things to the people, he went to Capernaum. A Roman officer there had a servant who was very dear to him; the man was sick and about to die. When* *the officer heard about Jesus, he sent some Jewish elders to ask him to come and heal his servant. They came to Jesus and begged him earnestly, "This man really deserves your help. <u>He loves our people and he himself built a synagogue for us.</u>" So Jesus went with them. He was not far from the house when the officer sent friends to tell him, "Sir, don't trouble yourself. I do not deserve to have you come into my house, neither do I consider myself worthy to come to you in person. Just give the order, and my servant will get well. I, too, am a man placed under the authority of superior officers, and I have soldiers under me. I order this one, 'Go!' and he goes; I order that one, 'Come!' and he comes; and I order my slave, 'Do this!' and he does it." Jesus was surprised when he heard this; he turned around and said to the crowd following him, "I tell you, I have never found faith like this, not even in Israel!" The messengers went back to the officer's house and found his servant well.*

The woman in Matthew 15:22:

- *A Canaanite woman who lived in that region came to him, "Son of David!" she cried out, "Have mercy on me, sir! My daughter has a demon and is in a terrible condition* (Matthew 15:22 *GNB*).

The centurion in Matthew 27:54 (*GNB*). It's interesting to notice that the first person to recognize that Jesus was the Son of God after His death was a Gentile.

- *When the army officer and the soldiers with him who were watching Jesus saw the earthquake and everything else that happened, they were terrified and said, "He really was the Son of God!"*.

Cornelius, another centurion is found in Acts 10 (*GNB*).

- *There was a man in Caesarea named Cornelius, who was a captain in the Roman army regiment called "The Italian Regiment."*

Gentiles were permitted to enter the synagogues, but they had to sit in a section that was partitioned off, separating them from the rest of the congregation. There were able to see and hear everything perfectly. Let's just say that this was a manifest form of religious and ethnic racism that sprouted from a misinterpretation of the admonition in the law about mixing with other nations lest they be contaminated by their gods.

- *You shall be holy and belong only to me, because I am the LORD and I am holy. I have set you apart from the other nations so that you would belong to me alone* (Leviticus 20:26 *GNB*).

Ephesians 2:11-15 (*ASV*) makes reference of this partition of separation that was in the synagogue because of the law.

- *Wherefore remember, that once ye, the Gentiles in the flesh, who are called Un-circumcision by that which is called Circumcision, in the flesh, made by hands; that ye were at that time separate from Christ, alienated from the commonwealth of Israel, and strangers from the covenants of the promise, having no hope and without God in the world. But now in Christ Jesus ye that once were far off are made nigh in the blood of Christ. For he is our peace, who made both one, <u>and brake down the middle wall of partition</u>, having abolished in the flesh the enmity, even the law of commandments contained in ordinances; that he might create in himself of the two one new man, so making peace.*

This same misapplication of the law was the reason that John Mark abandoned the first missionary journey, because Paul's ministry had a primary function of also reaching the Gentiles. This, naturally, included immersed interaction and involvement with Gentiles in their homes and social activities.

- *Paul and his companions sailed from Paphos and came to Perga, a city in Pamphylia, where John Mark left them and went back to Jerusalem* (Acts 13:13 *GNB*).

Unlike Saul of Tarsus (Paul) and Joseph of Cyprus (Barnabas) who had been raised around Gentiles and were accustomed to associating with them, Mark was raised in Palestine in a strictly Jewish culture and society. Remember, this happened shortly after Paul and Barnabas's encounter with governor of the island of Salamis, Sergius Paulus. At this point in time, the church had not fully accepted non-circumcised Gentile believers; that occurred in Acts 15. Mark was also unsure if they actually could be saved being uncircumcised – he yet considered them unclean and was sure that he too would be contaminated. This is also the reason that Paul refused to take him on the second missionary journey.

Was Luke a Jew?

Was Luke a Jew or a converted God Fearer? There are strong arguments for and against Luke's Jewishness. One of the evidences for him being a Gentile is that in Colossians 4:10-11, mentions Aristarchus, John Mark, who was Barnabas' nephew, (and now wholly accepted by Paul's ministry) and Jesus, also known as Justus, as the Jews that were with him at the time. He goes on to mention the Gentiles that were with him and then he mentions Luke… who was not mentioned with the Jews. Paul also does not include Tychicus and Onesimus, mentioned before in verses 7–9, as being Jews.

For me, the most compelling evidence for him being a Jew is Luke's intimate knowledge of temple practices. More than any other writer of the Gospels, Luke showed such an intimate knowledge of the temple when he described the announcement to Zacharias concerning the birth of John the Baptist. Luke described the rotating selection of the Levitical priests for service according to their families. He also described the position of the priest before the altar of incense, where the angel appeared to Zacharias (Luke 1:8–20). Though this information could have been obtained via interviews as did much of the other that makes comprises his marvelous Gospel, none of the other synoptics written by Jews offers such insights. I say this with special interest to the Gospel of Matthew, the Gospel written especially to the Jews.

This is a good argument, but I personally tend to incline towards the understanding that Luke was a Gentile from Troas. I believe that his letters to Theophilus, the Gospel of Luke – the Gospel to the Greeks, and the Book of Acts, were written with the mindset of one Greek Gentile, a converted God Fearer, to another Greek Gentile. Some believe that it was a code to all Greek believers – this also very possible. Nevertheless, it is still a God Fearer's message to other Gentile believers.

Now I brought this out to say that I believe that Luke was one of the most famous God Fearers that believed and received the hope of the Gospel under Paul's ministry when he passed through his city.

- *So <u>they</u> traveled right on through Mysia and went to Troas. That night Paul had a vision in which he saw a Macedonian standing and begging him, "Come over to Macedonia and help us!" As soon as Paul had this vision, we got ready to leave for Macedonia, because <u>we</u> decided that God had called us to preach the Good News to the people there. <u>We</u> left by ship from Troas and sailed* *straight across to Samothrace, and the next day to Neapolis* (Acts 16:8-11 *GNB*).

My point is this, unlike the situation in Acts 14:15-17, the Apostle was not talking to a bunch of people on the streets that were ignorant of the Word of God and had no knowledge of the One True God. Paul ministered over a base, albeit an incomplete base, of a consciousness of the holiness of God. This conscience was deeply inculcated in sincere and devout Jews. This awareness and the teachings that gave it birth were a great advantage that, under normal circumstances, we do not enjoy in our society. This makes evangelism and church planting on our streets and in our cities today a far cry from Paul's method of church planting. We are dealing with two radically different cultural and ambiental situations.

Don't You Understand That They Don't Understand?

My wife and I worked for decades as church planters on the mission field. We focused our efforts in virgin territory. We took the Gospel to people who live in cities, towns and villages where there was no testimony of the Gospel prior to our arrival. Sometimes I had to minister for six months to a year to the same people before they began to remotely understand the truth of God's true character and our state and obligation before Him. Sometimes it was a year before they finally understood enough to make an intelligent surrender to Christ – but, when they did, we have seen that they have been true and eternal decisions!

When I work with Muslims here in Europe (particularly in Spain), sometimes it takes a year for them to even understand that in a city of twenty-thousand inhabitants, there are perhaps one hundred Christians. This is not uncommon in Spain. They have been indoctrinated to believe that all Europeans and Westerners in over-all are Christians… just as we erroneously believe that all those who live in Arab countries are Muslims. Don't laugh, just about everybody in Europe and the American countries usually think the same thing. How many times have you had to convince a non-Christian that they were not really Christian? Millions of people in "evangelized" countries believe that they have the right to go to heaven and they do not even know who Jesus Christ really is. It's that they do not understand that they don't understand.

While I lived and ministered in such circumstances, I received numerous visits from churches and ministries that sent groups on short-term missions trips. These well enthusiastic and intentioned groups would go out to evangelize. The majority of the times they didn't speak the native tongue of the people that they intended to evangelize. At times, I would see that they would have some dude or another cornered. I knew or had at least seen them around town and know them to be genuine clowns… not the ha, ha, funny type of clowns, but the sinner that really thinks that he's a player because of the wine, women and wild lifestyle that seem to be their mantra. They would share a gospel of their four flaws, I mean laws, with this impious, incarnated demon while he sat there, smoked a cigarette and blew smoke into their faces. One of his pagan friends would pass by while they were talking to him and he would shout an expletive at him in greeting saying, "Dude, how ya' doin' you son… ¡_bk♞⇧Dek⬤҉Hb♎!!?!".

The foreign believer would simply see two friends greeting one another, smile and also greet the passer-by, and sincerely continue to share a gospel. After sharing for about five minutes with them, they would ask if they wanted to pray and receive Christ. Wow, in his understanding he thinks, who wouldn't? Why I carry him around on a cross on a chain around my neck every day! I even have a tattoo of him on my back! Wanna see it? These two are not only speaking two different languages physically, but spiritually. The young heathen snuffs out his cigarette, repeats the prayer of faith and *"receives Christ"*. Forty people *received Christ* that day and these beautiful and well-meaning brethren return to their homes rejoicing.

A week later I find this guy in the street, (he's never even stopped by the church yet) and he asks me, "Hey, who were those funny foreigners that were with you last week? What the heck were they talking about anyway? I knew they were talking something about the Bible and God and stuff, But I couldn't really make heads or tails of anything!" *Of course he couldn't understand anything!* But they had gone home convinced that they had evangelized the streets of "X" country. Do you really think that Christ or the Apostles evangelized the world like that? I tell you, Brothers and Sisters, doing these things we fall far short of the Biblical message and method.

CHAPTER 12
CONFESSING JESUS CHRIST AS LORD

————— ❧ —————

- *You call me Master and Lord and you say well: for so I am* (John 13:13 *DRB*).

Y ou might say, *"But, Brother, what you've said in the last two chapters just can't be. Doesn't the Bible say that all we have to do is confess Christ as Lord? If that man repeated the prayer and confessed Christ as Lord, how can you say that he didn't have an encounter with the Lord?"* Thank you for asking, because that's an excellent and fair question.

A King or an Elected Official

Concerning this confession, one of the problems that we have today is that we really don't know the meaning of the word "Lord". In American countries (and many others as well) we know not what it means to have a king and to live under the authority of a true monarchy. Even in many countries that still have kings; their kings rule under a constitutional monarchy and are more figureheads and beloved personalities than true sovereign authorities (I have lived in such a country for many years now).

Therefore, having a "kingdom" has little context in our world. We think of a king simply as some kind of political authority. This is why, today, a majority hold their faith or concept of Jesus (though it be a false concept) as if He were a prime minister, president, governor, mayor or even as a janitor to go around and clean up after them. They live as if He were an elected official that they could impeach and remove Him from power if they don't agree with his injunctions. Once they even tried to assassinate Him. That failed miserably- He ended up coming back alive and getting out of the grave after being dead for three days!

John Emerich Edward Dalberg Acton (what a name!), simply known as Lord Action, was a historian and moralist in the nineteenth century. In 1887, he wrote a letter to a Bishop Mandell Creighton in which he made a remark that to me is quite a quotable quote. He said, *"Power tends to corrupt, and absolute power corrupts absolutely. Great men are almost always bad men."*

A true king is one that holds absolute power in his hands. In almost all of the past civilizations, the kings of the people were often considered as demigods or deities of sorts. The people truly believed that they were gods who had authority to come and reign over them. Many times, they were just egotistical bullies or spoiled brats who couldn't read or write. Nevertheless, the power of life and death that they wielded brought the people to their knees and made them subservient. Their word was law; the people lived or died according to their whims. No human being should have that kind of authority! This is why God did not want Israel to have a king because He was already their King and He reigns over the universe with justice and love.

Speaking of Israel, watch out for Salomon—and he's one of the good guys! This young man was a genius, but he must have also had a temper[1]. So one of Israel's most powerful kings writes us about how life and death could hang on the thing thread of the king's mood.

- *The wrath of a king is as messengers of death: but a wise man will pacify it* (Proverbs 16:14 *KJV*).
- *In the light of the king's countenance is life; and his favour is as a cloud of the latter rain* (Proverbs 16:15 *KJV*).
- *The king's wrath is as the roaring of a lion; but his favour is as dew upon the grass* (Proverbs 19:12 *KJV*).
- *The terror of a king is like the growling of a lion; whoever provokes him to anger forfeits his life.* (Proverbs 20:2 *ESV*).
- *A king that sitteth in the throne of judgment scattereth away all evil with his eyes* (Proverbs 20:8 *KJV*).

This is why the Bible tells us to pray for kings (and those in power).

So when we speak of Jesus Christ as King, we have to receive the word *king* in the most radical sense of its definition and with all of its implications and potentials. Such is His authority and Lordship. In this, we can see that the Word of God is not just a *good idea* or some kind of suggestion for humanity. Christ is God, the King of kings and the Sovereign of the universe. The kings of this world shall hear the word, *"Abrek!"* shouted to them and in absolute terror; they shall bend their knees before Him.

How then, are we going to present Him to the world in such a way that we ask people if they would like to *receive Him* or not? Once again, consider the Scripture that says, *"Though God has overlooked those times of ignorance, he now commands everyone everywhere to repent"* (Acts 17:30 *ISV*). (Hey! He didn't say, *"Please* repent"!) The truth is that people do not receive Christ. In His infinite love and mercy, it is Christ, who receives *us*, the hopeless and condemned sinners. Dude, you do realize that you're talking about a King here, don't you?

He's A Lion And A Lamb

Imagine; some despot "general" in a conflicted third world country with his army and tanks. He comes up to the mud hut of a humble villager and demands that the owner present himself immediately. The villager leans out the window and shouts, "I don't want to! As a matter-of-fact, I have neither the time nor the desire to pay the least amount of attention to you! Get lost!" I assure you that after such an answer, there would not be a trace of the hut nor of its owner left in the wake of the army.

"But, Brother, this is different", you might say, "because Jesus is a King that reigns with love". Yes, but is this is why you think that you can treat Him however you want and escape unscathed? Do you actually believe that the thrice-holy God would tolerate such insubordination? Have you forgotten what happened to the angels and the antediluvian world – that is to say Noah's world or what happen to Sodom and Gomorrah?

- *For if God did not spare angels when they sinned, but threw them into the lowest hell and imprisoned them in chains of deepest darkness, holding them for judgment, And if he did not spare the ancient world but protected Noah, a righteous preacher, along with seven others when he brought the flood on the world of ungodly people. And if he condemned the cities of Sodom and Gomorrah and destroyed them by burning them to ashes, making them an example to ungodly people of what is going to happen to them* (II Peter 2:4-6 ISV).

There is no doubt that He is a King of love, but the same Bible says, *"...For our God is a consuming fire"* (Hebrews 12:29 *KJV*). This epistle also warns the laid-back sinners saying, *"For if we sin wilfully after that we have received the knowledge of the truth, there remaineth no more sacrifice for sins, But a certain fearful looking for of judgment and fiery indignation, which shall devour the adversaries"* (Hebrews 10:26-27 *KJV*).

The Lord Jesus Christ told the following story:

- *...A prince went to a distant country to be appointed king and then to return. He called ten of his servants and gave them ten coins. He told them, 'Invest this money until I come back.' But the citizens of his country hated him and sent a delegation to follow him and to announce, 'We don't want this man to rule over us!' "After he was appointed king, the prince came back. He ordered the servants to whom he had given the money to be called so he could find out what they had earned by investing. The first servant came and said, 'Sir, your coin has earned ten more coins.' The king told him, 'Well done, good servant! Because you have been trustworthy in a very small thing, take charge of ten cities.' "The second servant came and said, 'Your coin, sir, has earned five coins.' The king told him, 'You take charge of five cities.' "Then the other servant came and said, 'Sir, look! Here's your coin. I've kept it in a cloth for safekeeping because I was afraid of you. You are a hard man. You withdraw what you didn't deposit and harvest what you didn't plant.' The king told him, 'I will judge you by your own words, you evil servant! You knew, did you, that I was a hard man, and that I withdraw what I didn't deposit and harvest what I didn't plant? Then why didn't you put my money in the bank? When I returned, I could have collected it* *with interest.' "So the king told those standing nearby, 'Take the coin away from him and give it to the man who has the ten coins.' They answered him, 'Sir, he already has ten coins!' 'I tell you, to everyone who has something, more will be given, but from the person who has nothing, even what he has will be taken away. But as for these enemies of mine who didn't want me to be their king–bring them here and slaughter them in my presence!'* (Luke 19:12-27 *ISV*).

Okay, now that's scary! Don't you know that Jesus told this parable in reference to Himself? In this parable, He is the Prince and the kingdom that He came to receive is the one that He wants to establish in us. He wants to reign over us. Either we can submit to Him or we are counted as rebels.

The Prophesied Prophet

There is another thing that people forget about, and that is that Moses prophesied about Christ's coming in Deuteronomy 18:15. He repeats the prophecy in verse 18, but look at what Moses prophetically says right after the reiteration of the prognostication. Now remember, this is in reference to Jesus Christ:

* *I will raise them up a prophet out of the midst of their brethren like to thee: and I will put my words in his mouth, and he shall speak to them all that I shall command him. And he that will not hear his words, which he shall speak in my name, I will be the revenger* (Deuteronomy 18:18-19 *DRB*).

Roughly two thousand years after Moses' prophecy, Peter quotes the prophecy in Deuteronomy 18:18-19 and he interprets it this way,

- *For Moses truly said unto the fathers, A prophet shall the Lord your God raise up unto you of your brethren, like unto me; him shall ye hear in all things whatsoever he shall say unto you. And it shall come to pass, that every soul, which will not hear that prophet, shall be destroyed from among the people* (Acts 3:22-23 *KJV*).

The Good News Bible says, "*Anyone who does not obey that prophet shall be separated from God's people and destroyed.*" Wow! Is that sobering enough for you?

I Am The I Am That I Am

How easy it is to forget that the terrifying God that made the mountain shake with thunder and lightning, smoke and voices and the sound of trumpets, and shook the earth with His voice was the same humble carpenter from Nazareth. Jesus Christ was the one that spoke to Moses from the burning bush, He is the Great I AM (Exodus 3:14).

Believers have the promise of forgiveness when we repent. Never the less, we would be under some delusional impression if we think that God is obligated to forgive the sinner. When something is taken for granted, it is given little or no value and expectancy destroys gratefulness. But I don't think that Peter had that warped understanding of who God was or remotely thought that way when he rebuked Simon the warlock in Acts 8:22 (*KJV*), "*Repent therefore of this thy wickedness, and pray God, if perhaps the thought of thine heart may be forgiven thee*". The ISV goes a tab bit farther and says, "*if possible*" instead of "*if perhaps*".

Paul also exhorts us hold as precious the incredible mercy that God has had on us:

- *... do you think you will escape God's judgment? Or are you unaware of his rich kindness, forbearance, and patience, that it is God's kindness that is leading you to repent? But because of your stubborn and unrepentant heart you are reserving wrath for yourself on the day of wrath, when God's righteous judgment will be revealed* (Romans 2:3-5 *ISV*).

- *Consider, then, the kindness and severity of God: his severity toward those who fell, but God's kindness toward you—if you continue receiving his kindness. Otherwise, you too will be cut off* (Romans 11:22 *ISV*).

The Tale of a Man Named Cruz

I want to tell you about a man named Cruz (Cross) that might help to illustrate my following point. Back in the mid '80s I had a discipleship-training institute in the church I pastored in a certain country in Latin America. I had a group of about twenty young people who were ministerial aspirants in the school. One of the obligations that they had was to go out and evangelize house to house in the surrounding villages on Sunday afternoons.

On one occasion, they were in a village that was close to a heavily wooded area. The inhabitants of the village cautioned our young evangelists not to go near the wooded area because a man named Cruz lived and roamed those parts. Everyone warned saying, "If you go in there, Cruz will kill you!" Now, in that region where we worked, when they said, "someone is going to kill you", that meant ... *that someone was going to kill you!* They were not idle words. It turns out that this was a very dangerous wanted man. Counted in his victims was even an eight-year-old child. The federal police had a Wanted, Dead or Alive search out for him ... which mostly meant that they wanted him dead. Hearing this, most of the disciples said, "Got it, no problem, we're fine right here chatting with you nice folks." I said most of them … All but one acquiesced, and his name was Eusebio (nicknamed Chevo). He was our youngest disciple and a quiet lad of about fifteen year old at the time.

Chevo thought, Cruz is mine! I'm going after him to win him for Christ! So he left directly for the forest in search for him, but he figured that this wanted man would find him first. After a while, Cruz came out of hiding heavily armed and with a frightening weapon point at him with mortal intentions. Chevo showed him his hands and said that he only had a Bible with him. Cruz sized him up, and after hearing his intention to talk to him about Jesus, Cruz conceded and led him to a place where they could talk without being surprised. They shared a lengthy conversation in which Chevo talked to him about the righteousness of God and the corruption of man and the eternal judgment. Chevo asked him if he could return the following week accompanied by other young people from the discipleship school and Cruz surprisingly said yes.

For about two months, those in discipleship visited Cruz every Sunday sharing the power of the cross to redeem the truly repentant sinner and the joys of the glory of God in Christ Jesus. They all fell in love with Cruz and he opened himself more and more to the truth and power of the Gospel as they took him food and clothing. At last, they brought him to an absolute crossroad in which he had to choose between life and death, blessing and cursing. He knew that he had to make a decision for Christ and confessed to Chevo, "If I give my life to Christ, the federal police are going to kill me and I cannot defend myself!" He knew that if they found him they were going to shoot him on the spot. In that region, if a criminal was trapped in such circumstances, their saying was that they would always fall on a pillow; meaning that if they died, they would surly take at least one with them.

To this, Chevo answered him, "You have two choices before you.

- One: However you want to look at it, you will not die with gray hair. In the path that you have chosen to live without Christ, you will die violently – and then you will go to Hell.

- Two: *"Do not be afraid of those who kill the body but cannot kill the soul; rather be afraid of God, who can destroy both body and soul in hell"* (Matthew 10:28 *GNB*). Yet there is life and forgiveness in Christ. You will face Christ and be judged for your sins one way or another. It is better to die and rest, trusting God and knowing that you have repented of your sins. You will, surely die, but you will die and go to Heaven.

Cruz took a deep breath and while in profound thought said, "Fine then, I have made my decision. I recognize that Jesus Christ is the Lord and I surrender my life to Him. I understand that by doing this, I have signed my own death certificate". Three days later, the federal police found him, and Cruz threw down his weapons and died of at least thirty gunshot wounds while embracing, close to his heart, the Bible that our young people gave him. Even though Cruz died because of his past crimes, his sins were forgiven before God. He, in a very real sense, was a true witness for Christ, because it literally cost him his life to submit to the Lordship of Christ.

Who Is the Lord?

I was raised to address men that were my elders as *sir*. If asked something, and the answer was yes or no, the correct way to answer was, "Yes, sir" or "No, Sir". The word sir, comes from *sir* derives from the Middle French honorific title sire. The word, *messier*, gave rise to, *my lord*. In fact, the Old French *sieur* is itself a contraction of Seigneur meaning 'lord'. In Latin countries, it is not as masked as in Anglophone countries. They just come right out and say, *"Buenos días, Señor (Lord) Alberto"*. It is also a respectful term. In Spain, it is more common to say, "Don Alberto", which is the same thing because its etymological origin is from the Latin word *dominus* or lord, master. In fact, in Portuguese, an older language than Castilian, the term is *Dom*, as in *Dom Alberto*.

In English, we have the term *"mister"*. It sounds respectful and courteous–and it is. Nevertheless, the English word "Mister" comes from a sixteenth century variant of the old English original unaccented word "Master", or Lord. As you know, even today in the United Kingdom, when the Crown knights a person, they are henceforth known as "Sir John Doe". Of course, nobody today would greet Sir Paul McCartney, Sir Sean Connery, Sir Elton John or Sir Anthony Hopkins thinking they are their masters and owners with absolute authority over him or her ... well, some fans of theirs might; but that would just be weird.

All of that makes it so that today everybody wants to be lord. No problem. We even have landlords and slumlords ... hum, that can be a problem. As a-matter-of-fact, all of this is a problem. Because sadly enough the same is true with people's concept of Christ. Most that call Jesus Lord or think of themselves as Christians also do not consider Him to be their master or owner. This is because they do not understand the word, *Lord*.

This is why I think that many do not understand the importance of the Lordship of Jesus Christ. To understand this you must have a correct exegesis of the Scriptures. It is necessary to take into account various idiomatic and historical aspects so that we might come to correct conclusions about what certain verses are actually saying. We must take into consideration the context, the occasion, the receiving audience of the writing, the culture, and the people involved in the situation or subject together with the linguistic situation.

Are You a Witness?

With this in mind, let's examine the verses that we use to support our modern doctrine of "Confess Christ as Lord". First, I want to ask you a question. What did Christ mean when He said, *"But when the Holy Spirit comes upon you, you will be filled with power, and you will be witnesses for me in Jerusalem, in all of Judea and Samaria, and to the ends of the earth."* (Acts 1:8 *GNB*). Was He simply saying that we would be able to go out and talk to people about Jesus everywhere? I don't think so, because without the Lordship of Christ over our lives, if we try to do that, God would just say, *"... How dare you recite my statutes or speak about my covenant with your lips!"* (Psalms 50:16 *ISV*).

This is because, in Greek, the word, "witness" is the word, *"martus"* (μάρτυς), and it's translated *"witness"* twenty-nine times. The word implies, in a legal and historical sense, that one is an observer of a particular act or event. This word is used only twice with this particular inference. The most interesting rendering of the word is that it is the term most commonly used as martyr. In my opinion, this is the definition of the word that I find most adequate and in agreement to its original use in Acts 1:8. This definition carries a strong implication of a witness being one that is willing to give his life, with or without a violent end, for what they have seen or heard.

Paul calls Stephen "a witness" in Acts 22:20 saying, *"Even when the blood of your witness Stephen was being shed, I was standing there approving it and guarding the coats of those who were killing him"* (Acts 22:20 *ISV*). The King James says, *"And when the blood of thy martyr Stephen was shed, I also was standing by, and consenting unto his death, and kept the raiment of them that slew him"*. Brothers and Sisters, this is the same Greek word for witness that is used in Acts 1:8!

Now the interesting thing about Stephen is his name. It is a Greek name pronounced, *"Stephanos"*; it means, "a crown". We have many names in the Bible that are given to people, places and things, because at the time if the writing, they were known as such. But many times they were given those names after the fact of the even in which they were mentioned. For example, the use of the name *"Bethel"* in Genesis 12:8 and 13:3. This place actually did not receive the God-ordained name until Genesis 28:19, but when Moses wrote the account, everybody knew the place as Bethel – he just filled them in on what it was originally called later.

I believe that the same is true with Stephanos. What his name originally was is very probably not as important as the powerful role that he played in the history of the church as its first martyr; just as Barnabas is not generally known by his birth name of Joseph (Acts 4:36). Think about it, Jesus said, *"be thou faithful unto death, and I will give thee a crown of life"* (Revelation 2:10 *KJV*). His life was a graphic illustration of what it meant to be a true witness! Right after Jesus says this, three verses later, He mentions another faithful witness, Antipas, saying, *"I know where you live. Satan's throne is there. Yet you hold on to my name and have not denied your faith in me, even in the days of* <u>*Antipas, my faithful witness,*</u> *who was killed in your presence, where Satan lives"* (Revelation 2:13 *ISV*). The KJV says, *"… my faithful martyr…"*

Twice the Right

Does the Lord have the right to ask us to give up our lives for Him? (The only way that question even makes any sense is if you don't understand Lordship.) If you understand who Jesus Christ is and the significance of His divine titles, you know that the answer is unequivocally, *yes*, without a doubt! In the first place, He is our Creator. Being that as it is, this automatically makes Him our Master and Owner. After this, He has bought us to rescue us from Satan and from perdition. This gives Him a double irrefutable right to ask anything that He wants of us.

- *Forasmuch as ye know that ye were not redeemed with corruptible things, as silver and gold, from your vain conversation received by tradition from your fathers* (1 Peter 1:18 *KJV*).

This, by itself, gives Him all legal right to demand everything of us. You say it doesn't sound fair? Well, you would only say so because you don't know how lost you really were–either that or you're still lost and just don't know it, Hell is real, Brothers and Sisters! If Jesus is who He says that He is … and He is. Paul was right when He says, *"For our light affliction, which is but for a moment, worketh for us a far more exceeding and eternal weight of glory"* (II Corinthians 4:17 *KJV*).

- (Romans 8:18 *KJV*) *For I reckon that the sufferings of this present time are not worthy to be compared with the glory which shall be revealed in us.*

If it were just any man who would have asked Richard Ruler to give all of his material goods to the poor to follow him, it would have been a calamitously preposterous request. But Christ, being God Almighty in the flesh, was well within His rights when He, did not request, but commanded Richard to leave all and to follow Him. Why? As I said, because He is Lord.

Do You Like It?

So often people ask me if I like living in or going to all of the different places of the world where the Lord takes us. My honest answer is, "What does it matter if I like it or not? God has never asked me if I like it or not. It just so happens that happiness is not His highest purpose for us. It's not about us, but about Jesus. Do you remember that nifty, but true little cliché? (Hold that thought. I'm going to get back to it.)

Can you imagine God asking Paul, 'How'd you like Lystra?' or 'What do you think? Would you like to go to Philippi?' Where would you like to go?' The truth is, it just so happens that I love where God puts us, but only because God has placed or sent us there.' (Well… there have been a couple of places that I didn't like at all! Nevertheless, it still doesn't matter). Do I have preferences? Yes. Is that really important? No. What is important is if it's the will of God or not."

As I have said, the truth is that it's a bit difficult to answer that question because the answer, unintentionally, comes out harsh. It's not that I am trying to be difficult, but I have no other worthy answer to such a question. I suspect that people take me wrong because they probably do not understand or are not considering the Lordship of Christ. If Christ is truly the Lord of my life, what does what I want or like have to do with anything? Did the apostles or martyrs of the church want or like what happened to them? Did Joseph or any of the prophets like what happened to them? When does the Word of God begin to apply to our lives? When will we begin to take this seriously and not play church or religion?

One of the problems that arises because of our lack of knowledge of the Lordship of Christ, manifests itself when we pray, "Lord, show me you will". That is not a biblical prayer! That still puts you in control! It's like you're watching TV with the remote in your hand and if you don't like what you see, you just flip to something else. Jesus told us to pray, "*Thy kingdom come. Thy will be done in earth, as it is in heaven*" (Matthew 6:10 *KJV*). Now that's Lordship. There is no place there for your opinion. You're not asking God to show you something and give you the choice if you like it or not. Thy will be done is saying, "Here I am, Lord. Do with me whatever you and … and you don't have to ask my permission".

If you want the raw truth, believers, it's either this, or are they simply words when we say, "Lord, Lord?" God loves us, but doesn't care a flea's wing if you like it or not. This type of comment is harsh and conflictive to us because it contradicts our concept of God… the concept that permits us to live according to our whims and caprices.

Why do we feel that we have the right to be the spoiled children of the kingdom? Throughout history, beginning with our Brother Stephanos, how many followers have suffered horribly simply because they were servants of Christ? How many have sacrificed so much more than even the majority of us that have left all to take the Gospel to distant countries? I fear that with these modern attitudes, when we encounter, face to face, with faithful servants in eternity, we will bow our heads in shame. The Lord never asked them if they wanted to suffer or not.

Was Paul Kidnapped?

A great lie that we have believed today is touching the thought that the priority of God is our happiness. Hear me out; this is an incredibly erroneous concept that has been born due to the twisted gospel that is being announced today. The priority of God for His people, His subjects, is and has always been our obedience. Remember, He is King and we are His subjects, He is the Lord and we are the servants.

Many years ago, my family, about ten of those in our discipleship program and I were kidnapped and held hostage for about three days by some hit men from a drug cartel who had just been in a shootout in which several people were killed. While running from the federal police, three of them ran into our building and held us hostage for three days. The rest is a very interesting story. I will just briefly say that by the third day, we had led two of them to Christ and a day later, they were killed in an ambush.

Did you know that once Paul was also kidnapped? Paul went up to Jerusalem *"bound in the spirit"* (Acts 20:22). He was a yielded vessel, so God just came, tied him up and as he was dragging him away said, "How about a trip to Jerusalem?" In his own words, he said, *"And now, behold, I go bound in the spirit unto Jerusalem, not knowing the things that shall befall me there"*. The Lord didn't ask him if he wanted to go... because it didn't matter. Paul, and anyone who has really made a pact with the Lord, said, from the day that they submitted to the Lordship of Christ, "What you want for my life infinitely supersedes anything I might want." Paul understood the Lordship of Christ.

How "Kurios"

The Greek word for Lord is, "Kurios". It is derived from the word, *"kuros"* (supereminence). In the Bible, this word is defined: supreme, maximum in authority, owner, controller, one that holds the power of decision over another person or object; master. It is a title given to: God and the Messiah, and in political terminology: the sovereign, prince, boss, the Roman emperor; It is a title of honor that expresses respect and reverence that servants use to greet their masters. When God wanted all to call Jesus Christ Lord, He had all of this in mind.

It's interesting to note that the New Testament refers to Christ as Savior around twenty-three times while it refers to Him as Lord more than six hundred times[4]. Don't you think that this is a clear indication of how God wants us to see Jesus Christ? If this is so, how is it that most of the sermons that we hear of Christ speak of His ministry as Savior and not of Him as Lord? This is especially true of evangelistic sermons. In no way do I wish to give the impression that I am belittling His role as our Savior; without the Savior, we have nothing. What I want to do is to reclaim how indispensable it is to be submitted to His Lordship.

Zarlatry

Now, with this bit of linguistic background in mind, let's look at history. As mentioned, throughout history diverse civilizations have considered their monarchs as deities. Japan considered their emperor a god until as recently as the end of the Second World

War. This is why so many Japanese young men gladly gave their lives for him. The Russians held their tsars as the heirs of Caesars throne. As a matter of fact, tsar is Russian for Caesar, and, in a large sense, Caesar was considered a deity by the Romans. It was actually called, the Imperial cult. There existed a certified offer of what was known as *"cultus"* to an enthroned emperor. This recognized his office and rule as divinely accepted and constitutional. A deceased emperor that was esteemed worthy of the honor could be voted a state divinity by the senate and thus be exalted in what was called an act of divinization or *"apotheosis"*. This is really the same thing that the Catholic Church dose when someone is elevated to "sainthood" – even the process is similar. It is no wonder they call themselves "The Roman Catholic Church". In the Roman Empire, *"Apotheosis"* served to put moral, political and religious influences on imperial rulers and allowed seated Emperors to claim association with a revered pedigree of imperial divinities. Conveniently, unpopular or unworthy precursors were omitted.

The Case of the Philippian Jailer

In the days of the Early Church, the Roman Empire dominated a large part of the known world. To ensure their power, in every principal city of the Empire, minus Palestine, the Romans placed an image of Caesar. This practice was largely avoided in Palestine, with the exception of official government buildings and personal property of Roman officials. The Jews in the diaspora were also legally exempted from certain parts of this practice, for Judaism was a recognized religion by the Roman government.

Periodically, the local government officials would summon all of the subjects of the surrounding areas to the central plaza where they had the effigy. The officers took note as all came before the deified political figure and bowed their knee to confess that Caesar was Lord. Refusal to do so was heavily castigated and counted as tantamount to treason. Failing to submit to this edict was done with the price of blood because it was a way to isolate potential rebels. The Caesars were so protective of their Crown that they frequently slaughter their own family members to assure that their positions were secure and due homage was paid to them.

Being that Philippi was a principal city of Macedonia, a Roman colony; the Imperial Cult was officiated there. Philippi was a place that hosted an image of Caesar. The Philippian jailer knew full well what non-submission to Caesar meant, for surely he had cruelly punished many who did not bow the knee and confess Caesar as Lord. Look at what he did to Paul and Silas. Under Roman law, when a rebel was captured, his family often also suffered the same chastisement due the guilty individual. The penalty was almost always some form of death. If they didn't kill you, the Romans knew how to make you wish that you were dead, and let me tell you that almost dying is a real drag!

Therefore, when the Apostles said, "... *Believe on <u>the Lord Jesus Christ,</u> and thou shalt be saved, and thy house*" (Acts 16:31 *KJV*), to the Philippian jailer, they were, in essence, saying, "We invite you and your family to die with us for Jesus." Being Jews, Paul and Silas could have gotten out of the veneration of the image, but not the part about the confession of Caesar as Lord. But not the jailer or his family couldn't get out of any of it! What the jailer heard was, "*Believe* on the *Lord Jesus*_Christ, and thou shalt be *saved*, and *thy house*". For him, to be a believer was, in the purest sense, to be a witness, that is to say a martyr. Now, it's alright to make a dangerous decision for yourself, but who would make such a dangerous decision lightly knowing that you put the heads of your loved ones on the chopping block too? *"Believe in the Lord Jesus Christ"* for this man did not mean the same thing as it might to some dude walking down the street in today's cities.

The Value of the Confession of the Philippian Jailer

For this reason, Paul, addressing the Philippians, said,

- *Wherefore God also hath highly exalted him, and given him a name which is above every name: That at the name of Jesus every knee should bow, of things in heaven, and things in earth, and things under the earth* (Philippians 2:9-10 *KJV*).

He not only quoted an Old Testament verse that affirms that Jesus Christ is God; he quoted a Scripture that was a direct challenge to the Imperial Cult. Let's take a look at what Paul was quoting from Isaiah's prophetic writings:

- *Look unto me, and be ye saved, all the ends of the earth: for I am God, and there is none else. I have sworn by myself, the word is gone out of my mouth in righteousness, and shall not return, that unto me every knee shall bow, every tongue shall swear* (Isaiah 45:22-23 *KJV*).

Once again, here the GNV captures a clearer sense of this Scripture saying, "... *Everyone will come and kneel before me and vow to be loyal to me*".

Under these perilously threatening circumstances, they demanded that these people should bow the knee and confess that Jesus Christ was the Lord and the only true God. The people, to whom Paul ministered, lived under these conditions. Do we have anything in our society that demands such a life and death commitment because we confess Jesus as Lord? In most western countries, No! Therefore, the average "Joe" can't possibly mean the same thing by simply confessing that Jesus is Lord, nor can it have the same impact in his life without a deeper orientation of the Gospel.

The Confession of the Romans

The famous verses quoted to inspire people to confess Christ as Lord and affirm that they are saved are from Romans 10:9-10,

- *That if thou shalt confess with thy mouth the Lord Jesus, and shalt believe in thine heart that God hath raised him from the dead, thou shalt be saved. For with the heart man believeth unto righteousness; and with the mouth confession is made unto salvation* (Romans 10:9-10 *KJV*).

In order to understand that the confession of the Romans had a far greater price to pay than our present situation in western society, we simply have to think of who they were. THEY WERE ROMANS! They were in the very same city that Caesar was. We're talking about Rome, the city where the Coliseum was found. You know, the place where they eventually let the Christians go out and play with the lions! It was probably not far from their neighborhood. For crying out loud, the Catacombs exist today because they confessed Christ as Lord! They were acutely aware of the cost involved in confessing Christ as Lord. For the believers of the Early Church, confessing Jesus Christ as Lord was equivalent to being a *witness*; that is to say, a martyr. It was practically a death sentence in itself. Therefore, they clearly understood that this was a question of life or death. The cross wasn't a nice piece of jewelry for them, it was a reality.

The truth is that it's an insult to the shed blood of our brethren to compare our interpretation of these verses to what these beloved "witnesses for the Lord" had to go through to confess Christ. For the first believers the "trial of our faith" was if they could withstand deadly persecution or not. I personally think that Paul's thorn in the flesh was getting beat up and almost killed everywhere he went (II Corinthians 12:7-10 *ISV*) *"That is why I take such pleasure in weaknesses, insults, hardships, persecutions, and difficulties for the Messiah's sake, for when I am weak, then I am strong."*

Today there are many countries in which the persecution is as real and present as it was in biblical Times. In most western countries, we enjoy diverse forms and degrees of religious freedom. In some western countries, the opposition is political, problematical and oppressive. Oppression and certain forms of persecution can arise from families and certain sectors of society, but in the majority of the cases, these assaults are legally frowned upon and prosecuted by law. Other than that, it usually amounts to personal insults and being ostracized by friends and family. By contrast, for the Early Church, persecution was usually nothing short of death.

Nevertheless, in the west today, Christianity is presented, basically, as a way for people to escape their problems that, in their majority, are caused by their sins. For the believers of the Early Church, they were inviting the problems to come look for them when they confessed Christ as Lord. The *"trial of our faith"* today is mostly because of the abundance of our unbelief or self-centeredness. People "suffer" from "trials" like, "Why doesn't God make my problems go away?" or, "It's so hard to be a Christian because of all the temptations out there." Under these circumstances, the Christian life is only difficult if you love sin or self, more than you love God. If a person does not have in mind to die to his own flesh, it is in vain to tell him, *"And it shall come to pass, that whosoever shall call on the name of the Lord shall be saved" (Acts 2:21 KJV)*. It serves no purpose to call on the Lord if it is not with an attitude of total surrender and submission to His Will. Didn't the Lord Himself say, *"Why do you call me, 'Lord, Lord,' and yet don't do what I tell you?"* (Luke 6:46 *GNB*).

Chapter 13
Preaching Repentance from Dead Works

------ ∞ ------

- *Jesus looked at him and loved him. Then he told him, "You're missing one thing. Go and sell everything you own, give the money to the destitute, and you will have treasure in heaven. Then come back and follow me* (Mark 10:21 *ISV*).

Jesus Christ, being the Eternal Father according to Isaiah 9:6, always saw things from the eternal point of view. This is why He told Richie Ruler that he must separate himself from his riches or his riches would separate him from God and eternal life. Was it right for Him to ask such a thing of him? The Bible specifically says that it was a command born of divine love, the utmost and incomparable love of the universe. Surely, the Lord saw that the sin of avarice that Richie had would eventually lead him to misery, death and finally Hell itself.

All for the Love Of Money

- *But they that will be rich fall into temptation and a snare, and into many foolish and hurtful lusts, which drown men in destruction and perdition. For the love of money is the root of all evil: which while some coveted after, they have erred from the faith, and pierced themselves through with many sorrows* (II Timothy 6:9-10 *KJV*).

Many years ago, when we ministered in Latin America, I knew of a businessman who died in a fire in the building that housed his business. He had managed to escape, but when he was outside, he thought about the money he had in his safe and went back in to retrieve it. When they recovered his carbonized remains, they discovered that the money in the safe was in perfect condition. The worst part of it was that it was a miserable quantity to begin with. Worse still, two weeks later, the national currency suffered a debilitating devaluation and the amount that he died for could not have afforded him a new pair of socks! What in the world was he thinking! Did he think that his money could buy him life? This brings to mind another greedy man that Peter rebuked saying, *"May you and your money go to hell, for thinking that you can buy God's gift with money!"* (Acts 8:20 *GNB*). By the way, that's an excellent translation of this verse. The, *"go to hell"* part, is the same Greek word that is used in I Timothy 6:9 for "perdition".

I knew of a man, many years ago, who was the captain of the security guards for the Homeland Security building in Los Angeles. He made close to five thousand dollars a month; which was an excellent salary back then. One day he was caught stealing money from a lady's purse by the same security cameras that he controlled. It was a federal offense because it took place on federal property so He went to a federal prison. The dumbest part of this whole debacle was that the total amount that he robbed was about thirty dollars–from a poor lady who cleaned houses to feed her family! He lost his honor, his job, his house, his car and any respectable future he might have had-for thirty dollars!

One night a bunch of airheads stole a pick-up truck from an intimate friend of mine. They later found the vehicle abandoned by the side of the freeway with smoke coming from under the hood. It turned out that the thieves had broken into a house, but didn't find anything worth taking but a big heavy safe. It is fairly certain that taking the safe wasn't planned, because they couldn't get it open, so those geniuses decided to take the safe with them. There was just one detail; they didn't have a get-away car. So, here they are walking down the street carrying this huge safe between the two of them until they saw my friend's family four-door pickup. They hotwired it and off they went... until the smoke started to come out from under the hood. They abandoned the truck, but soon were found by the Highway Patrol walking down the freeway. The officer just stopped to see if they needed help for he had seen the abandoned and smoking pickup. Of course, their guilty consciences got the better of them and they ran. They were investigated, and they were subsequently arrested and convicted for breaking and entering and grand theft auto. It turns out that the safe was empty and the smoke that was coming from the engine of the truck was because, my friend's dad, an old-school gentleman from Mexico, always placed a blanket over the motor at night to keep it warm.

Here, I have given you only three, of the millions of mindless cases of lives that fell into ruin because of the love of money; and these are the lightweight cases! Things start out bad and go downhill from there. The most horrible crimes in history have been committed against individuals and entire nations for the love of money and the power money can bring. People either love money for power, or they love power so they can have money. Countless millions have perished with bloody deaths because of the love of money. Jesus Christ had every right to demand Mr. Rich to leave his avarice, because such a horrendous thing has no place among His true followers. It's not that it is a sin to be rich, but we are talking here about covetousness and the love of money.

- *For what shall it profit a man, if he shall gain the whole world, and lose his own soul?* (Mark 8:36 *KJV*).

Everything Is Ready

Jesus had prepared the heart of Mr. Ruler to receive the ultimatum of the Gospel. He had revealed the incomparable goodness of the father towards the sinner. He reminded him of the law and applied it to his life in the most practical way. Now his listener was ready to know what he should do to inherit eternal life. It was necessary to repent and to believe. By insisting that Richard sell all and give to the poor, the Lord was indicating the sin of covetousness that was in his heart. He had to turn his back to his earthly treasure in order to possess heavenly treasures. The Lord had placed His finger on the area where he had to begin his process of repentance.

This is the heart of true repentance. The New Testament word translated "repentance" is the Greek word "*metanoia*" which means "a change of mind and direction". For our covetous Mr. Ruler, a change of mind would translate into leaving his riches. Jesus was demanding that he change all of his priorities, revolutionize the philosophy of his life and turn his back on his soul's idol. Paul could say,

- *But all those things that I might count as profit I now reckon as loss for Christ's sake. Not only those things; I reckon everything as complete loss for the sake of what is so much more valuable, the knowledge of Christ Jesus my Lord. For his sake I have thrown everything away; I consider it all as mere garbage, so that I may gain Christ* (Philippians 3:7-8 *GNB*).

That which was highly appraised before his conversion, is now held in disdain by the apostle. He had experienced a change of heart and mind. He now knew, from personal experience, what repentance was.

Nice, But Worthless Words

What would you think if one fine morning I would come up to you and say, *"Faamunuia oi ele Auta"*? You might just want to answer, "Oh yeah? Well so's your mom!" But, that greeting simply means "God bless you" in Samoan.

The Bible says in I Corinthians 14 that when we speak in the presence of others, that we should speak in such a way that we are clearly understood by all. Everything should be done for the edification of the hearer.

- *Take such lifeless musical instruments as the flute or the harp—-how will anyone know the tune that is being played unless the notes are sounded distinctly? And if the one who plays the bugle does not sound a clear call, who will prepare for battle? In the same way, how will anyone understand what you are talking about if your message given in strange tongues is not clear? Your words will vanish in the air! There are many different languages in the world, yet none of them is without meaning. But if I do not know the language being spoken, those who use it will be foreigners to me and I will be a foreigner to them* (I Corinthians 14:7-11 *GNB*).

We Christians speak a language that non-Christians do not understand. At times, we think that they have understood us, but in reality, they haven't. It is normal that we would have a different language, because the truth is that we really are from another

Kingdom and we speak the tongue of our nation. It also happened during the earthly ministry of Christ that even His own disciples often did not understand His words or purposes.

However, the Bible says, *"Here we are, then, speaking for Christ, as though God himself were making his appeal through us. We plead on Christ's behalf: let God change you from enemies into his friends!"* (II Corinthians 5:20 *GNB*), or as it says in the KJV, *"Now then we are ambassadors for Christ ..."* An ambassador is a representative of his native country or kingdom and the national leader that sent him. It would be a backwards nation that would send an ambassador who didn't even speak their country's language. Being such our case, as ambassadors with the universe's most important message, must do as the apostle said, *"Seeing then that we have such hope, we use great plainness of speech"* (II Corinthians 3:12 *KJV*). This actually means that we should speak the truth with such frankness that it leaves no doubt about what we are talking. We must talk with intelligible words that communicate the message of our King.

Our ears have grown accustomed to hear sayings like, "Accept Jesus as your personal Savior". These words might sound precious to a Christian, but they are foreign and inadequate for the instruction of a raw sinner in the way of eternal life for they completely pass over all of the essential elements of the Gospel, principally repentance. This part of Evangelical preaching is quickly disappearing from the pulpits of our churches even though the New Testament is full of such preaching.

Life Assurance

When Jesus began His public ministry, His message was, *"... The time is fulfilled, and the kingdom of God is at hand: repent ye, and believe the gospel*" (Mark 1:15 *KJV*). When He encountered the Samaritan woman, His Gospel opened her eyes to her adultery. After time with Jesus, Zacchaeus turned from his thievery to become a philanthropist. Now He calls upon Richard Ruler to repent of his lust for material gain and prestige.

The apostles preached the same message. The men that knew Christ and sat at His feet for three years understood the Gospel. They went out and "... *preached that people should repent*" (Mark 6:12 *ISV*). On the day of Pentecost, Peter urged the stricken hearts saying, "... *Repent, and be baptized every one of you in the name of Jesus Christ for the remission of sins...*" (Acts 2:38 *KJV*). While he preached in the temple, after the healing of the lame man, the message of the Gospel was, "*Repent ye therefore, and turn again, that your sins may be blotted out, that so there may come seasons of refreshing from the presence of the Lord*" (Acts 3:19 *ASV*). Peter was unabashedly obeying the Great Commission of our Lord. The only account that gives us the doctrinal content of the commission that we were commanded to preach is Luke 24:46-47. In this passage, Jesus insists that "... *in his name the message about repentance and the forgiveness of sins must be preached to all nations, beginning in Jerusalem*" (Luke 24:46-47 *GNB*).

He Didn't Make Many Friends

Christ really didn't make many friends with His messages or ministry style and John the Baptist made even fewer. John called the people all kinds of reptiles and things. Still, both had something else in common concerning the content of their messages–repentance. Every time that the disciples saw large multitudes following them, Jesus went and "ruined" everything with His exigencies. He always ran the crowds off with conditions like,

- *... If anyone wants to come with me, he must deny himself, pick up his cross every day, and follow me continually, because whoever wants to save his life will lose it, but whoever loses his life for my sake will save it. What profit will a person have if he gains the whole world, but destroys himself or is lost?* (Luke 9:23-25 *ISV*)

or

- *In the same way, none of you can be my disciple unless he gives up all his possessions.* (Luke 14:33 *ISV*).

Today, the most popular pastors would give Jesus the kind suggestion to read Dale Carnegie's fine book on, *How to Win Friends and Influence People.* He would have been much more popular if He would have limited His discourses to subjects like, abundant life, joy, peace and other nice things that He was going to offer the people. But no, He had to go and start demanding all kinds of stringent conditions to fulfill in order to be one of His disciples.

A Little Missing Detail

Today people are correctly instructed to confess their sins and ask forgiveness, but many evangelists and pastors forget to tell sinners to repent. This is like, instead of having the "Great Commission", we have the "Great Omission". As a result, this misinformed generation thinks itself capable to continue in their old way of life and just have Jesus on the side, like a fire insurance policy for Judgment Day. Just imagine the salesperson on a used car lot with a thunderously loud colored sports coat on trying to sell that product: "What a deal! The treasures of Earth and Heaven! You can enjoy the pleasures of sin AND reap the benefits of eternal life all in one package! Who could refuse such a bargain?

Friend, the Old Testament never offered anything like that." (Well, neither does the New.)

- *By faith Moses, when he had grown up, refused to be called a son of Pharaoh's daughter, because he preferred being mistreated with God's people to enjoying the pleasures of sin for a short time. He thought that being insulted for the sake of the Messiah was of greater value than the treasures of Egypt, because he was looking ahead to his reward* (Hebrews 11:24-26 *ISV*).

Sadly, sinners have not been grieved or challenged, as was Mr. Ruler. They must understand that they have to abandon their life of sin in order to have eternal life, or with their eyes wide open, know full well that they have chosen to continue in sin, fully aware that they have chosen sin and death over righteousness and eternal life. It would be the cruelest of deceptions to think that you are going to heaven only to end up in hell. We must be as clear as Moses was in His declaration of truth when he said, *"I call heaven and earth to record this day against you, that I have set before you life and death, blessing and cursing: therefore choose life, that both thou and thy seed may live"* (Deuteronomy 30:19 *KJV*).

This forgotten little detail is the fulcrum of the promises of God in the Gospel. The Scriptures always couple true repentance with forgiveness of sins; they are almost inseparable. We might understand that natural sequence, but we cannot expect the sinners to have the same extension of comprehension. When Christ commissioned Paul, He told him that he was to go to the Gentiles, *"You are to open their eyes and turn them from the darkness to the light and from the power of Satan to God. So that through their faith in me they will have their sins forgiven and receive their place among God's chosen people"* (Acts 26:18 *GNB*).

The mere confession of sins is not enough. There must be clear evidence of a turning from darkness and Satan to a new walk in righteousness and transformation in the allegiances of the heart. Christ was saying to Richard, *"You cannot be a slave of two masters; you will hate one and love the other; you will be loyal to one and despise the other. You cannot serve both God and money"* (Matthew 6:24 *GNB*). We cannot deceive ourselves by thinking that God will save someone that continues to serve the world. To confess, "I have sinned because I have loved sin and the world", while harboring full intentions to continue down the same path is not repentance. To obtain eternal life, Mr. Rich had to determine to both confess and abandon his sin.

- *He that covereth his transgressions shall not prosper; but whoso confesseth and forsaketh them shall obtain mercy* (Proverbs 28:13 *JPS*).

Even though a contrite confession is an essential part of repentance, it is not the all of repentance. A transformed mind that gives the fruit of a definite turning from sin is the heart and soul of true repentance.

A Logical Conclusion

Nonetheless, it is still a wonder that repentance is not duly preached today. How can a person return to the One of whom they are ignorant? How can a sinner be freed from sin if they cannot see their sins? The righteousness of God's law has not been revealed to them to convict them of sin. You might easily lead a sinner to some sort of a guilty conscience because they feel like their life is about to go down with the Titanic. However, a majority of the grief is because things didn't work out for them as they desired, not because they are sorry that they ever sinned and defiled themselves before the presence of a holy God. As I said before, most criminals are sorry because they were caught and now face punishment. If they had gotten away with it, would they be equally as repentant? Probably not ... They'd probably be out bragging or partying in celebration.

Get your friends thinking about life after life and what's beyond the grave and you can always awaken the fear that what might await them is possibly not very good. Then if you throw in the suggestion that their imperfect lives are responsible for the impending threat that hangs over them, you will succeed in finding them open to "accepting" Jesus as the "personal liberator" from those undesirable consequences. Even the rich man in Luke 16:19, (let's go ahead and call him Richard Ruler's brother), when he found himself in the flames of Hell, had a great desire to support the Great Commission and the sending of missionaries. He wanted to send Lazarus to his father's house to preach to his five brothers. But what a bummer! He waited just a tad bit too late for the eternal and spiritual things of God to become so all-important to him (see Luke 16:27-28).

As I was saying, at this point you can't really call them to repentance. They lament the fact that they are in danger of going to Hell, but they are not yet truly conscious of the fact that they have personally violated the laws of a holy God. Of course, they see their sin as if it were just a big mistake, but that wasn't really their fault. "I'm only human," they might say. "In fact, nobody is perfect. I never harm anybody else. Honestly, I'm really not that bad.... You should see some of the things that my friends do! Wow! Why just the other night we were ..." – Wait a minute, Friend, your sins occasioned the death of Jesus Christ! He died for your sins!

That's not harming anybody else?–They do not yet understand that their sins are treason to the highest scale against the King of kings! At this point, their repentance is solely for themselves. This is not what God is talking about in Zechariah. Truly stricken sinners *"... shall look upon me whom they have pierced, and they shall mourn for him, as one mourneth for his only son, and shall be in bitterness for him, as one that is in bitterness for his firstborn"* (Zechariah 12:10 *KJV*).

Of Course

There is no doubt that Mr. Rich would have joyously received Jesus to get a free "get out of hell" card, sans repentance, that is offered with the gospel preached today. Of course he would give a token admittance to having sinned and was separated from the glory of God (even though he wouldn't be talking about the same thing that Paul mentioned in Romans 3:10-18). It would have been easy to receive eternal life with no commitment whatsoever. What he didn't want to do was to leave his greedy materialistic lifestyle to have eternal life; but that's is exactly what Jesus required of him to show the fruit of his repentance.

Churches are full of people that profess to be Christians but have never truly repented – nor do they even know what true repentance is; yet they want to have eternal life. People will crowd the altars or stand in line to "accept Jesus as their personal savior", yet have no concept of what *"selling all"* would mean when applied to their lives. No one has ever told them that there is a condition to fulfill in order to have the treasures in Heaven... that condition is repentance. As a result, the converts of this gospel are as worldly after their "decision" as they were before, because their decision was filtered through the sifter of repentance.

The Things We Say!

I get a blast out of oxymorons and redundancies! Most of the time we use them quite naturally. Here are a few: "act naturally", "a little pregnant", "altogether separate", "awfully good", "boneless ribs", "soft rock" and, one of my favorites, "there are no such things as absolutes". Here is one of my favorite redundancies, "He's a born- again Christian," as if there were any other kind. Do I have to remind anybody that Jesus said, *"I am telling you the truth: no one can see the Kingdom of God without being born again."* (John 3:3 *GNB*)?

The term *carnal Christian* is also oxymoronic. Some believe that Paul was speaking of carnal Christians, a clear oxymoron, in I Corinthians 3:1 when he said, *"And I, brethren, could not speak unto you as unto spiritual, but as unto carnal, even as unto babes in Christ."* The Greek word for carnal is *sarkikos*, which means: *temporal, animal, unregenerate,* and *carnal*. Wait! Did I just say, *unregenerated?* That simply means not born again. How, pray tell, are they going to be Christians if they are not born again? If we say that this is possible, then, beyond the shadow of a doubt, we are preaching another gospel.

- *We know that the person who has been born from God does not go on sinning. Rather, the Son of God protects them, and the evil one cannot harm them* (I John 5:18 *ISV*).

I Corinthians 3:1 Paul was saying that it was necessary to speak to them like they were still pagans, not even born again, or like they were baby Christians that understood little. He was not saying that babes in Christ were carnal. The Bible does not contradict itself… it contradicts us! If we are to interpret this verse to say that carnal Christians exist, then there is an evident contradiction to what Paul said in Romans 8:4-9 and 8:12-13.

- *That the righteousness of the law might be fulfilled in us, who walk not after the flesh, but after the Spirit. For they that are after the flesh do mind the things of the flesh; but they that are after the Spirit the things of the Spirit. For to be carnally minded is death; but to be spiritually minded is life and peace. Because the carnal mind is enmity against God: for it is not subject to the law of God, neither indeed can be. So then they that are in the flesh cannot please God. But ye are not in the flesh, but in the Spirit, if so be that the Spirit of God dwell in you. Now if any man have not the Spirit of Christ, he is none of his."... "Therefore, brethren, we are debtors, not to the flesh, to live after the flesh. For if ye live after the flesh, ye shall die: but if ye through the Spirit do mortify the deeds of the body, ye shall live.*

A New Kind of New Creature

Imagine going over to your friend's house, and there is some kind of "critter thing" sitting in a corner and giving off a dull green glowing vapor. It also has about five eyes, a forked tongue hanging out of its open mouth, scaly skin, horns running along its spine and six legs – two of them with hooves. When you ask him, "Dude! Where did you find the chupacabra? Is that your dog? What the heck happened to your dog, Man?" Your friend casually answers, "Oh nothing, he's okay. I just started to feed him some stuff that I find and bring home from the plant where I work. He likes it and it's cheaper to feed him that way." Oh, did I mention that the plant where your friend works is a nuclear plant?

In the same way, as a result of being fed this mutated gospel, we have the phenomenon of the formation of a new science-fiction-type beast called "the carnal Christian". In an attempt to explain this abnormality that is rapidly becoming the norm, it is said that they have accepted eternal life, but have not yet been able to leave their sin. They have permitted Jesus to be their savior, but they have not yet given Him their lives. Now, I really got to hand it to them, that is creative! So creative, in fact, that God didn't even think of creating something like that! Of course, it goes without saying that God knows nothing of this monstrosity known as being saved without having repented. Illegitimate children will never enter into the kingdom of God; all must be born again by faith toward God through Jesus Christ or Lord and repentance from dead works.

Three Kinds of People

What a lot of people don't understand, is that there are three kinds of people who hear the Gospel:

The careless sinner: He cares nothing for the things of God. He loves his sin and the here and now. Eat, drink and be merry–for tomorrow we die!

The convicted sinner: The Word of God has begun to burn in his soul; he knows that it's real and the truth. He even knows that the Christian life is correct, that church is good and probably attends faithfully. He knows that Christians are the children of God; he is almost in total agreement with it all. I likes it. He fears, or more accurately stated – is afraid of God. He is aware of everything and probably even speaks *Christianese*; But that doesn't mean that he is born again … because he is not.

The true convert: this person has experience the complete brokenness of his soul because they have heard the Word of God, have received it wholly and believed in their heart. This Word has

239

penetrated their soul, and the Spirit has driven them to the hatred of their sins, true repentance and the new birth.

- *For having sorrow in a godly way results in repentance that leads to salvation and leaves no regrets. But the sorrow of the world produces death. See what great earnestness godly sorrow has produced in you! How ready you are to clear yourselves, how indignant, how alarmed, how full of longing and enthusiasm, how eager to seek justice! In every way you have demonstrated that you are innocent in this matter* (I Corinthians 7:10-11 *ISV*).

In an attempt to repair defective evangelism, the church has adopted follow-up programs that are equally as defective. Said programs defend the doubtful conversion experiences by trying to convince the "converts" that they are saved when the Holy Spirit Himself has not given them the security of their salvation.

- *The Spirit himself testifies with our spirit that we are God's children* (Romans 8:16 *ISV*).

This is why confusion invades these poor souls when sincere counselors attempt to convince them with Scriptures of their salvation. Some argue that it is their duty to give them, or at least convince them of the security of their salvation. However, I vehemently present to you that that is not our job at all! That is strictly the work of the Holy Spirit, and if we insist on trying to do His work, we will convince people of a lie and provoke spiritual abortions. (I will enter into more details about this in chapter 16.) People think that because the hearers are sincerely interested in things of God and that they have repeated "The Prayer" that they are now Christians, but the work of regeneration has not taken place in their lives.

The Rudiments

- *Wherefore leaving the doctrine of the first principles of Christ, let us press on unto perfection; not laying again a foundation of repentance from dead works, and of faith toward God, of the teaching of baptisms, and of laying on of hands, and of resurrection of the dead, and of eternal judgment (ASV).*

This verse in, Hebrews 6:1-2, says that the doctrine of repentance from dead works is one of the foundational doctrines. In fact, it is the first principle in the list of indispensable teachings. Who is the person that thought that they had more authority than the Word of God to remove this doctrine? We have absolutely no right to reduce the requirements that God has place in order to enter His kingdom. Christ has not invented another gospel for the twenty-first century. Yet the sad truth is that this fundamental teaching has all but disappeared from the presentation of the modern gospel and has been replaced with an easy confession. If this is what has happened to the foundation, what is to become of the structure that is to be built thereupon? What shall be the end of those souls under its influence?

Paul testified publicly and from house to house about repentance towards God and faith in our Lord Jesus Christ.

- *I never shrank from telling you anything that would help you nor from teaching you publicly and from house to house. I testified to both Jews and Greeks about repentance to God and faith in our Lord Jesus (Acts 20:20-21 ISV).*

This was the central message when the Holy Spirit visited the church with His power. It is time to return to the preaching of repentance from dead works. The prodigal son could not return to his father while he yet embraced prostitutes and Mr. Rich could not enter Heaven embracing his riches and avarice. In the same way, men should be confronted with the ultimatum that Christ gave to Mr. Richard Ruler: Repent or perish at the hands of a Holy God whose laws you have transgressed and criminally despised. Cast your sins away from you as a despicable thing.

CHAPTER 14
FAITH IN THE SON OF GOD
(FAITH PART 1)

- *Jesus looked at him and loved him. Then he told him, "You're missing one thing. Go and sell everything you own, give the money to the destitute, and you will have treasure in heaven. Then come back and follow me* (Mark 10:21 *ISV*).

I saw an interview with Paul McCartney right before the death of his wife, Linda. This man really impressed me – I mean, apart from the fact that I was a crazy Beatles fan since 1963–he impressed me with his concept of family and other ideals that he personally espoused. One refreshing thing that he mentioned particularly caught my attention. He said, "In our twenty-eight years of marriage with Linda, we have only been separated a total of eleven days – and those because of unavoidable situations." He continued by saying that all should take into account that if they saw him, assume automatically that it was because his wife was also nearby. She, quite literally, was always with him.

In the same way, faith and repentance are inseparable. Where you find one, you will find that the other is not far away and in the heart of the true convert, the two have joined. True repentance can only be brought to pass in a life through faith.

Christ placed a choice before Richie just like He places a choice before each one of us. We cannot remain in the valley of decision, we must decide between Jesus Christ and the broad way that leads to Hell, going your own ways and thinking your own thoughts or receiving the mind of Christ. Mr. Ruler couldn't abandon his materialism because he lacked faith in the Son of God. His philosophy of life had established riches as a high priority on his scale of values. His way of thinking was built upon the admiration and desire for riches.

- *For they that are after the flesh do mind the things of the flesh; but they that are after the Spirit the things of the Spirit. For to be carnally minded is death; but to be spiritually minded is life and peace. Because the carnal mind is enmity against God: for it is not subject to the law of God, neither indeed can be (Romans 8:5-7 KJV).*

A Case of Mistaken Identity

I know of a case of a fine young man that traveled to another city to complete his university studies. A short while after he arrived, he was walking down the street when a man came up to him from behind and shot him point-blank in the back of the head while shouting, "I finally found you, you coward!" When he fell to the ground, his assailant saw his face and shouted horrified, "My God! What have I done? You're the wrong man!"

Many people think that they don't believe in God, when, in reality, what they do not believe in is their concept of God. The same is true for many of those who say that they do believe in God. They really don't believe in the God of the Bible but hold faith in their own, self-conceived concept of God. A person can have a very mistaken idea of another person and think a multitude of negative things about him or her. Yet when they get to know the person that they had perceived to be this malicious villain, they find that they almost missed the privilege of having them as one of their best friends. In the same way, people often say that they do not have faith in God when what they really don't have faith in is the caricature that they have made of God.

We All Have Faith

There is not one person on the face of the earth that does not have faith. Without faith, it is impossible to live cogently in this world. You, quite literally, would be a wide-eyed maniac in a straightjacket, locked away in a padded room somewhere, completely incapable of dealing to everyday life in this present world. It is impossible to fulfill common and menial day-to-day tasks – even something as simple as sitting in a chair, without the employment of faith. It is impossible to maintain any type of relationship, personal, social, business or otherwise, study any subject, be it science, history, mathematics, or read any book without faith. To me, anyone who says that they don't have any faith and go to restaurants, are hypocrites or are completely ignorant and have absolutely no idea of what they are talking about. This is why I say that unbelief is the true fountain of ignorance and in the best of cases only gives birth to pseudo-intellectualism. The Bible says many thing about this, but one verse in particular comes to mind:

- *... without faith it is impossible to please God, for whoever comes to him must believe that he exists and that he rewards those who diligently search for him* (Hebrews 11:6 *ISV*).

Being that we all have faith, what is it that becomes the great obstacle for humanity? This is where I would answer and say that it is found in the object (or objects) of our faith. Can the object of your faith offer a real remedy for the question of eternity that we all face? Misdirected faith will only conclude in our destruction. Some people want to believe in God, but their concept of God is so distorted that they have actually believed in something altogether different. Their faith ends up being a violation of the first commandment. As I said in chapter 11, to have a false concept of God is sin. How is it possible that the serpent managed to convince the woman to eat the fruit of the tree? She had allowed the devil to elaborate a false concept of God in her mind. It is from there that all of our problems have stemmed.

Make Us a god!

Let's take the case of the children of Israel. After they had been freed from four hundred years of cruel slavery in the midst of an idolatrous people, Israel found itself in the Sinai desert. Moses had gone up Mount Sinai to chat with God. Well, the prayer meeting lasted a tad bit longer than normal and forty days later the people began to mumble and grumble. "Hey", they said, "this Moses guy is eighty years old. He went up into that mountain forty days ago. He took no food or water.... Why heck, he didn't even take the granola-flavored manna bars I offered him! I think that the old guy went up there and died or something." For me, the most alarming thing about this situation is the comment that summed up the conclusion of the general populace.

- *When the people saw that Moses took a long time to come down the mountain, they gathered around Aaron and told him, "Come here and make us a god who will go before us, because, as for this fellow Moses who led us out of the land of Egypt, we don't know what has become of him* (Exodus 32:1 *ISV*).

Make us a god! This comment is indicative of a totally con-venience-seeking mentality completely willing to believe in gods made according to their own likes and whims. Instead of following the biblical account of the creation where God makes man in His image, what we have is man, making God in his image. The Greeks and the Nordics did the same thing with their concepts of the gods. These gods had no true ideas of morality, righteousness or injus-tice. They committed the same sins that the people who created them did. The only difference between the gods and humans was the powers that they possessed. Since the fall, mankind has always believed that power is god. This is why people seek power through money, fame, politics, witchcraft, and so forth. They simply want to be gods unto themselves.

Serious Aberrations of Faith

Paul, in his tremendous expose on atheism, agnosticism, pan-theism and polytheism along with other "isms" in Romans 1:18-32 (*ISV*), clarified the reason for these forms of rebellion; sin and aberrations of faith.

- *For God's wrath is being revealed from heaven against all the ungodliness and wickedness of those who in their wickedness suppress the truth. For what can be known about God is plain to them, because God himself has made it plain to them. For since the creation of the world God's invisible attributes—his eternal power and divine nature—have been understood and observed by what he made, so that people are without excuse. For although they knew God, they neither glorified him as God nor gave thanks to him. Instead, their thoughts turned to worth-less things, and their senseless hearts were darkened. Though claiming to be wise, they became fools and exchanged the glory of the immortal God for images that looked like mortal human beings, birds, four-footed animals, and reptiles. For this reason, God delivered them to sexual impurity as they followed the lusts of their hearts and dishonored their bodies with one another. They exchanged God's truth for a lie and worshipped and served the creation rather than the Creator, who is blessed forever. Amen. For this reason, God delivered them to degrading passions as their females exchanged their natural sexual function for one that is unnatural. In the same way, their males also abandoned their natural sexual function toward females and burned with lust toward one another. Males committed indecent acts with males, and received within themselves the appropriate penalty for their perversion. Furthermore, because they did not think it worthwhile to keep knowing God fully, God delivered them to degraded minds to perform acts that should not be done. They have become filled with every kind of wickedness, evil, greed, and depravity. They are full of envy, murder, quarreling, deceit, and viciousness. They are gossips, slanderers, God-haters, haughty, arrogant, boastful, inventors of evil, disobedient to their parents, foolish, faithless, heartless, and ruthless. Although they know God's just requirement—that those who practice such things deserve to die—they not only do these things but even applaud others who practice them.*

They Put Horns on God

In just about every home with pre-school aged children, you will usually find crazy looking drawings with alien-looking creatures labeled Mommy and Daddy hung on the fridge with magnets. Some parents glow with pride – other grin and bear it.

I love art. Fine paintings, photography, sculptor, music, in short, all that is fine art, I enjoy. One of my favorite artists is the famous painter and sculptor, Michelangelo. He is accredited for having elaborated some of the finest artistic works in history. The majority of his work focuses of biblical personalities. However, one in particular catches my attention; it's a sculpture he did of Moses. Michelangelo put horns on Moses! I don't know if he was secretly (or not so secretly) expressing his anger at Moses for hearing God on that Decalogue thing or not, but, really? Horns? I don't know, Mike … Anyway, if you ever go to Rome, you can see that sculpture of Moses with goat horns on his head. I wonder what Moses would have thought about that? I don't know, but I have a pretty good idea of what God thought about it when they put horns on Him!

Here's how the story goes … The children of Israel went and had a god made according to how they understood things. The Egyptians had all kinds of gods that looked like dogs, cats, cows, and a bunch of other animals. So, the children of Israel decided that that wasn't such a bad idea and said, "I want one of those!" What they did was worse than what Michelangelo did! They put hooves and horns on God! Anyway, it turns out that when man refuses to submit to the One True God and worship Him in Spirit and in truth, he will always make himself a god after his own imagination and likes; he doesn't even bother with image and likeness... too boring.

The major problem that people have with the God of the Bible is not the question of believing in the historical testimonies of the Bible, because if a person believes in God, this automatically precludes that anything is possible. The problem is found with God's moral dictates. For them, instead of repenting of their malicious ways, it is much easier to just reinvent God and turn Him into someone or something that exists according to their likes and dislikes and, in this way, gladly permit their favorite sins and lifestyles.

Heralds for the Antichrist

Satan has always tried to divert the worship, praise and honor that only God deserves so that he might be the final recipient. He has always coveted that which belongs only to God. This sinful and egocentric goal was what caused his fall and brought about the fall of man. Remember when he said, *"for God doth know that in the day ye eat thereof, then your eyes shall be opened, and ye shall be as God, knowing good and evil"* (Genesis 3:5 *JPS*).

This same attitude will facilitate the entrance of the Antichrist into the world. The Greek word *"anti"* (ἀντί) means, "instead or in the place of". The desire of the Antichrist will be to establish himself as God in the place of God. Paul explains the nature and goals of his overt motives warning us,

- *... not to be so quickly upset or alarmed when someone claims that we said, either by some spirit, conversation, or letter that the Day of the Lord has already come. Do not let anyone deceive you in any way, for it will not come unless the rebellion takes place first and the man of sin, who is destined for destruction, is revealed. He opposes and exalts himself above every so-called god and object of worship. As a result, he seats himself in the sanctuary of God and himself declares that he is God* (II Thessalonians 2:2-4 *ISV*).

The spirit of the Antichrist is already in the world convincing people that they are gods. People, today, have so much faith in the ideologies of the "New Age" teachings; which are not at all, new, but have been around since the Fall. The word on the street is, *"Have faith in yourself"*. Psalms 12:4 describes this mentality saying, *"... those who say, "By our tongues we will prevail; our lips belong to us. Who is master over us?""* The Bible, in recognition of this spirit as the spirit of the Antichrist, says, *"But every spirit who does not acknowledge Jesus is not from God. This is the spirit of the antichrist. You have heard that he is coming, and now he is already in the world"* (1 John 4:3 *ISV*).

I Believe In...

In Acts 5, we find that having a false concept of God cost Ananias and Sapphira their lives. Simon the warlock found himself severely rebuked for his false concept of God and it almost cost him his soul. Let me quit beating around the bush and get right to the point; every scandal and sin in the Bible from Adam to the Apocalypse is because of this equivocation. It is what I call "misplaced faith".

People place their faith in all kinds of things. They rest their faith in things like: themselves, other people, other people's opinion of them, politics, science, religion (be that orthodox religion or a cult), fame and wealth. They place their hopes in their job, profession, some noble "cause" such as, "we just have to save this rare species of cockroach and housefly because they're in danger of extinction", or any number of such useful ways to waste your life. I heard on the radio the other day that some dude was translating the New Testament into "Klingon"; you know, that famous extraterrestrial language spoken by 0.00000001 percent of the world's population ... (Yeah, there might be about sixty geeks out there that have actually learned to speak Klingon.) But, you never know, maybe one day we will be invaded by some bullies from another galaxy the just happen to speak Klingon and need to be evangelized. I read in a periodical about a guy had seen "Star Wars" six hundred times! When one of the actors of the movie was told of this, his only comment was, "Dude! Get a life!" (This particular actor had only watched the movie once.) Nevertheless, everybody is seeking a purpose, a cause and something in which to believe.

Clearly, one can dedicate their life to far more noble causes. Why just the other day I read about the famous Chilean cardiologist, Jorge Kaplan. In 1968, he carried out Latin America's third and the world's twenty-third heart transplant, which was his country's first successful heart transplant. He traveled worldwide giving seminars on cardiac and circulatory health. It was a noble cause and it was his life's defining purpose. Unfortunately and paradoxically, he died of massive coronary failure!

No matter what we do or hold as our outlining purpose in life, all things must be measured for their true value under the scrupulous light of eternity! What you theoretically believe or hold to be true might be a good thing. But the great question is the one that Mr. Richard Ruler had: "What must I do to inherit eternal life?" How you answer that question is what makes your faith and what you believe valid or invalid. By way of our choices and the decisions that we make in our lives, we manifest the evidence of the true object of our faith, if it is, in truth, Christ or the things and values of this world.

How do you measure the true value of any given thing – be it tangible or intangible. Is it measured by how much people are willing to pay for it? Can you measure it by that fact that people are willing to die for it? How can you know if something is truly valuable or not? I would present to you that the true measure of value of any given thing is *time*. In one year, or ten, or twenty or fifty or even one hundred years from now, just how valuable or important will that thing be to you that you are scrambling so much to hold on to now? What value will that thing hold for you on your deathbed? Outside of Christ, nothing holds eternal value.

- *For all that is in the world, the lust of the flesh, and the lust of the eyes, and the pride of life, is not of the Father, but is of the world. And the world passes away, and the lust thereof: but he that doeth the will of God abides forever."*[1] The entire world and its systems are summed up in the Bible as, *"Utterly pointless, says the Teacher, Absolutely pointless; everything is pointless* (Ecclesiastes 1:2 *ISV)*[2].

Faith Equals Obedience

Once again, it is necessary to clarify confused and erroneous concepts concerning faith. Faith is hearing and obeying the Word of God. In Hebrews 4, the words faith and obedience are synonymous.

- *For unto us was the gospel preached, as well as unto them: but the word preached did not profit them, not being mixed with faith in them that heard it. For we which have believed do enter into rest, as he said, as I have sworn in my wrath, if they shall enter into my rest: although the works were finished from the foundation of the world. For he spake in a certain place of the seventh day on this wise, And God did rest the seventh day from all his work,*

And in this place again, if they shall enter into my rest. Seeing therefore it remaineth that some must enter therein, and they to whom it was first preached entered not in because of unbelief (Hebrews 4:2-6 *KJV*).

A simple fact: The Hebrew words that we commonly as translate "faith" are ('êmûn - אמן), used once as "faith" but which we also see rendered as "faithful" and "truth". Also, with a more liberal swing to its meaning and usage is the word ('ĕmûnâh - אמונה), which too, is rendered as "faith" – one time, but is also used as, "steady, truth, office, faithfulness, faithfully, truly and stability". Therefore, we can conclude that the word "faith", as we understand the word, only appears two times in the Old Testament.[1] Notwithstanding, the entire eleventh chapter of Hebrews speaks of faith, using only Old Testament personalities. How did they demonstrate their faith if it were not through their obedience? James dedicated the second chapter of his epistle to the theme of the futility of saying that one has faith without the corresponding works that manifest it.

F–W = B–S

While traveling, my daughter Genesis found herself in an airport somewhere in Europe and saw a woman who had a beautiful dog on a leash. Up to that point, everything is nice and normal, but we all know that things can't stay that way; something has to get weird in order for things to continue being "normal". That's when she began to notice that this dog was atypically tranquil. As my daughter continued to peruse her magazine, she finally concluded that that dog *never* moved... at all! My daughter was overcome by her curiosity, so she approached the owner to ask about her "dog". The woman explained the animal had died several years ago, but it was such a beloved mascot that she could not imagine going on in life without her best friend by her side. My reaction is like, "Lady, maybe to need a hobby – like sucking your thumb or some other pastime… and while you're at it, get a live dog!" Now, I don't know about you, but in my mind, walking around with a dead animal on a leash is not quite the same thing as having a nice loving and faithful pet dog.

I don't know if James had something like this in mind (probably not) but it still reminds me of the verse where he says, *"For as the body without the spirit is dead, so faith without works is dead also"* (James 2:26 *KJV*). I can just imagine how unimpressed and bored that God is when we say that we believe in Him. James shows us the same boredom when he says, *"Do you believe that there is only one God? Good!* (Whoopee! Good for you.) *The demons also believe; and tremble with fear"* (James 2:19 GNB). The "demon" part really nails his sarcasm; a demon's faith is absolutely worthless. Nevertheless, they at least have the sense to tremble before God when humanity rambles on as if nothing is ever to become of their wayward impiety and arrogance.

Misplaced Faith

Is it possible to have misplaced faith even in the name of Jesus? Wow! Now that's a scary question! But, lamentably, yes, it is possible and let me explain. Just think about that question when you consider what Christ said.

- *When the Judgment Day comes; many will say to me, 'Lord, Lord! In your name we spoke God's message, by your name we drove out many demons and performed many miracles!' Then*

I will say to them, 'I never knew you. Get away from me, you wicked people!' (Matthew 7:22-23 *GNB*).

Just as a demon's faith is worthless, even though God was working through these people, it was to no avail for their own spiritual wellbeing. I believe that the reason for this is explained in Hebrews 4:2 (*ASV*): "*For we have heard the Good News, just as they did. They heard the message, but it did them no good, because when they heard it, they did not accept it with faith*". These mentioned here had a kind of faith; yet it wasn't the kind of faith that could save their souls. It was none other than misplaced faith. It was not a faith of obedience to the Word of God.

Do you recall those seven brothers in Acts 19:13-15 (*ASV*)?

- *But certain also of the strolling* (itinerant) *Jews, exorcists, took upon them to name over them that had the evil spirits the name of the Lord Jesus, saying, I adjure you by Jesus whom Paul preacheth. And there were seven sons of one Sceva, a Jew, a chief priest, who did this. And the evil spirit answered and said unto them, Jesus I know, and Paul I know, but who are ye?*

These guys were like some of the old-fashioned traveling faith-healing evangelists; only they were charlatans (I'll let you decide). Can you imagine those seven brothers running down the street hollering and screaming like a bunch of wimps, naked, beat-up, hair standing up and shooting out in all directions on their heads? Meanwhile, the demonized man goes calmly walking down the same street admiring his seven new suits – all seven which he happened to be wearing at that moment. Talk about misplaced faith!

Another Christ

Back to Richie Ruler: Christ didn't want him to have a mistaken idea concerning what this deal of eternal life was all about. He wanted to focus keenly on Richie's faith as well as the faith of those who witnessed the encounter. How did Jesus offer Himself to the guilty Mr. Ruler? Did He do so as a servant to his master? No, He demanded submission and obedience. In this way it was exceedingly clear in Richard's and the witnesses' minds that Christ was presenting Himself to them as their Master.

When you invite a sinner to "accept Christ", what kind of concept of Christ have you painted in their minds? One of a servant or one as the Lord? The difference between the two is as immense as the difference between the Creator and the creature. If you have engraved the image of Christ as a "Cosmic Busboy" or a god that exists to serve the whims and caprices of his creation, these people will not be believing in the God of the Bible. They might be invoking the name of Jesus, but it would be as if they were dialing and calling a wrong phone number. Let me tell you, many times someone is going to answer that call, but it's not going to be the person you think that you're talking to or with whom you want to talk.

What is going to happen is that the first time that this god does not fulfill one of their wishes (as if He were like a genie in a lamp), they will abandon him because, to them, their god has lied to them and failed them. The truth of the matter is that God never failed them, but misplaced faith in *their god* or *their false concept* of the True God has failed them. This is what I call, misplaced faith. People don't generally believe in God, they believe in their concept of God – that is to say, a god of their own creation.

Clear Demands

We hear Jesus' loving invitation to, *"come, follow me."* The Incarnate God has humbled Himself to come down and tenderly call the rebellious soul that loves money more than he loves Him. *"Come".* The invitation is given to the poor sinner that has fallen.

- *... into temptation and a snare, and into many foolish and hurtful lusts, which drown men in destruction and perdition. For the love of money is the root of all evil: which while some coveted after, they have erred from the faith, and pierced themselves through with many sorrows* (1 Timothy 6:9-10 *KJV*).

The Savior calls the transgressor of His law saying, *"Come. Believe in Me. Give me your mind, your love and your obedience."*

I have to say again that Jesus' invitation to Richard Ruler is antithetical to modern evangelism. More often than not, our sermons imply that Jesus is a personal savior that is only there to help people escape from their problems and perils. The picture that we often paint is one of a servant that is anxious and ready to help all those who simply submit a request for His aid to be their rescuer. Yet there is a silence when it comes to the fact that He is the Master that must be followed and the Lord that must be obeyed. In the Scriptures, the demands for those who desire to be disciples are clearly set forth from the beginning of the narrow way that leads to eternal life. It was never placed forth as a second step or an added consideration for those mature, on-fire believers. It's the prerequisite for entering in the strait gate.

Now, most assuredly, Christ is a very present help in times of trouble for all those who trust in Him. Nonetheless, He never hands out His saving grace to one that will not follow Him. If Christ would have said to Richard that he simply had to repeat a prayer and confess that He was Lord and to feel bad for not having lived a perfect life, without exacting from him faith, that is to say, obedience and repentance, we would be on point today. But, that is not what Christ did. If He would have assured the young Mr. Rich that He would give him heavenly riches and eternal life, even though he was not ready to surrender all of his wealth, it would have been inconsistent if not an open contradiction to the truth of all that He preached.

The sinner must know that Jesus will not be a Savior to anyone that refuses to follow Him as Lord. Christ would shun the twenty-first-century idea that the Lordship of Jesus over believers is optional in the Christian life. Christ will not be the Savior to those who refuse to follow Him as their Lord. Jesus' invitation for salvation is, *"come, follow me."* A practical recognition of Christ's Lordship, the surrender to His authority to follow Him. As I have said, to believe and to obey are ideas that are so parallel that the New Testament interchanges them. To believe is to obey. Without obedience, no one will see life. If you do not bow the knee before the scepter of Christ, you will not receive the benefits of the sacrifice of Christ.

Who's in Charge Here?

This man sincerely wanted eternal life and he would gladly have invited Jesus to enter his heart in order to receive it. However, Jesus did not wait for Richard to invite Him into his heart, because He has the keys to the Kingdom of Heaven and He will open those doors only to those who He deems apt to enter (Matthew 16:19). This concedes even less power of negotiation to the sinner, because after His resurrection, the Apostle John saw Jesus. Just look at John's reaction when he saw Him in His glory and hear what He said,

- *And when I saw him, I fell at his feet as dead. And he laid his right hand upon me, saying unto me, Fear not; I am the first and the last: I am he that liveth, and was dead; and, behold, I am alive for evermore, Amen; and have the keys of hell and of death* (Revelation 1:17-18 *KJV*).

So, seeing as Jesus has the keys of the Kingdom of Heaven and of death and hell, what kind of negotiating power does the sinner have? His entire fate is in the hands of the Son of God, "*I am Alpha and Omega, the beginning and the ending,... which is, and which was, and which is to come, the Almighty*" (Revelation 1:8 *KJV*). Are you getting this? Christ was offering Richard the terms of salvation: I will give you eternal life if you come and follow me. I will allow you to become my servant. Submit your mind to my teachings because I am the Great Prophet that was promised of old. Bend your knee to my commands because I am your King; these are the terms of the salvation that I offer. You take them as they are or remain outside of my Kingdom.

What's the Difference?

If Jesus would have been satisfied with an intellectual admission that He was the Savior, and the repetition of, "*The Prayer*", the New Testament would be a completely different book and Christianity would not be any different from Islam. In Islam, to become a Muslim, it is only necessary to confess and repeat a prayer that is quite literally the first verse of the Koran saying, "There is no god But Allah and Mohammed is his prophet." Aside from the names invoked, there is little difference between Islam and the prerequisite of modern evangelism. If that was the kind of Christianity that the Son of God offered to the world, John could not have written, *"If we say that we know him, but do not obey his commands, we are liars and there is no truth in us"* (1 John 2:4 *GNB*). Jesus' half-brother, James, would also have been in error when he wrote, *"Do you want proof, you foolish person, that faith without actions is worthless?"* (James 2:20 *ISV*).

The Selfish Seeker

- For all seek their own, not the things which are Jesus Christ's (Philippians 2:21 *KJV*).

Richie was caught completely by surprise by the fact that Christ had demands to be fulfilled in order to receive eternal life. It's like, everybody wants to go to heaven, but nobody wants to die! Well, in a way, that's quite normal. However, in this case, Christ was telling this young seeker to die to himself, something that He demands of all those who want to follow Him. Anyway, it turns out that for the majority of us, dying to self is a lot harder than dying physically – in this is manifested our selfishness and egocentrism.

I can prove to you that all marital problems are caused by selfishness. Proverbs 13:10 says, *"Only by pride cometh contention: but with the well advised is wisdom"* (*KJV*). This pride that brings contention also brings God's resistance. Look at what James says, *"... As the scripture says, God resists the proud, but gives grace to the humble."* (James 4:6 *GNB*). You want to be arrogant and always right in your marriage? It's because you're arrogant. All divorces – I'm saying that 100 percent of today's divorces–are the result of selfish actions. You can say the same thing about theft, rape, and drug addiction (be that with legal including alcohol or illegal drugs).

That also goes for any other problem that we can find evident in our world, be it poverty, war, disease or hunger. It all comes down to selfishness. Even the love of money is ultimately, selfishness. It is of little wonder that Christ would demand the death of our egotism.

The most despicable things occur when we try to cover our egocentrism with sheepskin and say that it's for the Lord. How many churches have been caught in scandals because ministers of the Gospel have been trapped in every sort of sin? It is easy to criticize preachers that have been caught in sin because everybody likes to make firewood out of fallen trees. It's just that the ministers are more visible as well as more responsible. But the sad thing is that it seems like church members malign ministers that have failed to fulfill their expectations, yet feel every right to continue to live their own lives in total self-centeredness. I should mention that there are as many bad witnesses amongst the members of the congregations as there are among the churches ministers. However, I will tell you why that is, and that the responsibility for a majority of the fault for this flaccidity falls principally on us, the ministers of the Gospel.

There Are Really Three Paths, Not Two

Looking at today's church you might be very inclined to think that the Bible promotes the existence of three paths in this life and not just two. You can always go down Broadway Boulevard. Why not? Most people do. But, you recognize that Broadway is only for the really bad people – the unrestrained sinners to whom nothing is off limits. Careless sinners that range from your loud-mouthed, macho womanizing beer-drinking lettered athlete, frat boy partying friend from your high school and college days to the serial killer. On Broadway are also the bad thieves that pull guns and break into homes and cars. You know, the really bad stuff. The congregation can steal the tithes and pirate videos and music-but only Christian music, not worldly music, why that would be sin to have that in your house. But, that's not the same thing as stealing from people or stores and stuff, that's different. Brother Prince you shouldn't be so legalistic!

Next is the narrow way. This is the path for pastors, missionaries, evangelists and other "servants of God". Oh, come on! You can't really expect everybody to serve God like they did in Bible days! Why that just wouldn't be practical! You have to be realistic, you can't be so heavenly minded that you're no earthly good, which I rarely find to be the problem. I usually find that people are so earthly minded that they are no heavenly good! Yet that is the standard that is promoted in the church by the hyperbolic exaltation of the spirituality of the clergy over the congregation – a division that was never meant to exist in this fashion in the New Testament church… but that's a subject for another book.

Finally, you have the medium road – it's like Goldilocks and baby bear's things: not too hot or cold, not too hard or soft, but just right. But Goldilocks would have been *busted* for breaking and entering and thrown in the can with the Broadway crowd! Yet that's the way it is with this third road. It's not too wide and not too narrow, but just right for everybody that doesn't want to fall into the other two categories. Nevertheless, Brothers and Sisters, this, in reality, is simply an extension of Broadway!

- *Question*: What is the difference between someone that says that they are a Christian yet lives a selfish life–and the selfish sinner?

- *Answer*: The religious egotist goes to church... and that's not even consistently true, sometime they don't even bother to show up there – and careless sinners might even think to show up Christmas, Mother's Day and Easter... or when there's food! Then, everybody shows up. Therefore, the real answer is: no difference at all!

Paul spoke of this problem several times in his letter to the Philippians. This church was very beloved by the Apostle and he warned them of spiritual plagues that he had seen in other places. These attitudes are foreign to Jesus Christ, and he can receive none that come to seek Him with such a mindset. Paul found it so difficult to find people fully submitted to the Lord to seek the good of others. I feel his pain as I read his words in Philippians 2:19-21.

- *But I trust in the Lord Jesus to send Timotheus shortly unto you, that I also may be of good comfort, when I know your state. For I have no man likeminded, who will naturally care for your state. <u>For all seek their own, not the things which are Jesus Christ's.</u>*

In Philippians 1:17, he even saw that some were trying to preach the Gospel with egotistical motives. That's what I was talking about when I said that some try to cover their egotism with sheepskin. I simply do not understand this! If you are going to live a slipshod lifestyle and simply seek pecuniary gain, leave the Gospel alone and go out and sell used cars or something! It's just plain evil to live like that and tell people that you are a Christian, and worse still to put yourself forth as a preacher! Do not muddy the waters for those sincere, thirsty lambs that might want to come in your wake and drink of that stream. Paul said, "*The others do not proclaim Christ sincerely, but from a spirit of selfish ambition...*" (Philippians 1:17 *GNB*).

Paul was continually faced with his demise. He lived under constant threat. He didn't want to die only because he had so much more to share with his beloved disciples. Not even his desire for life was about him, but rather, it was all about Jesus. The only thing he expected from this world was more rejection and suffering. (1:23-25) *"For I am in a strait betwixt two, having a desire to depart, and to be with Christ; which is far better: Nevertheless to abide in the flesh is more needful for you. And having this confidence, I know that I shall abide and continue with you all for your furtherance and joy of faith"* (Philippians 1:23-25 *KJV*).

Paul pointed out that egocentrism is contradictory to the person of Jesus Christ.

- *Don't do anything from selfish ambition or from a cheap desire to boast, but be humble toward one another, always considering others better than yourselves. And look out for one another's interests, not just for your own. The attitude you should have is the one that Christ Jesus had* (Philippians 2:3–5 GNB)..

If we seek first the benefits of the Kingdom of God, we will not be seeking the God of the Kingdom. Ironically, as a result will not have God, nor will we obtain the benefits or the Kingdom. Did not Jesus clearly say, *"Instead, be concerned above everything else with the Kingdom of God and with what he requires of you, and he will provide you with all these other things"* (Matthew 6:33 *GNB*)?

No Good Looking Girls In Our Church

When I was a new convert with the Jesus People back in Monterey, California (1971), I had close friend that was a Messianic Moroccan Jew, named Steve Stern, (now Dr. Steve Stern). He belonged to another Jesus People community across town. One day he said to me:

"You know what, Brother? I go to the most spiritual church in the area!"

"Oh yeah?" I replied, "Why do you think that?"

"Well," he continued, "It's just that there aren't any good looking girls in our church! They're all just plain ugly, and that's the sad truth! But here comes the spiritual part, our church is still full of guys and they are all seeking the Lord... I know that they are because they certainly didn't come to check out the chicks! Dude, I can guarantee you that if there's a guy there, he's there to seek the Lord!"

I know, I know, that's just messed up... but it's still funny... and true!

Anyway, perhaps we all might know somebody that started to come to church because of a girl and ended up have a true encounter with the Lord. What actually happened was that at some point in their journey, this person was confronted with the demands of Chris. The Holy Spirit revealed their spiritual wretchedness to them and they were finally broken before the Lord. Whatever the individual situation was for that person, they all had to release the ambitions and personal plans that they had held on to so tightly, and extend empty hands out to Christ seeking His mercy seeing only the profound need their soul had for Him and Him alone.

Following Shadows

The "eternal life" and "treasures in Heaven" that Richard ruler sought were only a part of the salvation that Christ came to bring. It was prophesied saying, "... *because he will save his people from their sins"* (Matthew 1:21). Though it is understood that salvation was for the spirit, soul and body, the Scriptures speak specifically of deliverance from sin. All of the other benefits are peripheral, and if a person focuses and seeks those fringe benefits, I fear that they will be seeking shadows and not seeking the One, who casts the shadow.

Someone might say, "But, Brother, if I follow that shadow, won't I end up where the Shadow Caster goes?" Well, that might be true only if you follow the shadow on a clear sunny day. With those ideal conditions, you should have no problem. But, what if bothersome things, like life and reality get in the way and night comes, or stormy and cloudy days are upon you and you can no longer see the shadow? They most certainly will come, and when they do, you will be lost and disoriented.

This is what happens to many that quit going to church. (I didn't say, *"They stopped following the Lord"*, because they most probably have never known Him.[1]) They were of those who followed the Lord's shadow when all of a sudden, a great tempest arose and everything crumbled around them. Christ knew that there would be people that would try to follow Him simply because there would be benefits. I believe that He had this in mind when He concluded the Sermon on the Mount in Matthew 7:24-27 (*GNB*).

- *So then, anyone who hears these words of mine and obeys* (believes) *them is like a wise man who built his house on rock. The rain poured down, the rivers flooded over, and the wind blew hard against that house. But it did not fall, because it was built on rock. But anyone who hears these words of mine and does not obey them is like a foolish man who built his house on sand. The*

rain poured down, the rivers flooded over, the wind blew hard
against that house, and it fell. And what a terrible fall that was!

All of this is classified as misplaced faith. Do you have true faith to follow the Lord? Brother, it is far more than a mere recognition of a series of historical facts. It is truly following Christ. How strange do these teachings sound to our people? We are accustomed to emotional sermons with little content or sermons that inform us just how much Jesus wants to serve us and help us to live our lives and go our merry ways.

A Decision

This is one of the reasons that around 1984, I decided to carry out "an experiment". At that time, I was ministering in Latin America and had been part of a team that formed a church that grew to over 1,000 people. Nevertheless, I was disillusioned with what I perceived as a lack of true fruit. So, I decided to move to a totally un-evangelized region of our country of residence at that time.

Few people are presented with the privilege of evangelizing virgin territory. Let me tell you that it is very, very difficult and at times life and death dangerous. To carry out this experiment, my family and I went through adventures that most people only see in the movies. Civil wars (an oxymoron), and drug cartels were rife and in vigor all around us. Going into that territory was like throwing rocks at a hornet's nest... Take my word from personal experience, you *do not* want to throw rocks at hornets nests-don't ask ...

Anyway, the people were completely ignorant of the Gospel, so I told myself, "I am going to completely empty myself of every-thing I have learned before this point of my life and ministry. The only thing I am going to try to preach and teach the unlearned are the messages that Christ preached. I'll put forth the demands of salvation just as He placed them in the Gospels. For me, that was radical, and I already told you that I was saved with the Jesus People. With us, radical was the norm! That being said, I also placed this prayer before the Lord, "God, I will not seek a big church nor multitudes. If you just give me five faithful men, I will dedicate myself to them in discipleship as Christ discipled those you gave to Him. I will ask of them all the things that He asked of His. I will treat the multitudes as Christ dealt with the multitudes that meandered aimlessly around Him. Afterwards I will simply wait and trust in you for the results."

In preparation, I spent at least six hours a day in prayer and intersession to break up the fallow ground. During that time, I read the entire Bible through several times as well as had a daily study-Bible meditation habit that covered at least ten chapters a day. I also had (and still have) a voracious personal reading discipline consuming, at one point, close to 300 books a year and reading four or five at a time. I simply wanted to see the results that Christ saw in the people of His day. If I failed, I failed and it was on me, but at least I would give it a try.

In about a year, I had a congregation of over 100 converted, broken, humbled and spiritually hungry people in the first congregation in that entire region. Our services were characterized with vibrant praise and worship and the relentless teaching of the Word. I was preaching in the streets and teaching in the services the demands of Christ over our lives just as I have been sharing in this book up to this point. The opposition was fierce and the persecution and ostracization of those faithful new believers was cruel. In spite of all of that, the hotter the fire of antagonism, the more on-fire these new believers became and the more that people came to Christ after having counted the cost of true discipleship (like William MacDonald teaches in his fine book).

My experiment lasted a total of five years and the number of these new believers continued to increase the entire time. In fact, I recently returned and was warmly greeted by welcoming crowds and many men of God that are now pastoring some of the more than 100 churches that are now spread across that region. So many teens, young adults and a large number of people that I didn't know, but knew me came out to greet me. They were people, or children of people, and in some cases even grandchildren of people that were in the crowds on the streets where I preach Jesus' hard callings and the things I am discussing in this book. Some of them were people that visited the church, and left deeply convicted and conflicted about their life's direction and later, surrendered wholeheartedly to Christ. They had fully understood the cost of the cross they were called to carry and now were faithfully serving Christ in the various churches or the region. I only know of a handful of people who were part of the church then are not following Christ today. However, I know of several hundred that heard the teachings and went away deeply convicted and surrendered to Christ later unbeknown to me.

We also saw countless spectacular and miraculous act of the Holy Spirit that, to me, were totally unexpected. I attribute these prodigious works to the fulfillment of Mark 16:17-18 (*DRB*), "*And these signs shall follow them that believe: In my name they shall cast out devils. They shall speak with new tongues. They shall take up serpents:*

and if they shall drink any deadly thing, it shall not hurt them. They shall lay their hand upon the sick: and they shall recover".

I personally, have never been particularly endowed with the power gifts. My wife moves in prophecy and praying for people to receive the Baptism in the Holy Spirit and healing. I pray and people get bored, but I teach and God moves. I'm a teacher, and I recognize my particular gift. During that time, I rarely laid hands on some to receive the Baptism in the Holy Spirit; the people began to receive it as I taught the Word without them understanding exactly what was happening to them. Many times the same thing happened with the healing of the sick. Before these experiences, if I would have been a cessationist and not believed that these marvels were for our day, after those years of revival, I would have had to change my entire theology and believe, as I do, that God is still doing the same awesome works that are found in His Word.

There was much violence all around us and I saw countless people killed; some right before my eyes. On several occasions, cartel hit men were hired and sent to the church to… let us just say, leave me "electrocardiographically disfuncional"[3]. The thing is they never counted on the Holy Spirit's presence in our services. While I led in praise and worship and taught the Word, the Holy Spirit would manifest Himself with power! They felt God's presence and it scared the devil out of them! They left the church running, ter-rified by what they had experienced and knowing that it was God. There were several similar incidents, but I found out about this one because two years later two of those cartel hit men surrendered to Christ and became members of the church.

We also had a large number of young people leave everything to prepare themselves for a life dedicated to preaching the Gospel in our discipleship-training institute. Many of those are faithful pastors today. Hundreds of people came to Christ in those five years and several churches were established throughout the region as missions of our church. Thousands more finally came to know what the Gospel was and what was required of them to come to Christ and have eternal life in towns and villages that previously had no knowledge of the Word of Life!

That's How It Happens When It Happens

My experience is not a unique and I know of others who have had results that are far more resplendent. Compared to some of these fellow laborers and friends of mine, I have little to say when I see the impressive fruit of their laborers. It just that this is a personal experience I can share with you. It's not something that God did with somebody else. I witnessed the conviction of sin and repentance that came over the people because of the exposition of the law and the Lordship of Christ. That's the only reason I have shared these testimonies. I have hundreds more.

Without a doubt, there was a variety of other elements that influenced this wonderfully fruitful harvest. Clearly, the Holy Spirit prepared the hearts and minds of the people. Without Him, nothing would have been accomplished. Nevertheless, I believe that a great part of this is a direct result of the faith in the Son of God that was born when the seed of the Word of God, exegetically expounded, was sown in their hearts in a practical way as I have been explaining. I share this experience because I discovered that the teachings of Christ, as He taught them would either give birth to true faith or chase insincere people away.

CHAPTER 15
SUFFERING FOR THE CROSS
(FAITH — PART 2)

—⚬⚬⚬—

- Those who do not carry their own cross and come after me cannot be my disciples (Luke 14:27 GNB).

I read once where three Christian athletes were in a race with about seven or eight other runners and one of the Christians ended up winning. In the post-race interview, the brother that won said that the Lord had helped him to win the race. The other two believers looked at each other and said, "Hey, what's the Lord got against us?"

Purified by Fire

Sometimes we Christians in the western hemisphere really think that we are God's favorite children. At least we sometimes express ourselves that way. At times, it even comes out in some of our doctrines. In this, we can see that our thoughts concerning persecution are that God would never let something like that happen to His children. If that's the case, why have so many millions of faithful believers had to give their lives in a bloody holocaust? I'll give a lesser-known example from the twentieth century:

Did you know that the word *"genocide"* was coined specifically to describe what we now call the, *"Armenian Genocide"*? In 1915, 1.5 million Armenian Christian civilians were slaughtered. The majority of Armenian diaspora communities were founded as a result of this carnage. Our beloved and departed Brother, Demos Shakarian and his family were a part of that diaspora as mentioned in his marvelous book, *The Happiest People on Earth*. In addition, also summarily executed by the same Ottoman government were a large number of other Christian ethnic groups such as the Assyrians and Greeks. True that it wasn't only Christians that were massacred during that time, but no Christians were exempted – they were eliminated automatically and unforgivably.

Today in Sudan, North Korea, and Malaysia, our brethren are suffering horribly simply because they will not refuse to be followers of our Lord Jesus Christ. Theirs is a faith that has been refined seven times in the furnace of affliction. It would do us well to know what they preach to their congregations in the face of such situations.

The reason I bring up persecution again is that it is necessary to understand that if, in truth, the faith that we are imparting to our hearers by way of our messages is capable of withstanding such bloody crossroads. As a result of the plastic gospel that we have today, the faith of many of our congregants cannot withstand everyday adversities that even pagans suffer. Okay, to be fair with this next question, I am fully aware that all hypothetical situations automatically exclude God's divine intervention. So I will only ask what you honestly think; could a majority of these pampered western Christians praise God in the midst of such death and fire? Bear with me, for we have the obligation to know if we are preaching a western, culturally and ideologically acceptable gospel that is foreign to the reality of the Eternal Gospel of Jesus Christ.

The Reality of Our Faith

On one occasion I was conversing with another believer who could not believe that God would ever ask His children to go through the tribulation and I said, "It's a reality of life in this world. Things can change in a matter of hours and all of a sudden, we are enemies of the State because we are believers. It would not be the first time in history to occur if this happened. Your faith, or lack thereof, could cost you your life or your eternal destiny!" Shocked, he replied, "Come on, Brother! Don't confuse me with the facts. They scare me." Like it or not, we must face the facts and search the Scriptures to see if we have believed a fabrication of our western (pop) gospel or the Eternal Gospel that Christ preached and entrusted to the first-century church.

I like to talk about positive testimonies, because they edifying and encouraging. Most of the time it's not worth it to speak of negative things because they always seem to come without being invited. Yet we cannot be like the proverbial ostrich, with its head stuck in the sand seeking refuge from danger. In reality, of you have chosen to preach the true faith in the Son of God, the enemy will attack as if he had an invitation to do so. If you can't take my word for it, you only need to read what happened to Christ because of His teachings. I'm speaking of His opposition before He went to the cross. Another tremendous example is the life of Paul. How many thing did this brother suffer because he preached the Gospel?

If you preach as clearly as Christ did, soon people will look at you as if you were the villain of the movie. Another thing that will come are the negative results for those who have believed the Word that you have preached. Almost all of the churches mentioned in Revelation 2 were suffering persecution.

- To the church of the Ephesians it was written, "*You are patient, you have suffered for my sake, and you have not given up*" (Revelation 2:3 *GNB*).
- To the church of Smyrna it was prophesied, "*Don't be afraid of what you are going to suffer. Look! The devil is going to throw some of you into prison so that you may be tested. For ten days you will undergo suffering. Be faithful until death, and I will give you the victor's crown of life*" (Revelation 2:10 *ISV*).
- To the church of Pergamum it was written, "*I know where you live. Satan's throne is there. Yet you hold on to my name and have not denied your faith in me, even in the days of Antipas, my faithful witness, who was killed in your presence, where Satan lives*" (Revelation 2:13 *ISV*).

The Offense of the Cross or Just Looking for a Fight?

Now, please bear with me and at least, hear me out while I illustrate my points. I'm going to rant a bit, but my intention is for the true global advance of the Gospel and not any other agenda.

Now there are two types of offenses: The first kind is *offenses of the flesh*. These are things that destroy more advances of the Kingdom than any other thing, and should be avoided at all costs. These offenses are usually the fruit of ignorance, immaturity, and sin.

The second kind are *offences of the cross*. If we are walking in the truth of the Gospel, these offenses are inevitable. The person who is offended by the cross is one who disagrees and says this it isn't so and claims to be wiser that Christ, the apostles, and millions of surrendered saints. I reiterate, we do not seek problems, much less do we seek to offend.

Just Who Said It Was So?

Christians offend people today, not because of the Gospel, but for our lack of wisdom. This is an offense of the flesh. We go around picking fights about things that have nothing to do with us. For example, today we rage because the church says that the world is changing the definition of marriage. But tell me, *since when does the world define anything for the church?* It does not now and never has. The *Bible defines everything* for the church.

To me, this just manifests the metaphor that the church is like a ship at sea. No problem with the ship being in the water. The problems begin when the water gets in the ship! When the world's definition of something that it knows nothing about bothers us so much that we feel persecuted, we have accepted the world as part of the church. Even when the world uses the same words as many Christians, it was still not talking about the same thing!

Jesus, Paul, and the Government

How would the western church have ever survived behind the Iron Curtain in Rumania, Russia, North Korea, or under Islam in so many other countries? With its present brainwashed western mentality the church feels that the government is its friend and owes them something. This is quite the contrary to believers under Rome and just about the rest of the world throughout history. This church would not survive!

It is interesting that both Jesus and Paul ministered under the very governments that ordered their deaths and they knew that they would be killed by them. The Roman government was also fiercely pro-gay. Quite a few of its Emperors were themselves gay. Yet we never hear them, ever, preach or talk against them!

They even tried to provoke Jesus to rail against the government and He wisely refused saying,

- *Tell us, then, what do you think? Is it against our Law to pay taxes to the Roman Emperor, or not?" Jesus, however, was aware of their evil plan, and so he said, "You hypocrites! Why are you trying to trap me? Show me the coin for paying the tax!" They brought him the coin, and he asked them, "Whose face and name are these?" "The Emperor's," they answered. So Jesus said to them, "Well, then, pay to the Emperor what belongs to the Emperor, and pay to God what belongs to God." When they heard this, they were amazed; and they left him and went away* (Matthew 22:17-22 *GNB*).

Paul was even more forward in his hands off policy on the government. Look at what he said to the Roman believers who were suffering under Caesar,

- *Every person must be subject to the governing authorities, for no authority exists except by God's permission. The existing authorities have been established by God, so that whoever resists the authorities opposes what God has established, and those who resist will bring judgment on themselves. For the authorities are not a terror to good conduct, but to bad. Would you like to live without being afraid of the authorities? Then do what is right, and you will receive their approval. For they are God's servants, working for your good. But if you do what is wrong, you should be afraid, for it is not without reason that they bear the sword. Indeed, they are God's servants to administer punishment to anyone who does wrong* (Romans 13:1-4 *ISV*).

I could care less what the government determines; it never decides what the church believes or decrees. It is neither our friend nor our enemy. To befriend it is like having a pet Tasmanian devil or python or something. Our lot is to just pray for their lost souls-and the whole lot of them are lost! The world can believe whatever it wants. It's the world! The people in the world want gay marriage; our shouting about it is not going to stop them… As I said, it is the world.

I agree, we do not marry gays. However, many of us believers, for biblical reasons, also don't marry divorced people. We claim that the world has changed the definition of marriage, but many in the the church changed it long before the world voiced its twisted opinion. By defending such frivolous acceptance of divorce and second nuptials for any reason, the church espoused the same warped concept of marriage as the world by our own making, and now we complain that they want to change it. It is simply the reaping of the fruit of our own making. This is a reiteration, for I have already explained about how our distorted concept of the Gospel has ruined our marriage testimony before the world in Chapter 3.

Now, About those Gays…

Whenever that New Testament speaks of gays, the author is talking to the church – not to the world. Clearly, it is not an acceptable behavior for the believer along with a long list of other unacceptable lifestyles. That is something that we can deal with in the same way that we would deal with an adulterer, fornicator or an addict who comes to the church. We have picked an offense that has nothing to do with the cross. Doesn't anybody remember what Paul said about this?

- *In the letter that I wrote you I told you not to associate with immoral people. Now I did not mean pagans who are immoral or greedy or are thieves, or who worship idols. To avoid them you would have to get out of the world completely. What I meant was that you should not associate with a person who calls himself a believer but is immoral or greedy or worships idols or is a slanderer or a drunkard or a thief. Don't even sit down to eat with such a person* (1 Corinthians 5:9-11 *GNB*).

Paul is talking to the church and not to the world!

Non-condemnation is not approval nor agreement with; it's simply non-condemnation. How are we to win the sinner if we spend our time, not leaving them convicted by the ministry of the Holy Spirit and the Word, but condemning them by spewing our vitriol and hatred? I wouldn't be attracted, would you? When my wife and I married, interracial marriage was still illegal in 17 states (mid-1970s). My own denomination published articles against it as unbiblical and I was even set aside for a few years. I would never have wanted to go to a church that condemned me for my marriage. Up until the late 1970s the Mormons didn't even believe that Blacks could be saved because they were cursed; that's why they were Black. You think I wanted to be Mormon? I am embarrassed to tell you just how recent it has been since my denomination or Christians in general have kind of started to change their erroneous ideas on race ... and many still haven't. It's a farce and a shame and it's a sheepskin over a curse.

Let's Take the Pill for Instance...

A generation ago, back in the 1960s... *yeah, yeah, yeah, I'm old enough to remember that.* Don't interrupt me, kid. Anyway, Protestants griped, big time, against the Catholics because they wanted "the pill". (It's strange that no one remembers that now.)

Well, we got the pill, but the Catholics complained and warned saying that it was just another form of abortion. So now, it is popular because Evangelicals pushed it. It's accepted by the world mainly because it was an agenda that we pushed and pushed hard to get accepted. That pill was just the forerunner of what we now have. Now the world wants to make the pill available for everyone, and we complain; but I say it's just inane and the fruit of our own doing for getting involved with things that do not concern us and truly being about our Father's business. Many of the problems that western churches have are summed up by the verse:

- *He that passeth by, and meddleth with strife belonging not to him, is like one that taketh a dog by the ears* (Proverbs 26:17 *KJV*).

It's Not the Cross

The fights that the church picks are carnally offensive and today merely carry out somebody's political agenda. They are not the Gospel and any persecution that they might incur are not because of the Gospel but are simply offences of the flesh. As far as the offence of the cross is concerned, it's quite the contrary. For the Gospel we preach is inoffensive to the societies of this world. Nevertheless, the Gospel of Christ convicted of sin or offended the whole world.

- *"... **Behold, I lay in Zion a stone of stumbling and a rock of offence: And he that believeth on him shall not be put to shame"** (**Romans 9:33** ASV).

It is hard for me to believe that Paul would have had many followers if he would have preached today's gospel. With all of the things that he suffered, I don't think that he had Antonio Banderas' good looks. (I don't know, maybe that's why he never married ...

Just messin' with you.) Anyway, imagine that they just dragged him out from underneath a pile of rocks because they had just stoned him for of the sermon that he preached. They are still stitching and wrapping him up, and all of a sudden he comes out with, "Accept Jesus, he'll make you happy and solve all of your problems."

I seriously doubt that that's how it went down, but he did manage to encourage them in the faith. Look what it does say,

- *Some Jews came from Antioch in Pisidia and from Iconium; they won the crowds over to their side, stoned Paul and dragged him out of the town, thinking that he was dead. But when the believers gathered around him, he got up and went back into the town. The next day he and Barnabas went to Derbe. Paul and Barnabas preached the Good News in Derbe and won many disciples. Then they went back to Lystra, to Iconium, and on to Antioch in Pisidia. They strengthened the believers and encouraged them to remain true to the faith. "We must pass through many troubles to enter the Kingdom of God," they taught* (Acts 14:19-22 *GNB*).

Now that's having faith in God and it's the kind of faith that God seeks! Today, people say that they arn't going back to the church because the pastor preached about tithes or some brother didn't greet them with a smile or a plethora of other insignificant reasons that people come up with. People think that having a headache is a trial and it's difficult to believe in God with so many "problems".

When Christ said to His disciples, *"These things I have spoken unto you, that in me ye might have peace. In the world ye shall have tribulation: but be of good cheer; I have overcome the world"* (John 16:33 *KJV*), He was talking about the coming persecutions that His followers were going to endure. Look at whom He was directing

His words. He was talking to His disciples. He wasn't talking about the things that we say today that are our tribulations: a marriage on the rocks, a rebellious child, troubled finances and the like. The majority of our problems are the results of our sin or lack of good judgment. Just consider the fact that all of His disciples, except for John, suffered martyrdom. They had the grave necessity to know that they had the promise of His peace and presence through everything that was coming.

Faith and Spiritual Warfare

It is true that Christ helps us in our daily struggles. Once again, that is a fringe benefit of unconditional total submission. But, if we are involved with our own lives in such a way that our prayers and all of our worries are all about us, and all of our problems are about things of this world, it's a great indication that we are living for ourselves and not for Christ and His Kingdom. This is the fruit of modern preaching and teaching. It inspires and encourages this kind of mentality. The results are a church that believes that the struggle that they have with their own sins is what spiritual warfare is all about.

The Bible teaches us that spiritual warfare is a heated battle against the powers of evil to snatch souls from the fire despising the garments stained by sin. Paul urged us to,

- *... be strong in the Lord, and in the power of his might. Put on the whole armour of God, that ye may be able to stand against the wiles of the devil. For we wrestle not against flesh and blood, but against principalities, against powers, against the rulers of the darkness of this world, against spiritual wickedness in high places. Wherefore take unto you the whole armour of God, that*

ye may be able to withstand in the evil day, and having done all,
to stand (Ephesians 6:10-13 *KJV*).

This battle begins in the spiritual realm and spills over into the physical. This war is quite literally battle of life and death. For Paul and the other apostles, as well as for countless thousands more since then, this bellicose encounter is much more than just an interesting subject. Demons are fighting to maintain their dominion over the souls of individuals as well as over entire nations as is mentioned in Daniel 10. All of this is much bigger than your struggle with sin and lack of self-control. These are serious problems when it comes to your authority over the powers of darkness. But, spiritual warfare is never simply about the matter of your personal sins, but about the eternal souls of the children of men that have never heard the truth.

Faith in Times of Adversity

The Bible says, "*If you are weak in a crisis, you are weak indeed*" (Proverbs 24:10 *GNB*), or as the *KJV* says, "*If thou faint in the day of adversity, thy strength is small*". God exhorted Jeremiah with the deeply impressive words saying, "*If thou hast run with the footmen, and they have wearied thee, then how canst thou contend with horses? and if in the land of peace, wherein thou trustedst, they wearied thee, then how wilt thou do in the swelling of Jordan?*" (Jeremiah 12:5 *KJV*). Wow!

This cowardice in the face of adversity is the reason that we don't have multiplied thousands on the mission field. Life is difficult in foreign countries and one can suffer multiple adversities and conflicts-yeah, as if something like that could never happen to those who don't go. Nevertheless, we have been taught the idea that God owes us a comfortable life without hindrances. True faith is manifested under fire. If, with these comparably small things the faith of so many in our churches is weakened, do they really have faith at all? Let a wave of persecution fall over the western church as it did to our New Testament brothers and we will see how many truly have faith. Having faith in the Son of God is much more than intellectual recognition of the existence of God and becoming a member of a church.

Look at Paul's faith. When Brother Ananias taught him those first days after his conversion, he told him that the Lord had said, *"For I am going to show him how much he must suffer for my name's sake"* (Acts 9:16 *ISV*). Paul received those words with resolved encouragement. He did not fear or get discouraged or say, "Suffering? Who said anything about signing up for suffering? As a matter of fact, I don't like pain because it hurts!" Why? Because he was braver than others were? No, but it was because he had true faith. Brothers and Sisters, this kind of faith is the work of the Holy Spirit.

My Own Experience

Please permit me to share briefly a few of the experiences that I have had in my ministry. I have no other way to continue talking about this subject without qualifying myself with credential worthy of the theme. For several years, we lived and ministered in a region in Latin America where the cartels grew and trafficked drugs. I evangelized mountain villages and people surrendered their lives to Christ. As a natural result, they set fire to their crops of drugs and planted corn. When that happened, I made some serious enemies with the cartels. In fact, at that time, they sold the drugs in the United States to finance their wars in Central America with American dollars. They held no qualms about killing some preacher.

For this reason, I have been trapped in ambushes and shot at from rooftops. Several hit men have been sent to eliminate me. I have been on five death lists – everybody else on those lists died the very week the lists were released. Once I was knocked out by a punch in the jaw that left me with a dislocated jaw for at least six months (That's actually a story that is quite funny, in retrospect, that is …) I have had my ribs broken by punches. I have had knives and guns placed under chin and on the side of my head numerous times. More than once, I have had people bust through the doors of my house with guns at the ready.

I have smelled so much death in tropical heat that my olfactory nerves learned to separate the sugar released by a decomposing body from the putrescine and cadaverine; which are the toxic, foul-smelling gasses we commonly associate with death. When that happens, and you literally understand the term, "sickeningly-sweet," then you know you've smelled too much death. The list goes on and just gets better and better. I heard so much gunfire, that at night, when I heard gunfire, I could tell, by the sound, if the bullet went into the air, hit a wall (and what kind of wall – brick or adobe), if it hit a tree or if someone just got shot – it makes a slightly different sound. All of this and the half has not been told.

I went through all of this with my family and I am not going to sit here and say that I went through those years with the courage of James Bond. No, in fact, I suffered many years of PTSD. There was absolutely nothing heroic about any of this. I was just doing what I had to do, to get done what needed to be done (Luke 17:10). I just want you to know that when I speak of such things, I am not merely speaking of theories. Some of my disciples and I have actually seen and smelled as much death and violence as some combat veterans-that includes having people die in your arms. My disciple Eusebio (Chevo) served as a missionary during the Liberian civil war. I went to spend time with him during his service there. None of these things happened to me because of personal problems, but because we were taking the Gospel where it was most needed.

What? Are You Going Or Staying?

Christ said that to be His disciple, it was necessary for us to consider well what we were going to do and to count the cost (Luke 14:28). Jesus' treatment of those who said that they wanted to follow Him was to tell them what to expect. To one eager man, Jesus said, "*...Foxes have holes and birds have nests, but the Son of Man has no place to rest*" (Matthew 8:20 *ISV*). It was as if He was saying, "*I will not deceive you. I am not offering you the end of your hard times or a bed of roses – if it were so, you would still have to know that even roses have thorns. I will not have you try to follow me under false pretexts. The road that you will have to choose is difficult and uphill. There will be storms along the way. There will be mountains of difficulty to climb and valleys of humiliation to cross. This is why I have symbolized it as carrying your cross, to show you the personal demands of a true disciple. I want you to come, but come with your eyes open, fully aware of the price that there is to pay.*"

Though unintentional, deception characterizes many modern invitations to Christ. People are reminded that they are sad, lonely discouraged and failing at life. Life is just a burden for them and problems have left them feeling claustrophobic because they are closing in around them on all sides and the future only offers a dark threat. Then the sinners are invited to come to Christ because He can change all of that and will put a smile upon their faces.

It's as if Jesus were presented as a cosmic psychologist who will fix all of your problems in one session on the sofa of His office. There is no setting forth of the demands of Christ and don't even think about mentioning some of Christ's words, like when He said, "... *If anyone wants to come with me, he must deny himself, pick up his cross every day, and follow me continually, because whoever wants to save his life will lose it, but whoever loses his life for my sake will save it*" (Luke 9:23-24 *ISV*). "Hey, don't worry about that now, we'll explain that later," we tell them. We don't want to scare them off. Go ahead and scare them off, for if they can be scared away, they never really drew near. Jesus scared the people off every time there was a multitude or He felt that they were following Him with ulterior and carnal motives. Let's look at a few of those examples:

- *But he turned, and said unto Peter, Get thee behind me, Satan: thou art an offence unto me: for thou savourest not the things that be of God, but those who be of men* (Matthew 16:23 *KJV*).
- *Jesus replied to them, "Truly, I tell all of you with certainty, you are looking for me, not because you saw signs, but because you ate the loaves and were completely satisfied* (John 6:26 *ISV*).
- *Many of his followers heard this and said, "This teaching is too hard. Who can listen to it?"* (John 6:60 *GNB*).
- *Because of this, many of Jesus' followers turned back and would not go with him anymore. So he asked the twelve disciples, "And you–would you also like to leave?" Simon Peter answered him, "Lord, to whom would we go? You have the words that give eternal life* (John 6:66-68 *GNB*).

Now, with these examples, Jesus spoke hard truths to the people. Yet He never worried about it nor begged the people not to go if they abandoned Him. He knew that if they did abandon Him it was because they had no faith in Him. If they had no faith, it was because the Father had not given them to Him. They had not yet experienced His work of grace.

- *All that the Father giveth to me shall come to me: and him that cometh to me, I will not cast out* (John 6:37 *DRB*).
- *He replied, "Every plant that my heavenly Father did not plant will be pulled up by the roots* (Matthew 15:13 *ISV*).

Our obligation is to preach the whole truth that Jesus Christ preached. It is not really our job to "save people". Saving people is God's part of our call to obey and announce His Word.

You're in the Army Now!

It's not surprising that many of those who "go to the altar" to prove this remedy that solves all problems of the modern gospel seldom remain in church. Their reaction is somewhat like that of a young military recruit. Perhaps he had dreamed of becoming a soldier since childhood. He was feeling his rebellious hormones and was tired of being under his parent's authority – he wanted his liberty, so he decided to join the army. (Yeah, how'd that work out for your plans of not being under somebody's authority and your precious freedom?)

The recruiter painted a very promising picture. You're going to see the world, Young Man! Then he explained about honor and fortune, job training and security. However, the first day at the induction center, the young man arrives feeling new emotions in his chest and with his eyes wide open in fascination with everything he is seeing. "Ah," he sighs, "my dreams are finally a reality. Now I can be my own man." Yeah, reality is about to stare him in the eye… quite literally. All of a sudden, he hears the incredibly loud and booming voice of his drill sergeant directly in front of him shouting, "HEY! *YOU WITH THE FACE!* WHAT ARE YOU DOIN'! WHO GAVE YOU PERMISSION TO THINK AND DAYDREAM ON MY TIME? YOU MISSING YOUR MAMA OR SOMETHING? WELL GET OVER IT OR SUCK YOUR THUMB AND COPE! GET OVER THERE AND GET IN LINE! NOW! WHAT'S THE MATTER WITH YOU, LADY; YOU GOT LEAD EN THOSE FEET? RUN! DO YOU WANT ME TO TEACH YOU HOW? THAT CAN, AND WILL BE ARRANGED! OH, A WISE GUY, EH! DROP AND GIVE ME 20!"

That is when he starts to understand that the reality of his new situation is nothing like it was explained to him-or at least nothing of how he was led to understand it. He begins to realize that his new norm is getting up before sunrise, long marches, hard work and the ineffable blood, fire and terror of the battlefield. That is always the truth of this situation; he was just lead to think that it would be different.

A few days after confessing Christ, the new "convert" wakes up to discover that their problems have only been multiplied. (Of course, we knew that the devil was going to make sure that happened all along.) Their family is giving them grief because of this "new religion" that they think is some kind of cult. Their friends have abandoned them and the workplace has become a torture chamber. The honeymoon is suddenly over. Now he thinks that he has been lied to by the evangelist and stops going to the church services. We've all seen it. In this we find a perfect example of the absence of true faith in the Son of God. There was never a true understanding of what the cost of discipleship really is. In this, also is fulfilled the Scripture that says, *"For we have heard the Good News, just as they did. They heard the message, but it did them no good, because when they heard it, they did not accept it with faith"* (Hebrews 4:2 *GNB*).

None of that ever mattered, because, even though this "convert" has gone his or her own way, they are still registered and counted as a statistic that proved the success of the recent evangelistic effort. This poor soul never showed up to be discipled for baptism or become a member of the church. They never gave testimony or did anything to serve Christ or edify the body of Christ with service. The only result was that the "convert" has embellished the reputation of the evangelist.

Integrity in Evangelism

Paul said, *"But if the truth of God through my lie abounded unto his glory, why am I also still judged as a sinner?"* (Romans 3:7 *ASV*). Integrity demands absolute transparency. Today's inquirer deserves to be treated like Mr. Ruler. It should be explained to them that the Lord, who we are called to serve, expects us to take up our cross. To help people contemplate the gravity of the decision that has been set before them, we would do well to tell them to stop and consider and not to enter blindly. For there is nothing frivolous about life or death, blessing or cursing. You are choosing a curse if you say yes and then do not continue. The Scriptures say,

- *When you make a promise to God, don't fail to keep it, since he isn't pleased with fools. Keep what you promise–it's better that you don't promise than that you do promise and not follow through. Never let your mouth cause you to sin and don't proclaim in the presence of the angel, "My promise was a mistake," for why should God be angry at your excuse and destroy what you've undertaken?"* (Ecclesiastes 5:4-6 *ISV*).

That Scripture is from the Old Testament, but this one if from the New.

- *If people have escaped from the corrupting forces of the world through their knowledge of our Lord and Savior Jesus Christ, and then are again caught and conquered by them, such people are in worse condition at the end than they were at the beginning. It would have been much better for them never to have known the way of righteousness than to know it and then turn away from the sacred command that was given them. What happened to them shows that the proverbs are true: "A dog goes back to what it has vomited" and "A pig that has been washed goes back to roll in the mud." (II Peter 2:20-22 GNB).*

James gives us this solemn notice,

- *Above all, my friends, do not use an oath when you make a promise. Do not swear by heaven or by earth or by anything else. Say only "Yes" when you mean yes, and "No" when you mean no, and then you will not come under God's judgment" (James 5:12 GNB). Even Jesus Himself said, "... No one who puts his hand to the plow and looks back is fit for the kingdom of God (Luke 9:62 ISV).*

Jesus also gave this example,

- *Whenever an unclean spirit goes out of a person, it wanders through waterless places looking for a place to rest but finds none. Then it says, 'I will go back to my home that I left.' When it arrives, it finds it empty, swept clean, and put in order. Then it goes and brings with it seven other spirits more evil than itself, and they go in and settle there. And so the final condition of that person becomes worse than the first. That's just what will happen to this evil generation! (Matthew 12:43-45 ISV).*

Contextually, Jesus is talking about what was going to happen to Israel if or when they rejected Him. But Jesus gives that example based on what actually happens to a person that thinks that they can play games with God by giddily coming and going. There are treasures in heaven, but they belong to those who take their cross here on the earth. Instead of warning the people and shaking off the frivolous followers as did Jesus, we energetically encourage all to, "Come on down to the altar and repeat 'The Prayer'".

The White Rabbit – A Real Problem

Not too long ago, while ministering in India, I had been preaching in a small village in an area where the Christians had suffered severe persecution. After the teaching a middle-aged man – who wasn't in the service but was hiding in a side room, came out weeping and confessed that he wanted to become a Christian. Standing right in front of me, he tearfully told me that he wanted to say something publically, first. I indicated that he could proceed. He, then began to ask his father, mother, wife and children to forgive him, for, as all knew, he was a part of the religious opposition that had been raining hell on the Christians and he had even encouraged the persecution of his own family.

I told him, publically, that I would pray with him, but would in no wise do so while standing. If he were to come before Christ, he must humble himself to the utmost and beg for His forgiveness. The brother fell down prostrate and his face before the Lord and weeping loudly began to confess his sins and ask for forgiveness! I spent quite a bit of time ministering to him as letting the Holy Spirit deal with his life. While doing the, which I might add, is going about the Father's business, one of the other ministers that had come with me from the England, leaned down and whispered in my ear, "Hurry it up, we've got to go." I was so shocked that I couldn't believe that I had just heard what I had just heard! Without thinking, I looked up and responded, "You're kidding, right? Are you mad? You want me to hurry up the work of God's Holy Spirit for your appointment with the plate? Look, if you have to go – Go! I will remain here for the night and figure out how to return to the city tomorrow – for this man's soul is far more important that your supper!" That night that man was gloriously saved and the entire village rejoiced.

We are more chained to the watch than Alice's White Rabbit. We are always, "Late, so late, for a very important date …" Though many today don't use watches, they still have their mobile phones and are even more enslaved to them. Our culture is ruled by the almighty hour and many times this directly affects our evangelism. We have become slaves of the watch and just do not have the time-or, at least the people that we evangelize think that they don't have the time. It's a real problem that we didn't have to deal with forty or fifty years ago, but we do today.

It's worse still when you consider that God cares nothing about our time or precious schedules; and He's right (as always). He has no watch, exists in Eternity and time means nothing to Him. He is concerned about us far more than we are concerned about ourselves because we don't understand the danger or severity of our plight! What would you rather lose? An hour or two here, or your entire life for an eternity in Hell?

No Small Challenge

Often our preaching, though it be biblical, finds no room in the agenda of the services of today's church or society. After the sermon, a public indication of the decision is on the program but it, because of our culture and with whom we have to deal, is time-restricted. *"This will only take a few minutes."* the responders are assured. But, if our time with them extends a bit, many times they begin to start looking at their watch or those who came with them begin to get impatient. Our intention is golden, because we understand that if people think that it's going to take a long time, they simply will not come or return.

Even though there is a sincere desire to see people give their lives to the Lord, our rushing desire to see this happen with our eyes takes priority over letting the Holy Spirit do the work that He wants to do in the lives of those who have heard the Word. The result is that though we have abortion, we end up provoking many spiritual abortions. This foments the indirect intention of avoiding discouragement of the faithful believers. Let me explain. All afternoon (and perhaps for quite some time before then) they have been praying, working and waiting to see, before their eyes, these precious souls accept Christ. We try our best to remove obstacles that would impede such expectations. Just think of what that would do to our evangelistic efforts. After all of our sincere and heartfelt work as well as the tremendous expenses involved in such efforts, not seeing the fruit of our labor can be quite discouraging! I know, been there – done that!

The White Rabbit syndrome is a real problem that we must deal with in our day and age. The solution might be different in every place. I just mention it here so that we might recognize it for what it really is: a problem that we must be conscious of and that must be dealt with. It is a major hindrance to the work of the Holy Spirit.

Confrontation

Think about it. There is no evidence that Mr. Ruler trusted in Christ or repented of his sins. Yet he was confronted honestly with the truth of the Gospel and its implications over his life. God did what He wanted to do in his life. The Word of God always accomplishes its purpose. Isaiah 55:11 says, *"So also will be the word that I speak—- it will not fail to do what I plan for it; it will do everything I send it to do."* Hebrews 4:12 says, *"The word of God is alive and active, sharper than any double-edged sword. It cuts all the way through, to where soul and spirit meet, to where joints and marrow come together. It judges the desires and thoughts of the heart."* If the Holy Spirit discerns that the thoughts and intentions of the hearer's heart are not acceptable, He Himself will send them along their ways sad just as Richie Ruler was. Why? Because the true faith in the Son of God was not found in them.

At least his personal counselor (Jesus) didn't mislead Richie into making a confession by way of pressure tactics. There was no manipulation using subtle psychological methods like a common used car salesperson. When he left, he knew what the answer to his initial question was. I am reminded of the wise words of an aged and seasoned "old school" African-American preacher of the true Gospel. He told me, *"Son, if I were a sinner, I would rather come to this church than any other that I know around here."* I scratched my head and asked, *"Why?"* He looked at me with those eyes wise with years of experience and replied, "Because at least if I'm a sinner in this church, I am fully informed that I'm going straight to hell for living in sin and turning my back on Jesus! Simply being a member ain't going to cut it here!"

CHAPTER 16
THE SECURITY OF THE BELIEVER
PART ONE

⸺⸙⸺

- *Shocked at this statement, the man went away sad, because he had many possessions* (Mark 10:22 *ISV*).

Jesus did not address the subject of security of salvation in this encounter with Mr. Rich. Yet, that in itself is informative. So many Christian workers feel compelled or are instructed to do the work of the Holy Spirit and give the assurance of salvation to others in their evangelism. All of this is part of a conjecture taken from the idea that when a person "comes forward", they have been saved. We think, "Surely, when a person repeats the prayer of the counselor with his mouth, he is sincerely calling out to God with his heart." Based on these dangerous presuppositions we place the precious souls that have trusted in us to inform them of the truth that leads to eternal life in the danger of eternal perdition. Richard Ruler asked Jesus a question and received His answer. He didn't like the answer and left sad, but that was his choice. Christ did not follow him to convince him of the benefits that would follow in an effort to change his mind.

Synthetic Security

We feel that it is our obligation not to let the people leave without repeating "The Prayer". The result is that shortly afterwards these poor souls begin to have serious doubts about their eternal state. The counselor reassures them that they are saved, but within the inquirers, there is absolutely nothing that gives them that assurance. The decisive factor is that, on top of the relentless anguish of the certain sense of impending doom that is upon them, they are given the solemn warning not to sin against God by doubting Him and calling Him a liar by doubting their salvation.

The practice of convincing people of the security of their salvation with one or two verses along with the warning, "Don't call God a liar" shows that even the "acceptance of the gift" depends not on if they have received it, but rather on if they have been received. I am inclined to label this, "the doctrine of synthetic security". This doctrine completely passes over the law and repentance and dilutes faith to "accepting a gift" and never mentions the death of our own self-will in submission to the will of God found in Jesus. Orthodox or traditional churches frequently hold their own version of synthetic security. The catechism classes replace the counseling rooms and the answers to the catechism replaces the repeated prayer. It is the same doctrine, because it assumes that the routine answers given by the aspirants, for acceptance by the church in class, are sufficient to assure one that they have been accepted by Christ, and have therefore trusted in Him. To doubt the conversion of the confirmed is inconceivable, unless, of course, there is some grave iniquity in the life of the confirmed.

Through this inference, people conclude that an intellectual recognition of a conjunction of strict doctrines gives the guarantee of salvation. This synthetic salvation also ignores the need for an interior experience of the grace of God. Though God, the law, repentance and faith have been beautifully defined, they remain without application. An honest confrontation with the exigencies of the Lordship of Christ and the cross we must carry in this life are avoided as if they were never demanded.

Jesus Christ was not looking for a way to end the interview with Mr. Rich with a bunch of concerted answers on some doctrinal issues or the repetition of a prayer. He loved this man's soul and wanted him to be spiritually united with his Creator by way of heartfelt repentance and true faith. Nobody wanted him to be saved more than the Lord Jesus did, but nothing could be done for him because he turned his back on the demands of Christ that would have led him to a true eternal relationship with God. The truth is that today we act as if we know more than Jesus did—that, or we just dismiss the teachings of the Word of God the same way that Richie Ruler did. Because, surely our churches would have registered this man as a tremendous convert.

Peace, Peace

- *Indeed, from the least important to the most important, they're all greedy for dishonest gain. From prophet to priest, they all act deceitfully. They treated my people's wound superficially, telling them, 'Peace, peace,' but there is no peace* (Jeremiah 6:13-14 *ISV*).

Years ago, I was teaching in a Bible school for regional pastors in Uganda, when a sincere pastor made a comment that, quite frankly, is innocuous and accepted as normal almost worldwide. He was discussing a virtuous young man who was a tremendous servant in the church and a gifted teacher of the Word. He went on to say that, since he was young and growing, he had him working with the youth. But he'd give him a year or two more in that ministry and then he would move him up to serious ministry. I almost came out of my seat and replied, "What do you mean by, serious ministry? Two of the most serious ministries that you have are children's and youth ministry, and that is not platitude! One out of every two Believers in the world are Believers to this day because they heard the Gospel in some form during their childhood or youth. The major statistics show us that at least 85% of all Believers were saved or were seriously evangelized by or before their 18th birthday! [5] The sick indication is that the only reason that people don't consider children and youth ministry as serious ministry, is because there is no money in them!"

With my head in my hands, I have to ask this very difficult question. "Is our easy evangelism partially motivated by the financial gain found in numbers?"

Without the shadow of a doubt, today's techniques would have given Mr. Ruler an artificial assurance of salvation before he left that encounter. There would never have been a doubt in the minds of the counselors about the salvation of that unfortunate client. After all, he did come forward, didn't he? He came running to Jesus, gave the right answers to the questions asked and he asked Jesus for eternal life. This young man was profoundly affected by Christ's message. Perhaps he wept, yet his soul was never saved.

Richard asked but did not receive, because he did not ask with true faith. Still, today the churches would have taken a lot of time to convince him that he did receive eternal life. Those who would give this avaricious man the security of his salvation would be fighting against the conclusions of God. To tell him that his petition for eternal life had been conceded, because God always grants salvation to those who ask Him verbally, would be a lie. If you don't love this person and want to send them to hell, tell him that. It would be the perfect deceptive trap and it works every time.

The Bible counts it as criminal negligence when we act as if the people's mortal wounds were only scratches. We would be the ones shouting, "Peace, peace". Such an offer of peace is false, yet it is given to hundreds of people by innocent and well intentioned believers. We can all shout that this is not what we want to do! Why of course not, I believe that quite the contrary is evidently true. We want the people to be saved and in the loving grace of Jesus! Nevertheless, according to Jeremiah 6:13-14, with these consolations and counsel, we classify ourselves as deceivers. No condemnation intended – I simply want to teach. I will repeat something I said much earlier; it is not our job to give the assurance of salvation. It is the work of the Holy Spirit to assure souls that they are children of God and belong to Him. The Believers of centuries past would have never used today's methods.

The Ancient Landmarks

- *Remove not the ancient landmark, which thy fathers have set* (Proverbs 22:28 *KJV*).

It is always good to ask, "What did the believers of yesteryear believe of the foundations of the faith?" What did John Bunyan believe about how one should get saved? Pilgrim's Progress certainly doesn't sound like, "Come forward and repeat this prayer." We would have had Pilgrim saved as soon as he left the City of Destruction! We have some fine documents and tremendous writings from the believers from the last five centuries. We can learn a tremendous amount from them. One of the frontal lobe failures[1] that young people suffer is that they think that they know far more than their parents or their elders. It always seem like that's the case. I have a saying, "Give jobs to young people… while they still know everything."

"The Westminster Confession of Faith" is one of those documents from yesteryear and is a fundamental text that declares all of the basic precepts of the Christian faith for the Evangelical world. This manuscript is like the cornerstone for the proclamation of what we know as sound teaching of the Scriptures accepted by teachers of the Bible from all Evangelical groups. Being that chapter 18 of this document declares the biblical and historical posture concerning the security of the believer so clearly, I believe that it is worthy of our focused attention:

1. Although hypocrites and other unregenerate men may vainly deceive themselves with false hopes and carnal presumptions of being in the favor of God, and estate of salvation (which hope of theirs shall perish). Yet such as truly believe in the Lord Jesus, and love Him in sincerity, *endeavouring* to walk in all good conscience before Him, may, in this life, be certainly assured that they are in the state of grace, and may rejoice in the hope of the glory of God, which hope shall never make them ashamed.

2. This certainty is not a bare conjectural and probable persuasion grounded upon a fallible hope; but an infallible assurance of faith founded upon:

- the divine truth of the promises of salvation,
- the inward evidence of those graces unto which these promises are made,
- the testimony of the Spirit of adoption witnessing with our spirits that we are the children of God, which Spirit is the

earnest of our inheritance, whereby we are sealed to the day of redemption.

3. This infallible assurance does not so belong to the essence of faith, but that a true believer may wait long, and conflict with many difficulties, before he be partaker of it. Yet, being enabled by the Spirit to know the things which are freely given him of God, he may, without extraordinary revelation in the right use of ordinary means, attain thereunto. And therefore it is the duty of every one to give all diligence to make his calling and election sure. That thereby his heart may be enlarged in peace and joy in the Holy Ghost, in love and thankfulness to God, and in strength and cheerfulness in the duties of obedience, the proper fruits of this assurance; so far is it from inclining men to looseness.

4. True believers may have the assurance of their salvation divers ways shaken, diminished, and intermitted. As, by:

- negligence in preserving of it,
- by falling into some special sin which wounds the conscience and grieves the Spirit;
- by some sudden or vehement temptation,
- by God's withdrawing the light of His countenance, and suffering even such as fear Him to walk in darkness and to have no light: Yet are they never so utterly destitute of that seed of God, and life of faith, that love of Christ and the brethren, that sincerity of heart, and conscience of duty, out of which, by the operation of the Spirit. This assurance may, in due time, be revived; and by the which, in the meantime, they are supported from utter despair.

The Work of the Holy Spirit

If we are faithful to do all that God has instructed for us to do in evangelism, we can trust God that the Holy Spirit will be even more faithful to do His part. Can you trust in God for Him to do His part? If not you remind me of an experience I had while driving down a dirt road in my pickup many years ago in Latin America. We were on our way, with a group of believers, to evangelize a village. We saw a woman walking down the road carrying a heavy load on her head. I stopped to offer her a ride, which she gladly accepted and climbed in the back with a few other disciples. As we continued on our way, I happened to look back and saw that the lady still carried the load on her head. We ask God to help us, yet we continue to try to carry the load all by ourselves without letting Him do His part.

D.L. Moody was a tremendous brother in the faith and an unequalled evangelist. However, he was the one that made the practice of pressuring the seekers to make an immediate decision for Christ. At that time, it wasn't a something to be counted against him. He was doing what he knew how to do with all simplicity and sincerity. He is accredited for countless decisions and his methods were innovative. He had large audiences and won souls on both sides of the Atlantic. Still, that doesn't mean that his methods were decrees of God; they were his tactics and at that moment they worked. But, since then, we have made a "Nehushtan" of his methods.

Many times the honest thing that we should do is to send the seekers home grieved and counting the cost. But our lack of faith manifests itself when we say, "If we dismiss the service without making an altar call, the people won't be saved," or, "What if they don't come back to the church?" If God is truly dealing with them, they will never escape! If they do not return, it is because they were not going to return even if you forced them to repeat, "The Prayer".

Brothers and Sisters, when the Holy Spirit is permitted to do His complete work, the person that surrenders to Christ will not have any need of human pressure tactics for the saving of their soul. The Holy Spirit is the one that gives assurance to those who have believed. In I John 3:24, the Apostle underlines what Paul said in Romans 8:16.

- *The Spirit itself beareth witness with our spirit, that we are the children of God (Romans 8:16 KJV).*
- *Whoever keeps his commandments abides in God, and God in him. And by this we know that he abides in us, by the Spirit whom he has given us. (1 John 3:24 ESV).*

The Spirit of God gives the blessed confidence of sins forgiven to those who examine themselves in the light of the Word of God. The Word says, *"Put yourselves to the test and judge yourselves, to find out whether you are living in faith. Surely you know that Christ Jesus is in you?–unless you have completely failed"* (II Corinthians 13:5 *GNB*).

There's Something Living in Me!

Imagine having something living in you without you knowing about it. That sound more like a horror flick than Christianity to me. If Christ lives in our hearts, He will let us know that He has taken up residence within us. If He didn't clearly let you know about it, don't you find that to be rather lowbrow and unrefined? Jesus is not some homeless squatter that somebody informs you that He is living in your house without letting you know.

Imagine this scene: You come home from work one day, tired, wearied, and ready to relax in your favorite recliner. All of a sudden, you see that there is a total stranger laid back in your chair with a cool drink of your favorite fruit juice in his hand taken from your refrigerator. He has recently showered and has your favorite robe and house shoes on. He's also munching on some cookies that your wife prepared for you last night. To top it off, with his mouth full of *your* cookies, he holds out one and says,

"These are great! You want one?"

Just a tad bit ticked off, you ask,

"Hey you! What are you doing here? Who are you?"

"Me?" asks the stranger pointing at himself.

"No, Wise Guy, I'm talking to my neighbor that happens to still be in *his own house*! Yeah you! What are you doing here?" you say, shouting now.

"Why… I live here", he answer with the gentlest of calm while he enjoys YOUR cookie.

"Oh yeah? Since when?"

I'll leave the conclusion to this situation to your own imagination.

When I pastored near Acapulco, Mexico, the pastoral residence was fairly large and it was connected to the back of the church property by a big patio between the two. We had the school of discipleship there and had at times up to thirty young people living with us. Frequently, the young people from the congregation would hang around until late at night singing, playing around and generally making their fair share of joyful noise. I never hung around until all of those who didn't live there left – I'd just disappear and go to bed. If I would have waited until they left, I would never have gone to bed, because they never left!

We had so much in-and-out traffic that many times I would wake up in the morning and I'd find some believers from the congregation or one of our pastors from the mountainous region had arrived during the night and was sleeping somewhere in the house. It didn't happen every week, but it was never unusual when it did happen, that I might even find some total strangers asleep on one of the beds in one of the dormitories. Once or twice, I have even found a drunkard asleep on the floor of the sanctuary! (At least I knew this guy. He was a harmless town drunk.) One way or another, I always found out who was in the house or had stayed the night somewhere on the property.

One of my Christian heroes was Bruce Olson[2]. He preached the Gospel to some aborigine tribes in the Amazon jungles of Colombia for many years. On one occasion, during a long trek through the jungle in the humidity and heat, he passed out from hunger. While unconscious, he had a dream in which he saw a butterfly fluttering around his head. Suddenly the butterfly landed on his face and went into his mouth! That's when he woke and found that he really did feel a butterfly fluttering around in his mouth! Or at least it felt like one. He opened his mouth and grabbed whatever it was fluttering around in there only to discover that it was a three-foot long intestinal parasite! It had come out because it was hungry. He said that from then on, he would always eat something because he didn't want to know what else was living down there. Now there's a horror flick for you!

But, Brothers and Sisters, *Christ is not a parasite*! It is rare or unheard of that we could have something so great living in us and not know it's there. Yet when we are talking about God, the Omnipotent of the universe, Father, Son and the Holy Spirit living in us, I would say that it would be IMPOSSIBLE not to know about it! John 14:23 dice, *"If anyone loves me, he will keep my word. Then my Father will love him, and we will go to him and make our home within him."*

I can understand it if a new Believer does not understand the new changes that God is working in their lives. It would be necessary to explain that. I can even understand that God had entered into the life of a new believer and them not being able to understand or explain what really happened to them. But, if I have to convince them that God is living in them and say that they would be calling God a liar if the say that it's not so, it could only be because God is not living in them and I am sorely mistaken to attempt to convince them otherwise. Don't you understand, that Christ loves us and will not torment us with doubts if, in truth, He was living in us? The security of our souls and the assurance of this fact is something the Lord has guaranteed with the seal of the Holy Spirit. With all clarity, tranquility and peace He will let us know that we have passed from darkness to light.

Candidates for Assurance

The promises of the Bible touching the assurance of salvation are not given without discrimination. They are given to those who have surrendered entirely to de exigencies of our Lord over their lives. Speaking of the necessity of this total change, Jesus turns to Mr. Richard Ruler and gives him this command, *"You're missing one thing. Go and sell everything you own, give the money to the destitute"*. Mr. Ruler's resistance to agree with Jesus on these terms excluded him conclusively from the promise, *"... you will have treasure in heaven."* (Mark 10:21). The Scriptures say, *"You need to be patient, in order to do the will of God and receive what he promises*" (Hebrews 10:36 *GNB*).

It's Worth It to Ask Questions

I have a saying: "The difference between a Christian and a sinner is that a sinner feels the need for sin and the Christian feels the need for Christ." I wouldn't hold this saying to the same height for a litmus test as the Scriptures, but simply ask yourself, "Do these words ring true for the new convert? Are they true for you?" This is why it is necessary to do a self-examination. In this auto-interrogation, we should ask the following questions:

1. Has your heart been bowed and broken by the grace of God to the point of joyful submission to the commands of Christ?

The carnal mind cannot find joy in the will of God. On the other hand, for the new creature, there is no joy outside of the will of God. This is why the Bible exhorts us, "*Do not conform yourselves to the standards of this world, but let God transform you inwardly by a complete change of your mind. Then you will be able to know the will of God–what is good and is pleasing to him and is perfect*" (Romans 12:2 *GNB*). So, for the new creature, seeking to be in the will of God is a spontaneous reaction and the most logical thing to do in life. It is easy for them to conclude that not to seek God's will is an obvious lapse of judgment.

- *Therefore, do not be foolish, but understand what the Lord's will is* (Ephesians 5:17 *ISV*).

Our joy is found in being able to be a servant of the Most High.

- *And whatever you do, in word or deed, do everything in the name of the Lord Jesus, giving thanks to God the Father through him* (Colossians 3:17 *ESV*).

Our desire is that others also might enjoy the fullness of life found only in total submission to Christ.

- *Greetings from Epaphras, another member of your group and a servant of Christ Jesus. He always prays fervently for you, asking God to make you stand firm, as mature and fully convinced Christians, in complete obedience to God's will* (Colossians 4:12 *GNB*).

Therefore, one of the major goals in the life of a new creature is to understand, desire and to do the will of God for our lives.

2. What are the things that can shake you or tempt you to take your eyes off God's will?

Paul said that he received nothing in the way of benefits from anything that the world had offered him when he compared them in the light of the glories of knowing Christ. His greatest goal was to know Him:

- *But whatever things were assets to me, these I now consider a loss for the sake of the Messiah. What is more, I continue to consider all these things to be a loss for the sake of what is far more valuable, knowing the Messiah Jesus, my Lord. It is because of him that I have experienced the loss of all those things. Indeed, I consider them rubbish in order to gain the Messiah and be found in him, not having a righteousness of my own that comes from the Law, but one that comes through the faithfulness of the Messiah, the righteousness that comes from God and that depends on faith. I want to know the Messiah—what his resurrection power is like and what it means to share in his sufferings by becoming like him in his death, though I hope to experience the resurrection from the dead. It's not that I have already reached this goal or have already become perfect. But I keep pursuing it, hoping somehow to embrace it just as I have been embraced by the Messiah Jesus. Brothers, I do not consider myself to have embraced it yet. But this one thing I do: Forgetting what lies behind and straining forward to what lies ahead, I keep pursuing the goal to win the prize of God's heavenly call in the Messiah Jesus* (Philippians 3:7-14 *ISV*).

As a natural result, he exhorted all true Believers to have the same attitude with the words, *"Therefore, those of us who are mature should think this way. And if you think differently about anything, God will show you how to think"* (Philippians 3:15 *ISV*). Everything that we do should be done with an open heart ready and willing to please the Lord.

- *With good will doing service, as to the Lord, and not to men* (Ephesians 6:7 *KJV*).

We all know that it is possible to be totally involved in church activities and still not have a heart that is right with God. Paul, in his experience discovered that, *"Some indeed preach Christ even of envy and strife; and some also of good will"* (Philippians 1:15 *KJV*). Here is something that I've never understood. With all of the millions of lost people that there are in the world, and the exorbitant costs to broadcast via radio and TV, why people would waste so much, effort, time and money just to blast other Christians? This is not to say anything about the wasted opportunities to minister to all of the lost souls that are turned away because they hear pure contentious polemic and not the Gospel. I think that that is what it means to preach with envy and strife.

3. What are the thoughts that dominate your mind?

The mind that has not been born again will find its joy in worldly meditations and will not recognize them as sinful. The mind renewed by the Spirit is grieved with unclean thoughts and strives to seek the approval of the Word of God over every one of them.

- *Instead, they find joy in obeying the Law of the LORD, and they study it day and night* (Psalms 1:2 *GNB*).
- *But he delights in the LORD's instruction, and meditates in his instruction day and night* (Psalms 1:2 *ISV*).
- *Let the words of my mouth, and the meditation of my heart, be acceptable in thy sight, O LORD, my strength, and my redeemer* (Psalms 19:14 *KJV*).
- Mem. *Oh how love I thy law! It is my meditation all the day* (Psalms 119:97 *ASV*).
- *For those who live according to the flesh set their minds on the things of the flesh, but those who live according to the Spirit set their minds on the things of the Spirit. For to set the mind on the flesh is death, but to set the mind on the Spirit is life and peace. For the mind that is set on the flesh is hostile to God, for it does not submit to God's law; indeed, it cannot. Those who are in the flesh cannot please God* (Romans 8:5-8 *ESV*).
- *The weapons we use in our fight are not the world's weapons but God's powerful weapons, which we use to destroy strongholds. We destroy false arguments; we pull down every proud obstacle that is raised against the knowledge of God; we take every thought captive and make it obey Christ* (II Corinthians 10:4-5 *GNB*).

4.) What are the things that stir up your most favorable emotions?

It's easy to find out which things that really excite you because they will be the object of the majority of your casual conversations. Jesus said, *"... for out of the abundance of the heart the mouth speaks"* (Matthew 12:34 *ESV*). It is also easy to know by way of the activities that consume the major part of your time. Paul said, *"I do it all for the sake of the gospel, that I may share with them in its blessings"* (1 Corinthians 9:23 *ESV*).

- *If ye then be risen with Christ, seek those things which are above, where Christ sitteth on the right hand of God. Set your affection on things above, not on things on the earth* (Colossians 3:1-2 *KJV*).

Religiously Dedicated, but Lost

When the deepest impulses and desires are for Christ in answer to these questions, we might confide that we have finally been born of God. Even still, religious enthusiasm is not valid proof of our having been accepted by God. I'll give you two examples.

Example 1: Saul of Tarsus is not the evil bad guy of the movie that we all imagine. He was a sincere Jew that wanted to keep the Jewish faith pure from all contamination. Unlike his elders, he sincerely wanted to please God as did Phinehas in Numbers 25:7-8 and, in his zeal for the Lord, destroy all those who would bring God's wrath over Israel by deviating from the faith of their fathers.

Think about it, after all of Israel's history of apostasy, judgment and repentance, Israel is finally in a place where an idolatrous Jew is almost unheard of. Yet, this itinerant rabbi from the Galilean region comes spreading his dangerously poisonous teachings. This is just another one of those things that could bring more judgment upon Israel just like in times of old.

Saul really thought that he was doing the will of God. Sure, he had his occasional doubts. Those times that he accompanied his teacher, Gamaliel, and the other elders to dispute with this Jesus of Nazareth, he found that Jesus had some arguments that were difficult to refute. Why that dying speech that that heretic they called

Stephen was also rather convincing. He was also seeing bothersome things in the Scriptures that really seemed to line up with this man's teachings and with what his followers were saying. It was an enigma that he had no answer for, and it disturbed him deeply. He also had no one of confidence with whom he could freely discuss these things. These things were like pricks goading his conscience day and night. But, they couldn't be right. Why is it that none of his elders or teachers saw or understood these things in the way he was beginning to see them? Who did he think that he was to doubt the understanding of such a wise man such as Gamaliel? All he ever wanted to do was to please God and to be so faithful that he could experience God's power, as did his forefathers in times of old.

In his effort to shake these things from his mind, he undertook a more daunting task. He had heard, from his elders about the spread of this dangerous doctrine in the Jewish communities in Syria. He would volunteer to go all the way to Damascus to purge the heretics and eliminate the refuge of these deviants that threatened the security of Israel. He was going to prove to God that he was faithful and truly loved Him and was going to be a guardian of the purity of His law!

He was in route to that ancient city that ancient city while, unavoidably, in deep meditation on the claims of the Jesus of Nazareth. Could he have actually have been the Messiah? Could he yet be? Those who followed him so gladly gave their lives claiming that this Jesus both died and was yet alive because he had risen from the dead! Bah! Preposterous rubbish! But was it really drivel? Do we not, as Pharisees, believe that the Scriptures teach the reality of the spirit world, angels as well as the resurrection of the dead? Is that so far from what we actually believe? But could this man that we saw die, a horrid and shameful death like a common criminal, could truly be the Messiah? Unthinkable! Or, could it actually be that we sent God's Chosen One, the One that we have been waiting for, for over four thousand years to His death in our calloused rejection of Him? Have we really been the ones who have rejected God Himself, by this action? It is all drastically disquieting and far too much to consider!

God is the one that sees all hearts and Christ's promise of, *"Blessed are those who hunger and thirst for righteousness, for they shall be satisfied"* (Matthew 5:6 *ESV*). Therefore, while on this lonely road with a motley crew of men determined to shed blood, Jesus Himself appeared to Saul and called him, for he had seen the sincere and earnest plight of his heart. When Paul was struck by the power of Almighty God and was cast to the ground by this Majestic Authority, he knew, without a doubt that it was God's doing. The God of his fathers was manifesting Himself as in times of old, just as he had long read and studied.

Then he heard the words that absolutely crushed his heart: *"Saul, Saul! Why do you persecute me?"* (In his mind, I can hear him saying, Oh no! Lord, what do you mean by saying that I am persecuting You? I love you and only want to please you. But, if I am persecuting you, that only means that I have been sorely and gravely mistaken about just who really are. So I must ask...[4]) *"Who are you, Lord?" he asked. "I am Jesus, whom you persecute," the voice said"* (Acts 9:4-5 *GNB*).

Paul's religious enthusiasm was not valid proof that he was accepted by God. In his case, it helped him to see the truth because he hungered and thirsted after righteousness in his sincere search to please God, as Malcolm X said, *"By any means necessary."*

Nevertheless, just as many religious people are lost, for they refuse to let God speak to them to show them something other than what they have already known.

Example 2: Our Mr. Richard, the young man that we have been examining in these studies. He would have put many Christians to shame with his faithful, yet ignorant, zeal to keep the law externally and to prepare himself for the next life. His discipline and moral concepts were impressive, yet he was not saved. Christ did not have his complete and unconditional allegiance.

When his interview with Jesus ended, Mr. Ruler had the information he requested. As I have said, he now had a correct orientation as to what God wanted of him. That he understood the truth of what Jesus said to him was evident in his reaction – he want away sad. If he would have considered Jesus' demand of him as ludicrous, he would have dismissed himself angry, mocking or any number of other emotional states, but not sad. "The Master is right," he must have thought. In that, he was in agreement with the Lord. "God is holy and I am covetous beast! The only way *for me* to have eternal life is to turn my back on my first love…, which I now know, is not God. In fact, I now know that my first love is my wealth and I have caused that to become a God unto me. If I am to have treasures in heaven, I must obey and follow the Lord."

Sadly, correct knowledge is not sufficient to save your soul. Neither should we dare to assume that the absence of heresy or immorality is a guarantee of security. He had to find, within himself, the evidence of a heart given to obey what the Gospel had revealed to him. He had to submit his life to the teachings of the Master.

A Changed Life

This young man's life was changed after his encounter with Christ, but not for the better. His conscience was sharpened because of the Word of God. Now he understood the truth and the righteous judgment of God was now a near tangible reality for him. Every one of his thoughts and actions were now judged in the light of this new knowledge.

He had turned his back on the Lord! He had rejected the God that he claimed to love so much so that he could live a life that he now understood to be sinful, selfish and rebellious against this God. Though others saw no need for his change and assured him that he was a good person, he knew the truth. His money was his identity, his estimation of self-worth and the reason he had so many other egotistical parasites for companions who were only with him because of his money. Jesus was the only one that didn't love him for his money. In fact, Jesus wanted nothing to do with his money – yet he had rejected Him. Were his "friends" actually friends? Would they "hang" with him if he had no money? Would he be their friend if they had no money? He had never considered these things before. Now such thoughts would not abandon his mind night or day. Now, when he was with his "friends" he saw then with new eyes of suspicion and distrust or open disdain.

He was now asking himself the question, "The life that I am now living, is it really life? Didn't Jesus say something like, "... *Watch out and guard yourselves from every kind of greed; because your true life is not made up of the things you own, no matter how rich you may be*" (Luke 12:15 *GNB*). If at any time my riches should fail me, would it befall me as it did to the young man in that story that the Master told saying, "*After he had spent everything, a severe famine took place throughout that country, and he began to be in need. So he went out to work for one of the citizens of that country, who sent him into his fields to feed pigs. No one would give him anything, even though he would gladly have filled himself with the husks the pigs were eating"* (Luke 15:14-16 *ISV*)?" When he sat with his friends for idle conversation and off-color humor, the smile of his face was plastic, for the Words of Christ burned in his mind, *"The good person out of his good treasure brings forth good, and the evil person out of his evil treasure brings forth evil. I tell you, on the day of judgment people will give account for every careless word they speak, for by your words you will be justified, and by your words you will be condemned"* (Matthew 12:35-37 *ESV*).

What a miserable life Mr. Richard must have lived after such a momentous contact with His Creator, his Master! I am sure that he was not able to arrive home, recline on his luxurious bed, and conclude that all would be fine with his soul when the Master had said, *"... Foxes have holes and birds have nests, but the Son of Man has no place to rest"* (Matthew 8:20 *ISV*). When he sat at his table and chewed on the finest cuts of selected meats, they tasted like paper because the Master had said, *"... My meat is to do the will of him that sent me, and to finish his work"* (John 4:34 *KJV*). He knew that he was not in the will of the Father. The Words of the Lord echoed in his mind, haunting him, *"He that is not with me is against me; and he that gathers not with me scatters abroad"* (Matthew 12:30). Christ had shown him His love and he had offered him eternal life and he had rejected it! If he did not repent he would end up eternally in the abode of the dead, but he was now a dead man that walked amongst the dead. Now he knew and understood what it would cost him if he did or did not repent. He was no longer ignorant of his sin.

- *If I had not come and spoken to them, they would not have been guilty of sin, but now they have no excuse for their sin* (John 15:22 *ESV*).

CHAPTER 17
WORTHLESS DECEIT
THE SECURITY OF THE BELIEVER —
PART TWO

—∞∞∞—

- *See to it, then, that no one enslaves you by means of the worthless deceit of human wisdom, which comes from the teachings handed down by human beings and from the ruling spirits of the universe, and not from Christ* (Colossians 2:8 GNB).

The Difference between Conviction and Condemnation

As seen in Mr. Ruler, the Word of God is a two edged sword: One edge will change your life for the better, but the other edge of the blade will do so in ways that will accentuate the curse. This is the same Word that we have today, yet it has not been ministered in the same manner. What are our results? Many lives are not changed or affected in any way. The people hear our preaching and leave giving no heed to what they have heard. None is convicted of sin as they continue in divergent ways. Perhaps they were in total agreement with what the preacher said, but saving faith was not engendered and fomented in their souls.

Some pastors, in their sincere attempts to correct this malady, simply manage to bring condemnation upon their listeners... not good. Condemnation comes from the devil and always brings confusion. People feel bad, but there is no clear definition as to why or how to resolve the imagined problem. Many times these well-intentioned preachers offer no practical solutions. In addition, their condemn brings guilt for things that the Word of God does not condemn. These vain philosophies and worthless deceits are according to the traditions of men and the world and not in harmony with Christ.

Conviction is very distinct and specific. It is the work of the Holy Spirit. It is the conviction of sin when one undoubtedly knows what has been done and the Word of God brings a clear solution. When someone repents of his or her sins, God Himself removes all guilt and the Lord Jesus Christ gives peace to the heart of the repentant. If we lack sincerity and true desire to face God, we might enter into confusion when there is conviction of sin. If we are sincere, there is never any confusion when the Holy Spirit convinces us of sin. We will know what's up and why.

- *This is all that I have learned: God made us plain and simple, but we have made ourselves very complicated* (Ecclesiastes 7:29 GNB).

As stated, condemnation is not based on truth and only results in confusion and there is no biblical solution that might bring relief to your problem apart from repentance and believing the truth. If there is condemnation in your life, it is because of your own inventions or things that man has placed over you, and that is not the work of the Holy Spirit. The only way to escape condemnation is to saturate ourselves with the Word of God and purge our minds of the teachings of man.

- *For the weapons of our warfare are not of the flesh but have divine power to destroy strongholds. We destroy arguments and every lofty opinion raised against the knowledge of God, and take every thought captive to obey Christ* (II Corinthians 10:4-5 *ESV*).

It is indispensable to have the security of the salvation of our souls. How are we to face eternity without it? This is why it is lamentable that so few truly understand security. Few take the doubts of those who have "gone forward" in our services to "receive Christ" seriously.

The problem does not consist in doubting the fact that God keeps His promises. For them there is no doubt that God will give eternal life to all those who repent and believe. But people have the discernment (a kind way of saying, "common sense") to know that *"going forward"* and repeating a prayer does not constitute faith, therefore honest and valid questions arise. For the majority of these inquirers, the questions, "Have we really repented and believed?" and, "Are we the recipients of the grace of God?" can save their souls if there is a wise and informed person there to counsel them.

Do You Know How to Do Good?

- *Learn to do good; seek justice, correct oppression; bring justice to the fatherless, plead the widow's cause* (Isaiah 1:17 *ESV*).
- *So then, if we do not do the good we know we should do, we are guilty of sin* (James 4:17 *GNB*).

Jeremiah the Prophet described the human heart with the illustrative and on-point words, *"The heart is deceitful above all things, and desperately sick; who can understand it?"* (Jeremiah 17:9 *ESV*). This is so because few people want to bare themselves honestly before God and themselves. People deceive themselves and willfully ignore the facts of their spiritual condition. However, the conscience is something from which we cannot hide. Paul, in Romans, tells us that God will judge us according to our conscience.

- *For whenever gentiles, who do not possess the Law, do instinctively what the Law requires, they are a law to themselves, even though they do not have the Law. They show that what the Law requires is written in their hearts, a fact to which their own consciences testify, and their thoughts will either accuse or excuse them on that day when God, through Jesus the Messiah, will judge people's secrets according to my gospel* (Romans 2:14-16 *ISV*).

Many times people approach me and ask questions about moral issues; is it right or wrong to do this or that? The majority of the times they already know the answers before they even ask the question, they just ask in the hope that I will give an answer that will be permissive to their flesh. They have already experienced the instruction of the Holy Spirit or the conviction of sins. In this, we can honestly apply what Paul said in Romans 14:22b, "... *Happy is he that condemns not himself in that thing which he allows.*" Didn't Paul inform us, "*For God has revealed his grace for the salvation of all people. That grace instructs us to give up ungodly living and worldly passions, and to live self-controlled, upright, and godly lives in this world*" (Titus 2:11-12 *GNB*). The Gospel is so clear and simple, but how many times do we turn a deaf ear when it comes to hearing the truths that are not convenient for our flesh. If a person says with their mouth that they want to seek the Lord, yet retain favorite sins hidden in their heart, they will always have doubts about their relationship with Christ and the security of their salvation. The Psalmist said, "*Were I to cherish iniquity in my heart, the Lord would not listen to me*" (Psalms 66:18 *ISV*).

We might not want to admit it, but we don't know everything; Yet God does. However, many well-intentioned Christians frequently attempt to override the dictates of the Holy Spirit in the lives of these seekers. We attempt to give consolation when God has not given it. Once again, Jeremiah sums it up perfectly saying, *"They act as if my people's wounds were only scratches. All is well, they say, when all is not well"* (Jeremiah 6:14 *GNB*). Any such consolation that we could give in these instances, at best can be described as a placebo. If the Holy Spirit has not given the assurance of salvation to them, it is because He is yet dealing with areas of their lives and it is to their benefit if we would counsel them to keep seeking the salvation of their souls and peace with God. It is a matter of them sincerely coming face to face with God and admitting the things that they are not submitting to Him.

Wait..., Did You Say, a Placebo?

Sometimes doctors have to treat patients who are actually hypochondriacs. Their only sickness is the one that makes them think they are sick-and they always think that they are sick. It is very tiring to constantly deal with them, yet when you have a hypochondriac, you constantly have to deal with them. It can wear on your patience. So it turns out that doctors have to be patient with these patients because you can never convince them that they are not sick – that there is nothing physically wrong with them. To resolve this problem, some genius came out with a pill that we call a placebo. It's just a sugar pill that has the appearance and presentation of a medication. The "critically ill" patient takes the miraculous remedy and almost always experiences *"recovery"*.

The placebo works if the infirmity is imaginary. There are occasions that placebos have been accredited for helping authentically ill people and this has provoked a plethora of investigations. Though such occurrences are not unheard of, these are the exceptions and not the rule. For if the person has a real sickness, or a physical wound such as a gunshot, a placebo would not only prove to be unhelpful, but dangerously life threatening. In the same way, man-made remedies prove to be useless and dangerous when it comes to resolving problems related to sin and its consequences. They can never give the security that a person has been forgiven and their soul has been eternally saved.

A Philosophy Class

Many years ago, while pastoring a church in Mexico, I was invited to be an adjunct professor to an educational faculty. They wanted me to teach a philosophy class in a college under the auspices of the Autonomous University of Mexico. I agreed to accept their offer for a year. During one of the class sessions thoughts about philosophy and religion came up. What Karl Marx said in his, *Critique of Hegel's Philosophy of Right*, is fascinating, and though I cannot agree with his conclusion, I cannot disagree with many things he presents in his argument. I want to quote the most well-known part of his discourse here:

> *Religious distress is at the same time the expression of real distress and the protest against real distress. Religion is the sigh of the oppressed creature, the heart of a heartless world, just as it is the spirit of a spiritless situation. It is the opium of the people. The abolition of religion as the illusory happiness of the people is required for their real happiness. The demand to give up the illusion*

about its condition is the demand to give up a condition, which needs illusions.–Karl Marx, *Critique of Hegel's Philosophy of Right.*

A fascinating and very interesting thought indeed! So, in the course of the discussion, it was natural that the subject of the existence of sin arose. In order to deliberate this theme judiciously, I first spoke to them about the possibility of Marx's implication that sin was merely the result of cultural conditioning. That is to say, to paraphrase Marx's idea that, "religion is an opium" and that sin does not really exist. We have merely been taught that it exists, and in doing so, an unjust and enslaving condemnation has been placed over our heads. I gave them various illustrations to reinforce this concept. One example that the students particularly enjoyed was that of the first Catholic missionaries to arrive in Japan. They discovered that there was no word for *"sin"* in that language; at least, for the language that they spoke in that part of Japan at that time. They really liked that concept and offered many favorable comments but no one debated what I was presenting.

Then I presented the antithetical argument of the very real possibility that perhaps the concept of sin was not a mere cultural imposition, but rather a reality that is patently recognized in the human heart. Returning to my example about Japan, I explained that even though the word *"sin"* did not exist, the concept most definitely did exist. They had the death penalty; they recognized adultery and fornication as wrong and there were words that were clearly not acceptable among decent folk. There were clear concepts of right and wrong, good and bad. What's more, how can they even use the term "decent folk" if there was no recognition of the difference between that which is go or bad?

One of the young men, in an attempt to defend his newly found philosophy, protested saying, "I believe that you were right when you said that it was merely a question of cultural inculcation. Because every time I go to mass, I do all that the priest commands me to do for penance and I never feel any better or free from guilt."

"Thank you very much," I replied, "Because you have just proven my objective by showing us that sin, most definitely exists independently from any human, sociological manipulation."

Perplexed with my affirmation, he countered, "Wait, how is that a contradiction to what I previously stated to prove a different point? Explain what you mean." They all objected and began to give opinions in favor of the nonexistence of sin. I loved it because they were all intrigued and involved in the discussion.

"It's easy." I responded, "Listen, though my example will be hypothetical, bear with me." They agreed. "If I tell you a lie and say, 'Hey! Don't move! There's a wasp on your shirt collar! Do not move!' You believe me and are frightened. Though you are afraid you, obediently, do not move in fear that the threatening vespine might attack. True?" Once again, they all agreed.

I continued, "Well, I faithfully come to your rescue, roll up a magazine and shoo the dangerous peck away. I assure you that the threat is now gone and you are free from being injured. Will you feel better?"

"Yeah, sure", they all agreed that they would feel relieved.

I continued by saying, "You feel better because the wasp was a lie; it was never there. Still, you thought that it was there – you believed my lie and for you, the wasp was real. I simply gave you a mental placebo and told you another lie that you also believed and now you feel better. One lie merely cancelled out the effects of another fabrication. However, what if there really was a wasp on your collar, if you knew for a certainty that there was a stinging threat near you and it was not a lie? You can hear it and feel its wings fluttering against your neck. You just saw it fly by you seconds ago and were terribly aware of this menacing presence. With this patent reality upon you, could one of my lies really make you feel better? No, because you know that that the threat is true."

They began to murmur amongst themselves discussing this new thought and finally agreed that I was right. Therefore, I told them, "Sin really exists and all of man's inventions will not take away the weight, stain and the guilt of sin." Then I went biblically ballistic on them. "When it comes to sin, there is no such thing as a spiritual placebo. The only thing that can remove the guilt of sin is the Blood of Christ applied by way of total faith in Him and repentance of the sin that incurred the guilt in the first place. A lie might resolve a fictitious problem, but a lie can never resolve a real problem – the problem of sin".

Man can never give the solace and peace that comes from the Holy Spirit's assurance of our salvation. The Bible says, *"Our God is a God of salvation, and to GOD, the Lord, belong deliverances from death"* (Psalms 68:20 *ESV*).

The Imperative Question

Being that we read about hypocrites and self-deceived people like Judas, the question, "What must I do to be saved?" is definitely imperious. This is a completely different question from, "How do I know if I am saved or not?" You can answer the first question with confidence, but only the Holy Spirit can answer the second with any kind of certainty. How many souls have been guided to a vain confidence by way of man-made evangelistic formulas? How many have been sent to their homes having their wounds treated as if they were scratches and consoled with the words *all is well*, when they should have been cut to the heart, grieved and disquieted?

When Richie Ruler retuned home yet in sin, his conscience was grieved and provoked by his rebellion. Perhaps he came to Christ later in one of the powerful moves of God found in Acts 2 and 3. Conceivably, he could have been one of those who were part of the crowd in Acts 4:32 where is says, *"The group of believers was one in mind and heart. None of them said that any of their belongings were their own, but they all shared with one another everything they had."* I would like to think so, and it is clearly not improbable. God has never given up on me and I am sure that the Holy Spirit continued to drill into Mr. Rich's conscience. Nevertheless, the placebo of false security only confuses the conscience and removes the conviction of sin before the Holy Spirit can do His work in the heart of man. This action of premature security seriously impedes the seeking heart from continuing to do so.

The Other Son

The interesting thing about Ishmael is that, though he was a son and was promised (Genesis 17:5-6), he was not the promised son (Genesis 17:19). The Quran says that God told Abraham to offer Ishmael as a sacrifice instead of Isaac. Actually, the Quranic account does not even mention Isaac. Interestingly, the Quran says that Abraham offered a lamb, instead of a ram as the Bible says. When I minister to Muslims, I never debate these points. Why? Instead of seeing it as a distortion of the biblical account and condemn the whole thing, which is foolish and would gain me nothing, I occupy this information to evangelize with the tools at hand. I simply tell them the Jesus is the "Lamb of God" that was offered for Ishmael. The Bible says that God loved Ishmael and miraculously intervened for him several times with angels to save his life. Yet the plan of God for the redemption of the world was through Isaac and not via Ishmael.

Some people avow that Ishmael was a work of the flesh, for it was Abraham's rush to fulfill God's promise over his life by his own means. I would kind of agree with that, because I understand what is being said. Yet I would also have to disagree for a multitude of reasons. One of them being that it was prophesied that Abraham would be the father of many nations. That logically concludes that he would have children who would father many nations and kings. This automatically assumes diversity, different ethnicities and people groups. Ishmael, Zimran, and Jokshan, and Medan, and Midian, and Ishbak, and Shuah were all a part of this promise. God did say that Abraham's children would be like the stars of the heavens and the grains of sand along the seashore. This speaks of heavenly descendants and carnal or earthly descendants. In another context, it is talking about Jews who are merely physical descendants contrasted to the spiritually born again people that are the children of the promised one, Jesus.

As for the natural Jews, as well as Ishmael, Zimran, and Jokshan, and Medan, and Midian, and Ishbak, and Shuah, all were born of a natural process and could be considered children of the flesh or as the grains of sand on the seashore. God had this in mind when He informed us, *"This means that the children born in the usual way are not the children of God; instead, the children born as a result of God's promise are regarded as the true descendants"* (Romans 9:8

GNB). Therefore, no matter how much Abraham loved Ishmael or his other children, God said to him of Isaac, "*... thou hast not withheld thy son, thine only son, from Me*" (Genesis 22:12 *JPS*). The child of the promise is what stood out in God's mind, for this would bring us Jesus. For us, this child is also the one born by true faith in Jesus. When spiritual children are born through the work of the Holy Spirit, God Himself will give them the assurance that they are children of God that inherit His promises.

My point in all this is that "*our*" gospel, which happens to be "*a*" gospel, has filled the church with Ishmaels. This carnally induced "White Rabbit" process is an effort to fulfill God's command, just as some say that Abraham sought to do with the other children. However, because of this man-powered rush, we have produced "converts" that are merely "*Ishmaels*" and the fruit of the flesh. But God is seeking "*Isaacs*", sons of the promise and the true work of God.

CHAPTER 18
PREACHING WITH DEPENDENCE ON GOD

———⟨∞⟩———

- *... How hard it will be for those who are wealthy to enter the kingdom of God!" The disciples were startled by these words, but Jesus told them again, "Children, how hard it is for those who trust in their wealth to get into the kingdom of God! It is easier for a camel to squeeze through the eye of a needle than for a rich person to get into the kingdom of God." The disciples were utterly amazed and asked one another, "Then who can be saved?" Jesus looked at them intently and said, "For humans it is impossible, but not for God. All things are possible for God* (Mark 10:23-27 *ISV*).

Nothing Up My Sleeve

On one occasion, while my wife and I were ministering in Japan, I was praying for the needs of believers who were lined up for personal ministry. I'm accustomed to seeing people fall down when prayed for, but I'm not used to it happening when I pray for people. Apparently this church was prepared for such, because they had "catchers" to receive the people that fell after being prayed for.

Finally, when the line had thinned down a bit, one of the "catchers" asked if I could pray for him. He was a well-educated, high-ranking officer and medical doctor in the US Marines. I reached up to touch his forehead and as I prayed, I felt him move forward. I looked up and saw him falling towards me. Well, all of these years living in Spain paid off, for like a good bullfighter, I nimbly stepped aside, *"olé"*, and let him fall full force, face first. He went down like a sequoia; Wham! I stepped over him and kept on praying for the people. After a few minutes, it occurred to me that it probably would have been a good idea to have caught him and eased him to the floor… but he was a pretty big dude! I looked back and he was still face down on the concrete floor-probably knocked out by the impact, I supposed. "Sorry 'bout that" I thought, "Well, I'll apologize to him after the service."

Unfortunately, I didn't get to see him after until the next day. When I finally saw him, straight away, I began to apologize. Perplexed, he asked me why I was apologizing. I explained what happened and he told me that he never felt a thing and had experienced a magnificently powerful time with the Lord while he was "down under the power" on the floor. He was extremely grateful for my simple prayer. Wow, nobody was more surprised than I was.

I totally believe in divine healing and the move of the power of the Holy Spirit, but I feel it intolerable when people fake, exaggerate or lie about healings or try to push you down while praying for you and then claim that it was the power of God when you fall. We can trust God for the movement of His Spirit and the manifestation of His mighty works, for He can do His awesome work without our tricks, lies and interference.

Can you trust God to move without trying to "conjure up" something? When we try to "help" Him, we just end up destroying everything that God really wants to do anyway. Do you remember when Paul talked about trying to glorify God by our lie in Romans 3:7? The results are not good for anybody… especially for the liar.

There are just as many ruses employed to try to trick the sinner into saying "The Prayer" now, and explain the scary details latter. By doing this, we are not giving the opportunity for the Holy Spirit to do His complete work in them and for them to count the true costs of following Him. Can you simply preach the Gospel with all of your heart, love, mind, soul, and strength and trust God to bring the results? Can you leave the results completely up to God? He can do it. How do you think that He did it in the church all of this time without all of today's gadgets and employments?

Therefore, the same question applies to our evangelism. Can you trust God completely for the results when you announce the truth of the message of the Gospel to the lost? Can you trust Him to do the complete work in their lives without any human manipulation? Yes, we are there, present in the lives of the sinners to whom we are ministering. Yes, we are there to urge them continually to flee from the wrath to come. However, we are not to promote our own schemes and agendas. Paul said, *"For what we proclaim is not ourselves, but Jesus Christ as Lord, with ourselves as your servants for Jesus' sake"* (II Corinthians 4:5 *ESV*).

That's Not Hard… That's Impossible!

It is impossible for man to save himself and it is equally impossible for you to save anybody: no matter how well intentioned you are. So even though Richard Ruler came running, he left sad and just as avaricious as ever. When Jesus said, *"How hard it is for rich people to get into the kingdom of God!"* He could just as easily have said, "Those who are easily angered", or "those who love sex, drugs and alcohol" or "those who love lies, love to lie and love to live lies". The point is not and never was about Richie's riches. It was all about his heart and what is was not willing or able to give so that he might serve and follow Christ with no anchors attached. This is also why Christ could have said, "How hard it is for those who have suffered abuse to enter into the kingdom of God!" for many times those who have suffered wrongfully, cherish their wounds and savor their bitterness and, even enjoy holding on to the hatred for those who have wronged them. When Jesus says to leave it all and follow me, he wasn't just talking about material things, He was talking about our hearts.

Christian Urban Myths

- *It is much harder for a rich person to enter the Kingdom of God than for a camel to go through the eye of a needle* (Luke 18:25 *GNB*).

Christians have tons of "Urban Myths"; I hear them all the time. I even hear them from the pulpit. One of these is the one about the rich man, the camel and the eye of the needle. The tale goes something like this, "There is a gate in Jerusalem called the eye of the needle through which a camel could not pass unless it stooped and first had all its baggage first removed. After dark or during times of eminent threat, when the main gates were shut, travelers or merchants would have to use this smaller gate, through which the camel had to be completely unloaded and enter crawling on its knees! A fun thought with emotional applications, but unfortunately unfounded!

This story has been around, possibly, since the nineth century, but not earlier. There is no evidence, archeological or historical for such a gate, much less so during Jesus' time or before. When such things are purported, we are robbed of Jesus' true intent and message. Jesus was using hyperbole: an exaggeration to show the impossibility or ridiculousness of something. A good example of that is, *"Why, then, do you look at the speck in your brother's eye and pay no attention to the log in your own eye?"* (Matthew 7:3 *GNB*). Yeah, that's definitely an exaggeration.

So what was Jesus saying to us when He spoke about the camel and the eye of the needle? Just as it is impossible for a camel to pass through the eye of a needle (literally), it is for a sinner to leave his sin and enter the kingdom of God. I love it when the disciples listening were shocked and said, *"Who, then, can be saved?"* For then Jesus had the opportunity to put in a plug in for the coming Holy Spirit and the grace of God by saying, *"What is impossible with man is possible with God."* It's the grace of God that has to do the entire work of God in us. It is totally impossible for us to do it even within ourselves, let alone to try to do it in somebody else. It's like we've come full circle, for once again we see, *"For it is God who is producing in you both the desire and the ability to do what pleases him"* (Philippians 2:13 *ISV*).

The Summer Is Past
- The harvest is past, the summer is ended, and we are not saved (Jeremiah 8:20 *ESV*)
- *For the time has come for judgment to begin with the household of God. And if it begins with us, what will be the outcome for those who refuse to obey the gospel of God? If it is hard for the righteous person to be saved, what will happen to the ungodly and sinful person?* (1 Peter 4:17-18 *ISV*).

These worrisome Scriptures do not seem to disturb or wake up many believers. Quite the contrary, instead of seeing the impossibility of man's salvation without the absolute work of God in his life, "easy believeism" formulas have been concocted to try to put things in man's hands and make the impossible seem easy to accomplish. Sure, we have to do our part, and that is to yield. But the reality is, that if God does not do the work, it will not get done! Jesus was informing His disciples that what was required of them was impossible for them to accomplish.

- *... Unless the LORD builds the house, its builders labor uselessly. Unless the LORD guards the city, its security forces keep watch uselessly* (Psalms 127:1 *ISV*).

The Counsel of the Wicked

What Jesus demanded of Richard was impossible for men to do under their own power. Apart from this, Richie had plenty of help to convince him that what Jesus had requested could never be done. Surely, the demons, constant, lifelong allies to all sinners, were there to whisper or shout in his ear thoughts like, "If you do that, how, then, shall you live?" Though his ear was far more open to hear that raspy voice that had counseled him his entire life, the still small voice of the Holy Spirit was there to remind him of Christ's words, "*So do not start worrying: 'Where will my food come from? or my drink? or my clothes?' (These are the things the pagans are always concerned about.) Your Father in heaven knows that you need all these things. Instead, be concerned above everything else with the Kingdom of God and with what he requires of you, and he will provide you with all these other things. So do not worry about tomorrow; it will have enough worries of its own. There is no need to add to the troubles each day brings"* (*Matthew 6:31-34 GNB*).

The enemy was also there to remind him of what others might think, "What will my family and Friends say?" Immediately the Holy Spirit answered his thoughts saying, ""*Those who love their father or mother more than me are not fit to be my disciples; those who love their son or daughter more than me are not fit to be my disciples"* (Matthew 10:37 *GNB*). But the father of Lies doesn't give up easily and comes up with, "They will call you mad; Mad, I say! They will think that you've lost your good senses!" The quiet voice replies, "*Blessed are you when others revile you and persecute you and utter all kinds of evil against you falsely on my account. Rejoice and be glad, for your reward is great in heaven, for so they persecuted the prophets who were before you"* (Matthew 5:11-12 *ESV*).

Finally, the Deceiver comes up with his trump card of an idea and says, "Surely they will send me to the madhouse and take possession and control of all of my goods!" Ah, those precious possessions... This cannot be! I cannot heed such a demand! Jesus cannot just say such a thing to me and not speak in jest! The voice of the Spirit continued to talk and remind him of Christ's words, "*And everyone who has left houses or brothers or sisters or father or mother or children or lands, for my name's sake, will receive a hundred-fold and will inherit eternal life"* (Matthew 19:29 *ESV*). Nevertheless, he had made up his mind to turn his back on the Master. Though his burdened conscience continued to reprove him, he would just have to grin and bear it, because, obey such a mandate, he could not. He would just have to risk his eternal destiny and hope that Jesus was wrong about all of this.

Not Humanly Possible

During biblical times, it was a common practice for the rich to be the owners of many slaves. However, in this case, Richie was found to be a slave of Satan, just as are all those who live enamored with this present world. His mind was perverted and contaminated with the world, his emotions and loves twisted and his will enslaved and subjected to lifeless things. He could not obey the mandates of the Gospel to repent and believe, his very nature roared against it.

We shouldn't think that he was more sinful that other men, because this is the common state of the person under the power of sin. Paul confirmed this in Romans 8:7, *"And so people become enemies of God when they are controlled by their human nature; for they do not obey God's law, and in fact they cannot obey it"* (*GNB*). Jeremiah also eloquently established the impossibility of man's ability to turn his back on sin when he said, *"Can an Ethiopian change his skin, or a leopard his spots? Then you who are trained to do evil will also be able to do good"* (Jeremiah 13:23 *ISV*).

I Know That It's True

I can take my own testimony as an example of how impossible it is for man to change his own life, and I'm sure that you can too. I surrendered to Christ at the early age of 17. Sin had broken my life to pieces. Now I look back and think, Wow! I was just a child! However, at that time I saw no hope where life was leading me. I say that life was leading me, for I certainly had no control over the sin that dominated me. Every day I would awake with a deep cry in my heart because I desperately wanted to change my life. To whom did I call? Who knew? I certainly didn't. I had never heard the Gospel and did not understand calling out to God. That, in itself, increases the desperation and the feeling that there is no hope in life. Shortly after Jesus saved me, I read Paul's words and they screamed TRUTH to my soul as to how much they applied to my life before Christ.

- *At that time you were apart from Christ. You were foreigners and did not belong to God's chosen people. You had no part in the covenants, which were based on God's promises to his people, and you lived in this world without hope and without God* (Ephesians 2:12 *GNB*).

Even though I had earned a full academic university scholarship and everything should have been looking like up, I was beginning to see life as disdainful, desolate and a downward direction deficient of any reason or purpose. The horrible guilt of my sins weighed upon me to the point that I welcomed death any way it could come. In my ignorance, I felt that if I died, I had nothing to lose. Repentance, for me, would have been totally impossible without the grace of the Holy Spirit!

That was until 7 May 1971, when the Lord Jesus Christ miraculously revealed Himself to me and I could hear and understand the Gospel. I fell upon the Rock and my soul was broken into myriads of pieces through repentance and the new birth. Since then I have had a completely new life and I know that I am a new creature. I personally know the truth of the words, *"without me ye can do nothing"* (John 15:5b). This is my personal testimony, but the truth is that, in a general sense, it is true that this is also the testimony of all those who have truly submitted their lives to Christ and have experienced the new birth.

None Righteous, No Not One

Richard came running proclaiming his own righteousness, but Christ wanted to show him that righteousness is only found in Him. This is the reason He said, *"Why do you call me good? No one is good except God alone"*. He wanted to prove to Richie both he and his own righteousness are as it says in, Isaiah 64:6: *"But we are all as an unclean thing, and all our righteousnesses are as filthy rags; and we all do fade as a leaf; and our iniquities, like the wind, have taken us away"* (KJV).

Paul said, *"For I know that nothing good dwells in me, that is, in my flesh. For I have the desire to do what is right, but not the ability to carry it out"* (Romans 7:18 *ESV*). This means that the good desire to seek God is not naturally found in us. The Bible says that in the beginning, God sought man. It wasn't man that was seeking God – he was running from Him! *"But the LORD God called to the man and said to him, where are you?"* (Genesis 3:9 *ESV*). Jonah showed us just how useless it is to try to run from God, yet man continues to try to escape his God even to this day.

There was nothing pure or natural in the element of Richard's character to be able to respond favorably to Christ's entreaty. This describes all of humanity; *"The LORD saw that the wickedness of man was great in the earth, and that every intention of the thoughts of his heart was only evil continually"* (Genesis 6:5 *ESV*). Humanity is *"dead in trespasses and sins,"* (Ephesians 2:1). The Bible does not say that we were almost dead or about to die. It says that we were dead! A dead man does not have the ability to do anything! This biblical truth is completely against the idea of the world that states that man is essentially good. Sin has killed us! *"Sin found its chance, and by means of the commandment it deceived me and killed me"* (Romans 7:11 *GNB*).

Jesus came to give us life. If Christ called Richard to repent and follow Him that means that He was also going to provide the capacitating grace so that he might be able to comply. Free will kicks in after grace is applied and then Richie would have the ability to obey or disobey, accept or reject. Without grace, we are enslaved to do only that which is contrary to God. Jesus Himself said, *"No man can come to me, except the Father which hath sent me draw him: and I will raise him up at the last day"* (John 6:44 *KJV*).

The resistance to God's grace that Mr. Ruler demonstrated was irrefutable evidence that he was a rebellious criminal worthy of death. Without the grace of God, this young man was incapable of taking a step of faith, it was necessary that he be born again to enter the kingdom of God – a work that is entirely of God and nothing of man. But alas, he was also incapable of choosing the new birth on his own accord. Jesus said that all those who have believed in Christ, *"who were born, not of blood nor of the will of the flesh nor of the will of man, but of God"* (John 1:13 *ESV*). Richard was not an exception.

The Noninvolved God?

Modern evangelism has been developed with the supposition that God has done all that He is going to do or can do to save man and will do no more. The image is fomented in the minds of men of a God that sits idly on His throne while observing the decisions of sinners concerning His Son and their salvation. They don't take into account that the Holy Spirit is in the world to convince of sin, reveal Christ and regenerate sinners. According to them, all of a sudden these dead, lost, chained, enslaved, blind and deaf sinners are going to have all of this power in and of themselves to overcome the devil and exert their own will. Paul said, *"in meekness correcting them that <u>oppose themselves</u>; if peradventure <u>God may give them repentance</u> unto the knowledge of the truth"* (II Timothy 2:25 *ASV*). This is a very thought-provoking Scripture. Do you grasp what has been stated here? This verse explains three important things.

First, we must notice that it is God who reserves the choice to concede repentance to the sinner; it is not the sinner who has the power to do anything in this situation. I like where it says that that sinners "oppose themselves", an interesting way of stating it. The Greek word for this phrase is, *"antidiatithemai"* (ἀντιδιατίθεμαι), and it means, "to set oneself opposite, that is, be disputatious and argumentative:–that oppose themselves". It doesn't say that they oppose God, for what harm can they do to God? He holds the keys of life and death as well as our eternal destiny in His hands. When people go against God, they are ultimately causing infinite damage to their own souls. Remember how Jonah understood this truth after his own rebellious romp through a monster's intestinal tract by saying, *"They that observe lying vanities <u>forsake their own mercy</u>"*? (Jonah 2:8 *KJV*).

Second, the sinner has a darkened understanding and is incapable of reasoning spiritually to understand these things;

- *For the message about the cross is nonsense to those who are being destroyed, but it is God's power to us who are being saved* (1 Corinthians 1:18 *ISV*).
- *The natural person does not accept the things of the Spirit of God, for they are folly to him, and he is not able to understand them because they are spiritually discerned* (1 Corinthians 2:14 *ESV*).

I'd like to point your attention to the fact that it says, *"if per-adventure God may give them repentance unto the knowledge of the truth"*. The word, "peradventure" is the Greek word, "may'-pot-eh" (μήποτε) – and contrary to the modern, pushover concept of God, this word enforces the Old Testament concept of God that life and death is in His hands and He will gran it to whomsoever He wills. It means, "not ever; or perhaps, not at all, or whether or not". This is the same thought I have already mentioned when Peter said something similar to Simon the Warlock in Acts 8:22.

The third thing I would like to point out is that sinners are slaves of the devil. The slave doesn't just get up and leave whenever he wants; the sinner must be set free! No man can set himself free; this is the work of Jesus Christ. God is the one that does all of this; it is not of us! We must depend on the power of God and let Him do the work. Paul says that, *"God may give them repentance"*. Once again, we will return to the Greek with the word, "give". It is the Greek word, *"dido̅mi"* (δι´δωμι), and can also be translated, "to grant, bestow, bring forth, commit, deliver (up), give" and a fair number of other renderings.

Summing this up, we see that salvation comes only from God and has to do with us receiving the grace of God that enlightens our darkened understanding, thus granting us the ability and the power to submit to God and to be free from the devil–if we choose, by employing our now-released freewill to obey or reject.

There can be no doubt that that receiving so great a salvation is an act of free human will. But, how is it possible, that said, can we come to trust in the Lord? We are all born with an aversion to the truth, a natural repulsion towards God and attraction to be free from His law. It is our rebellious nature. Our will, working in collusion with our mind and emotions, are inclined to refuse the truth of God, to despise reconciliation with our Creator and live in mockery of His commandments. How, then, can man choose an entirely new direction for himself if his nature is chained to such a destiny? That would be as easy as imagining a color that one has never seen! Of his own accord, how could Richard Ruler sell all and obediently follow Christ? His entire being protested such a decision. Yet much of our evangelism concepts continue to assume that man holds within himself the native ability to repent and believe. *"For humans it is impossible"*

"Then who can be saved?" remains a pertinent question. But Jesus gives a clear and positive answer. *"For humans it is impossible, but not for God. All things are possible for God"* Though no man can find in himself the needed resolution of an ability to repent and believe, God can change the heart.

- *And I will give you a new heart, and a new spirit I will put within you. And I will remove the heart of stone from your flesh and give you a heart of flesh* (Ezekiel 36:26 *ESV*).

This is the promise of God, He is the one that gives new life. We can only repent, believe and receive when the grace of God has done its work in our lives.

God Makes It Possible

Faith is an act of the heart quickened by the power of the Sovereign God.

- *For by grace you have been saved through faith. And this is not your own doing; it is the gift of God, not a result of works, so that no one may boast. For we are his workmanship, created in Christ*

Jesus for good works, which God prepared beforehand, that we should walk in them (Ephesians 2:8-10 *ESV*).

To the measure that God works in man, and is allowed to work in him by man operating his free will and submitting to the grace that is impelling him to do so, man is enabled to follow Christ. Though Richie had the responsibility to follow, he would never have chosen to do so unless the Lord had given him a new inclination; that is to say, unless God, in His mercy, would grant him a change of heart. Faith is the result of a spirit that has been regenerated by the Holy Spirit. Repentance is also the action of a man that has received this gift of faith. This being true, repentance can be considered as a gift from God. Observe what it says in Acts 5:31, *"God has exalted to his right hand this very man as our Leader and Savior in order to extend repentance and forgiveness of sins to Israel"* (*ISV*).

The interesting thing about this verse is the use of the word *"give* or *extend"*. In the Greek, this Word is *didomi*, which means: 1.) To give (now, that was deep) 2.) To bring to light, 3.) To offer by extended hand, 4.) To bring to pass, 5.) To minister, 6.) To offer, 7.) To have power, 8.) To place or put 9.) To show, 10.) To permit, 11.) To smite or strike with the palm of the hand. (I had to think about that one, but came to the conclusion that God was saying with that, "Boy, if I have to slap you 'up-side' the head to get you to understand..." Anyway ... moving right along...

If My People

However you want to interpret or translate this word from the autographs, tells us that all of the power of repentance falls in the hands of God Himself. By this, we can understand that the power of repentance of sin is a gift from God granted to man by way of

His grace. This reduces us to such a state before God, where we are totally at His mercy and are not even capable of repenting of our sins to save our souls without the help of God!

Are you getting this? Where, then, is this person who thinks that he is going to see if he is wants to "accept" Christ or not? I don't see that man is in the position to do anything but cry out to God for mercy! This leaves sinners completely bowed and face down, prostrate before Him under the power of the Holy Spirit pleading for the grace of God. He should then seek God for his salvation. His only hope is to call out to God so that He might do for them what they cannot do for themselves.

That is the old-time Gospel and what the Bible preaching and believing churches have historically believed for centuries. We can easily see this in old time Methodist, Baptists, Presbyterians, Pentecostals and others. Once again, check it out and read of their histories. Read about John and Charles Wesley, Charles Finney, Peter Cartwright, George Whitefield, Evan Roberts, William and Catherine Booth and so many others that have preached the Gospel. Read about the messages they preached and just how they preached them. This is the message that John Bunyan was conveying in *Pilgrims Progress*, a book that Evangelical believers have embraced for centuries. It is recognized for its excellent exposition and understanding of what salvation is and is not, as well as the plight of the sinner in his quest for salvation.

What then is our obligation? I will answer that in two words; preach THE GOSPEL and pray! You can even call them forward to pray, but instead of leading them in a prayer, chase the White Rabbit away and have an old-fashioned altar time for them to cry out to God on their own for as much time as they need. If they have to do it repeatedly, let them do it until they know that they have gotten ahold of God. Again, one of the major problems that keeps this from happening is the grave lack of the true conviction of sin, because the Gospel that convicts of sin is not being announced.

This is the part of the people of God; it is God's part to do everything else! Can you trust in God for the salvation of the lost? This is why Paul said, *"I planted the seed, Apollos watered the plant, but it was God who made the plant grow"* (1 Corinthians 3:6 *GNB*). The people that don't preach the truth of the Gospel and do not pray for the work of the Holy Spirit in the lives of the sinners are those who place the lost in danger of total destruction. This is why God has commanded His people to pray, this is the way that the Holy Spirit can free the lost after we have preached the truth of the Gospel to them. The only way a sinner can exercise repentance is if the Sovereign Lord would remove his heart of stone and replace it with a heart of flesh.

A Slave to Sin

I read of a rivalry between two dukes who were brothers. They fought over an inheritance that included sovereign dominion over a vast territory. One of the brothers won the conflict and had a special palace built for his defeated sibling. Though he earnestly avowed that he would not execute, exile or imprison his brother, no one ever saw him again.

The people protested because they suspected that the victor had indeed executed or imprisoned his brother. Together with other nobles, he was accused of being a cold-blooded despot. How could he just kill his own sibling? In his defense, the victorious duke was able to prove his innocence and that he would never do such a thing. He could quickly proved that his brother was accommodated in the finest of residences with servants and all of his desired commodities. He had acquired the finest of chefs for him to prepare the best of his preferred cuisines as well of any need that he might possibly have. He could come and go whenever he so desired for there were no bars no locks to impede his exit or entrance and whosoever wanted, could visit him at will. Perplexed at this, they inquired, "Why, then, do we not see him as we did before? He simply and calmly told the masses, "Come and see."

Those who agreed accompanied him to a moderately sized, luxurious palatial residence. All of the doors and windows were of normal size and, as promised, without bars or any such confining elements. The mystery was resolved when they came into the presence of the defeated duke himself. The supposed prisoner was a grossly obese subject and was not ambulatory. Even if he could walk, he could not leave his residence because the doors, being of normal size, were too small for him! His liberty, or lack thereof, was found in the self-control that he did not possess. He was a glutton! His brother, knowing this, provided him with the best of everything and his opponent could not say not. If he could just say no and deny himself, he would not die, but live and obtain his much desired freedom. He was a captive of his own lusts! From what we know, this duke died self-imprisoned and enslaved to his own wants.

Can Elephants Fly?

When Richard asked, *"What must I do?"* Jesus clearly informed him what he need to do to follow Him. When the answer was given, he didn't find himself capable to comply with the conditions placed before him for eternal life. It wasn't that Jesus barred his way; the Lord urged him to do so. It was not some external force that blocked his way to repentance and faith; it was his own evil heart that made it impossible. It is easier to ask an elephant to fly than to ask an avaricious man to sell everything and give it to the poor. It is easier to ask a hungry lion to spare the lives of tender lambs of the flock in their stead eat vegetables.

The Prophet Isaiah foretold the ministry of Christ with the words,

- *A voice cries: "In the wilderness prepare the way of the LORD; make straight in the desert a highway for our God. Every valley shall be lifted up, and every mountain and hill be made low; the uneven ground shall become level, and the rough places a plain* (Isaiah 40:3-4 *ESV*).

Richard began by claiming his own righteousness. In a way, he was bragging about just how good he was and, we could say that he was like a high mountain. Christ proved that he was a lowly sinner. He began as a mountain and was made low. Remember that Jesus said, "... *If you were blind, then you would not be guilty; but since you claim that you can see, this means that you are still guilty*" (John 9:41 *GNB*).

The disciples were shocked when they heard Christ's comment after His interview with Mr. Ruler: "*When the disciples heard this, they were completely amazed. Who, then, can be saved? they asked. Jesus looked straight at them and answered, This is impossible for human beings, but for God everything is possible*" (Matthew 19:25-26 *GNB*). Christ turned to His disciples and, in essence, said, "That is exactly my point. It is impossible for him to do so. But it is not impossible for God, because for God, all things are possible." The God of all possibilities can transform the twisted nature of His creatures.

There are multiple implications of this lesson. Though it is correct to reason with men to persuade them, even to plead with them to seek God and repent of their sins, we must understand that an answer on their part is impossible unless God grants them the grace to capacitate them to seek Him. They too, need to understand this truth. Our Gospel should be based on dependency upon the Lord. Our hope of obtaining results should be based upon His work in their lives and not in the power of man's will or any other faculty of the hearer or the messenger. God takes pleasure in resurrecting dead sinners by way of the foolishness of the preaching of the Gospel. Do believe this truth?

The Dead Shall Hear

There is an urban myth that says that hair and nails continue to grow after death. Not true-stated briefly, what happens is that the skin around the hair and fingernails will desiccate and thereby shrink and retract making hair and fingernails look longer as if they'd grown. Deeper logical explanations exist considering that in order for hair and nails to grow, the follicles that produce hair and the germinal matrix that produces nails need a constant supply of blood, oxygen and glucose as well as biotin. Death, the original and ultimate killjoy, puts a stop to the supply of blood, oxygen, glucose and biotin, and therefore puts a stop to fingernail and hair growth.

In death, nothing acts on its own except the degenerative process. The same is true with man. The sinner is dead in disobedience and sins. There is no way for the dead in sin to produce anything on their own but degeneration. For the dead to get out of their tomb of spiritual death on their own is as viable as the physically dead getting up of their own accord, and digging out if their graves and walking away. If you think that's easy, you've seen too many zombie movies!

But, why preach to the dead? When Christ went to Lazarus' tomb and cried, "Lazarus, come out" (John 11:43), we could have probably asked the same question. Why talk to the dead? How can a cadaver obey a command? Would you say that everything about Lazarus was dead except for his will in such a way that when Jesus said, "Lazarus, come out" his will could cause him to come back from the dead? I think that we can all agree that, in this setting, the free will aspect of Lazarus' "life" played no part in his obedience to Christ and coming out of the grave. I am sure that untold millions of the dead would have come out of their graves gladly and willingly. Wow! If that would happen, we'd have a real life horror flick on our hands! It was a sovereign act of God that gave new life to the four-days-dead, dead man. It had nothing to do with Lazarus' free will. ! God Himself had to quicken his ears to hear, his mind to understand and his will to obey His call.

- *Wherefore he saith, Awake thou that sleepest, and arise from the dead, and Christ shall give thee light* (Ephesians 5:14 *KJV*).

Some raise the objection that such an outlook would hamper evangelism; yet, it did not hinder the Lord. Jesus told us what would happen if we attempt to harvest fruit from plants that our Heavenly Father has not given: *"Every plant that my heavenly Father did not plant will be pulled up by the roots."* (Matthew 15:13 *ISV*). All of your labor will be in vain because it is a work of the flesh and not of the Spirit of God. It is not that God despises your love and sincere service for Him, but it is God and only God that gives the growth even though you have planted so sincerely and diligently and another has watered. You plant when you sow the Good Seed and you water with prayer and your faithful lifestyle. So it is that when Jesus spoke to Mr. Richard, He was speaking to a dead man whose will was as dead as his spirit and spiritual understanding.

- *... even when we were dead through our trespasses, made us alive together with Christ (by grace have ye been saved)* (Ephesians 2:5 *ASV*).

We have been limited to preach to the dead dry bones of the valley (Ezekiel 37). The Prophet Joel also spoke of such a valley saying, *"Multitudes, multitudes, in the valley of decision! For the day of the LORD is near in the valley of decision"* (Joel 3:14 *ESV*). As the Prophet Ezekiel of old, we have been placed in the valley of the dead of this world. This valley is filled with the sun-scorched bones of the dead. He tells us, *"Prophesy to the bones. Tell these dry bones to listen to the word of the LORD"* (Ezekiel 37:4 *GNB*).

God's purpose and will is that He would be freed to enact the resurrection of dead sinners by way of our preaching. We preach to bones that are dead and dry indeed and in whose marrow is not a fiber of free will. Nevertheless, when the wind of the breath of God blows over them, they will live and will become a great and powerful army that will faithfully follow the Lamb.

Correctly Understanding Our Purpose

Having this in mind, we can focus our attention on fervent prayer so that the power of God might cover us and minister His saving grace to the lost sinners who will hear the Word through us. This is what we, generally, have always believed when we pray for God to move in our services. The difference between what we believe and what we actually do is that after we pray and preach, we then move in aggressively to take the control from the Holy Spirit.

We say we will trust God, but we actually rely more upon the power of our manipulative and rush sales pitch tactics. We should leave the sinners in God's hands so that He might do His complete and perfect work in their lives. Our trust should not depend on whether we got the people to come to the altar or go to the counseling rooms and repeat "The Prayer", but in God's faithfulness to continue to work in their lives. His Spirit's loving hot pursuit will never let them "get away".

Back to That Brass Thing

Even though they might be a great blessing and we might see God moving and doing things with them, none of our tools will put flesh on those dry bones. They are not responsible for God having worked. As I said earlier, sometimes He works in spite of what we do and not because of what we do-and praise Him for that. Still, yes, we will give God the opportunity to utilize any variety of evangelistic methods available, it is just up to us to be sure and not to make a "*Nehushtan*" of said method.

For example, in the past, the Salvation Army used uniforms, ranks and acoustic street bands. Those were the secular rages of the day and they were very successful evangelistic tools of that time… today… not so much. It just ends up looking kind-of funny. The same thing happened with the Jesus People. I had never heard the Gospel before God reached me via that remarkable revival, so I'm extremely grateful to Him for that. It was great, effective, and powerful and definitely, a move of God, but the cloud continued to move, and those of us who were saved and chose to follow Jesus have moved along with it. To continue with a method or movement or ministry style because it once worked is neither obedience nor faith; it is nostalgia and not the work of God. It has become a *"Nehushtan"*.

Paul's counsel to Timothy, his young disciple, also teaches us that the only hope for both the preaching saint and the perishing sinner is found in God, and what a glorious hope it is.

- *And the Lord's servant must not be quarrelsome but kind to everyone, able to teach, patiently enduring evil, correcting his opponents with gentleness. God may perhaps <u>grant them repentance</u> leading to a knowledge of the truth, and they may come to their senses and escape from the snare of the devil, after being captured by him to do his will* (II Timothy 2:24-26 ESV).

This leaves those who desire to announce the truth of the love of God to those who oppose the Gospel, the hope of success that God might "grant them repentance". Good oratory skills, though they never hurt, will not convince the rebellious dead. I read Paul's writings and I think that he was incredibly eloquent. He was so impressed with his own oratory skills.

- *...and my teaching and message were not delivered with skillful words of human wisdom, but with convincing proof of the power of God's Spirit. Your faith, then, does not rest on human wisdom but on God's power* (1 Corinthians 2:4-5 GNB).

Nor will our ingenious methods, preparations, talents and presentations, or our precise theology break the heart of the dead in sin. Though none of this ever hurts and all that we do should be done to the best of our abilities, we must understand that if God does not impregnate all of this and continue with the work of His Spirit after we have done our best, it is all for naught. We have to get out of the way and let Him do what He does best: save the sinner for whom He sent His Son to die.

He loves them far more that we do, though we might love them greatly and have dedicated our lives to see them saved. We might even feel as did Paul in Romans 9:1-3, (a bit exaggerated I might add) but our love still pales in comparison to His for us. In fact, we wouldn't even love Him nor them if it were not for Him. The Word says, *"We love because God first loved us"* (1 John 4:19 *ISV*). Therefore, we are not talking about some narrow, by a thread hope here, because the words, *"... God may perhaps grant them repentance"*, is an infinitely more resplendent expectation than something like, "perhaps our tactics might convince them to come to church again".

Is there a possible danger in limiting the Gospel and its impact on humanity if we decide to trust and depend on God for the results of our evangelistic efforts? No way, José! I am sure that the people who are invited to our services have friends and family who are believers. If not, the continued watering of the Good Seed depends on faithful believers in our congregations. Let them continue to water the seed and let God give the increase and the resulting harvest will be far more abundant and healthy than if we use our synthetic fertilizers. Let's get out of God's way, we only hinder Him and we are obstacles to the sinner.

CONCLUSION

The Dog and the Porcupine

I've eaten a lot of weird thing in my years on the mission field and traveling and ministering in various countries. I'm quite sure I've been served dog, cat and a wide variety of rodents and reptiles. Once I was served putrid, seven-day dead goat – it smelled like road kill and probably was. Yet, for the people to whom I was ministering, it was a preferred dish that wasn't good until it wormed. They offered me the choicest selections. My wife lucked out that day and without knowing what was coming, had announced that she was fasting. Me and my big mouth! When they asked me if I like goat meat, I replied with an enthusiastic, *yes*! Then they brought that out. It was the most creative way to ruin a meal of goat meat that I have ever seen. Well… that was many years ago and as you can see, I lived to this point to be able to tell you about it.

So, if I were to ask you, "How many of you would eat a dog?" I'm sure that many would probably answer, "Ew!" Others might say, "Pass the salt." Though the dog be a best friend, honestly, in a tight, life or death pinch, Fido would make a fine meal! Hey, if it came down to it for Fido, you would be on the plate in a minute if he had anything to say about it. Though I love them as pets, dogs are filthy animals and a steady diet of dog meat is not highly recommendable. My wife once told me that if you ate cat meat, you would go crazy, because when she was a kid, a lady in her neighborhood ate cat and went crazy. I told her that she didn't go crazy because she ate a cat; she ate a cat because she was crazy!

Anyway, I knew some brothers who had gone up into the mountains to pray and fast for about two or three days. One of the brother's family owned a cabin in a remote region of a near-by mountain range and it seemed as if it was the perfect place for such a retreat. Unfortunately, they were blest with an opportunity to fast that turned out to be far more ample than previously anticipated. It turned out that a tremendous snowstorm unexpectedly blew in from the north and left them stranded and with cabin fever for close to two weeks.

When they were finally about to get out of the cabin, they were so hungry that they were willing to eat anything that had four legs as long as it wasn't a table or a chair. Lamentably, the only thing that happened to ramble along their path was a porcupine that just woke up from hibernating. Poor guy, they cooked him up in a broth... though "broth" is a generous gastronomical term for what they did. They actually just boiled him in melted snow. Anyway, they ended up even sucking the bones of that beast. Later they read up on porcupines to find out just what they had eaten and discovered that they had consumed one of the filthiest animals around, much worse than eating a dog or a cat. In their stomachs, you can find up to 1,500 parasites of the which, five of the same will almost kill a dog.

My Point Is This...

Now, bringing it back to our subject, what is it that I want to tell you with all of this talk about eating weird things? Just this little point: I thought of the porcupine being so unclean that it can withstand organisms so perilous that if this same invasive parasitic bacterium were found in a dog in a comparably insignificant quantity, it would be deadly. This is impressive when you consider that a dog's immune system can easily withstand one hundred thousand times more pathogens than a human can tolerate.

The point is this: the differences between our preaching today and Jesus' preaching are not insignificant; they are enormous! The principal errors are not questions of emphasis on peripheral issues, but on the heart of the message of the Gospel. If it would be a consistent error on just one of the mentioned areas, our deviation would be grave. But to overlook all of these areas:

- The attributes of the character of God,
- The law and grace,
- The call to bow to the Lordship of Christ,
- Repentance,
- True and biblical saving faith,
- The cross,
- The truth of the security of our salvation and,
- The dependency on God for the fruit of our labor.

Having systematically ignored these, our errors become lethal in their severity. Concerning the eternal salvation of our souls, we would be hard pressed to find subjects of greater cruciality in the Bible, for it is the principal focus of the Scriptures.

You might say, "But there are so many churches that have not paid attention of these things for years". I can only answer sadly, that if they have not yet died, they stagger from extreme illness as dying entities. Clearly, not all are in error and God always has His "seven thousand" that have not kissed Baal. Still there is a great number has fallen before this altar of easy believeism. More crucial still, few strive to recover the message of the Gospel because they assume that the evangelical tradition that they follow is sufficient. As far as the preaching of the true Gospel, true conversions and revival are concerned, a saying comes to my mind, "A generation has arisen that has 'not known Joseph,' and those who have known him have forgotten him as did the cupbearer in his comfort". As a result, great multitudes never examine their lifestyles under the searing and all-revealing light of the Scriptures.

Without a doubt, many evangelicals who practice the evangelistic shortcuts that have been mentioned are seeking to serve Jesus sincerely. Surely many have had an experience that which goes far beyond anything they can imagine or voice effectively. These errors do not negate the basic truths of the Word of God that are in effect in their lives. But sincerity and genuine conversion are not the only qualifications necessary for the work of an evangelist. The ability to communicate the biblical Gospel is essential. Please understand that the lack of such understanding in those who have still lead people to Jesus is the exception and not the rule.

Being that Evangelicals are honestly asking why God is not moving in their gigantic projects with His power, tells us that it's time to reexamine the content of the gospel that we are preaching. We should look beyond the numbers in the superficial result reports that we read and seek out the lasting fruit of such numbers. There exists no other subject that can take the place of the importance of the truth of the Gospel that Christ bequeathed to His disciples. It is time to rise up over our traditions do has Jude said and "... *earnestly contend for the faith which was once delivered unto the saints*" (Jude 1:3 *KJV*).

REFERENCES AND BIBLIOGRAPHY

Chapter 1–Learning from Past Errors

[1] *Bill Gothard*

Chapter 3–Truth and Traditions

NOTE: To you theologians out there, when I speak of the perfection of the Word of God, I am not talking about our vernacular translations. I am referring to the autographs of Scripture.

[1] *Why do you think that it didn't bother Jesus to cast out six thousand demons and put them into two thousand swine? All of those pigs killed committed suicide and somebody's business was totally ruined! I'll tell you why; what the heck were a bunch of Jews doing dealing in swine?!? They were not to have anything to do with this unclean animal. But in Decapolis (Ten Cities), there were communities that were predominantly comprised of Gentiles – and man, how those Gentiles like to eat pigs! But for the Jews it was like a Christian dealing in marijuana because the government has now legalized it!*

[2] TORRES, *Carmen Edith,* from the periodical *"El Nuevo Día"* Sunday November 8, 1998.

[3] CHANTRY, Walter J., *"Today's Gospel: Authentic or Synthetic?"* Publisher: Banner of Truth (July 1, 1970)

Chapter 5–Zeal Without Knowledge

[3] It turns out that this Singer was a spiritualist warlock.

Chapter 7–Christ is the Example

[1] – *"paidagogos"* (παιδαγωγός) *a boy leader, that is, a servant whose office it was to take the children to school; (by implication [figuratively] a tutor ["paedagogue"]):–instructor, schoolmaster.*

[2]–*For a righteous man falleth seven times, and riseth up again, but the wicked stumble under adversity.* (Proverbs 24:16 *JPS*)

Chapter 10–Such a Nice Young Man

[1] *In my opinion, the KJV offers the best translation for this verse.*

Chapter 12–Confessing Jesus Christ as Lord

[1] It comes out better in Spanish: *"El chico era un genio pero también ha de haber tenido su genio"*.

[1] *Strong's Concordance: gr. 3807*

[2] *for though a righteous man falls seven times, he will rise again, but the wicked stumble into calamity.* (Proverbs 24:16 *ISV*)

[3] *"For there is not a just man upon earth, that doeth good, and sinneth not."* (Ecclesiastes 7:20 *KJV*)."

[4] These figures might vary according to the translation used, but not much.

Chapter 16–The Security of the Believer (Part 1)

[1] *The executive functions of the frontal lobes involve the ability to recognize future consequences resulting from current actions, to choose between good and bad actions (or better and best), override and*

suppress socially unacceptable responses, and determine similarities and differences between things or events.

2 *Depending on how you translate the word in Job 39:12 and Deuteronomy 30:20, there are three possible appearances.*

3 OLSON, Bruce, *"Bruchko"*. Publisher: Charisma House; [Updated ed.] edition (June 1977)

4 *The parenthetical comments are mine and are not a part of the Scripture.*

5 BREWSTER, Dr. Daniel, *THE "4/14 WINDOW" Child Ministries and Mission Strategies*

Barna Research, *"Teens and adults have little chance of accepting Christ as their savior,"* Press release, 1999-NOV-15. Published in the 1999-OCT issue of Barna Reports, which can be ordered at: http://www.barna.org/cgi-bin/PageProduct. asp?ProductID=66

The Barna Research Group surveys demonstrate that American children ages 5 to 13 have a 32% probability of accepting Christ, but youth or teens aged 14 to 18 have only a 4% probability of doing so. Adults age 19 and over have just a 6% probability of becoming Christians.

Another survey — by the **International Bible Society** — indicated that 83% of all Christians make their commitment to Jesus between the ages of 4 and 14, that is, when they are children or early youth.

This data illustrates the importance of influencing children to consider making a decision to follow Christ. Because the 4-14 period is so large, many have started referring to the "4-14 Window." Many people serving as career cross-cultural missionaries have testified that they first felt

God calling them to missionary service during that 4-14 age period.

DR. JESÚS CARAMÉS TENREIRO'S RECOMMENDATION OF DR. PARKER'S BOOK, "SEVEN TIMES DEAD"

P eople do not commonly imagine that, while yet living, they are actually dead! The very possibility of thinking such a thing causes us to reason that we are alive; nevertheless, the author confront us with the fact that without Christ we are not only dead, but also dead in seven different ways! Prince goes further than the "simple" physical death; this is only one of the ways that man dies. He shows us that there are more, and all of them call us insistently. The passionate cry of the author is that, if we are to be free, we must have the experience and assurance that this last "sting of death" has been defeated in Christ.

Dr. Prince Parker takes us by the hand through each page, to the vision of the reality that so patently surrounds us, but he does so from a new viewpoint, from the perspective of the Word of God, the Bible. Not everything is as it appears, yet the cruelest part of deception is not knowing that you have been deceived. Prince demonstrates that the natural man seems to be alive, but we see, with new depth, that they are not only dead, but seven times so. This is the surprising title of this work. It brings out the contrast of what we conceive as life and contrasts it with what the Scriptures say. It situates us in the place where we become conscious of truth under the light of God's revelation. As Spurgeon said, "*The Bible is as a lion that defends itself; you only have to open the door*". Prince opens the door, and he does so with his experience as a missionary pastor, saying at one point, "*I have buried more people than I have married*". As a faithful witness, eloquent and objective about what is to befall us; he shows us that of concepts are often, absurd, irrational and unbelievable.

El lector, escuchará a Prince, que con ternura, pero con la insistencia apasionada de un padre, tal es el corazón pastoral, insta al cristiano a pensar y haciéndolo, recibir los aires frescos de la libertad que Dios ha querido y aún hoy, insiste en regalarnos. Y la alcanzaremos porque la lectura de este libro nos habrá de acercar más a Jesús.

The reader will be exhorted with tenderness, but with the passionate insistence of a father. Such is a pastor's heart: a heart that exhorts the Christian to think and act. Moreover, as they do, they find that they receive the fresh air of the freedom God has wanted to give us. We well get that freedom because, by reading this book, we will get closer to Jesus.

This opportunity is indispensable, that is why Dr. Parker redeems the time as he speaks to us in a frank manner. He exposes the reality of death that society, throughout history, has masked and converted into a subject of taboo and hides it is if it did not exist. In a contrary manner, Prince invites us to open our eyes to a heartless reality that smites humankind. The stench of death is not confined to the cemetery, but it surrounds Christless societies. The world is not sick, but dead, yet not dead in that, "your life here has ended", sense of dead. Rather, and this is the surprising part, since the very instant we were born, death was there to show us that which we do not want to see. It attacks us continually and robs us of all that which Christ desires to give us. Yet Prince exclaims, "Yes, we can defeat death!" Prince wants to provoke us and he manages to do so, because his writings will not leave you untouched. While showing us that man is most assuredly, seven times dead without God.

Prince is a theologian, but above all, he is a pastor. He knows how to "*keep it real*" and his life is a good example of dedication and passion for Christ in preaching the Gospel of God in Christ. He ministers using simple language. As pastor that is one with his flock, you can hear him saying: "think," "reflect," "decide". Words whispers with a loving and determined voice waiting for our reaction.

"The Seven Ways That Man Died" represents an effort to bring us closer to the Truth of God, confronting the curse of death with the blessing that God, in Christ, has placed at our disposal. If we can hear that "still small voice" which brings us peace, consolation, hope and freedom from beyond the grave.

Dr. Jesús Caramés Tenreiro
Rector of the Theological Seminary
Assemblies of God of Spain

DR. PRINCE M. PARKER'S MINISTRY

S ince 1973, Dr. Prince M. Parker has been a missionary to the Spanish-speaking world. He has been a pioneer in spreading the Gospel in various fields and has served as pastor of newly founded churches as well as established congregations. He is a professor and theologian and has been a professional musician in both secular and Christian environments having also been a pioneer of Spanish Contemporary Christian Music. Dr. Parker and his wife, Guillermina (Gina), have been married since 1976 and at the time of this publication, have been in ministry for more than 40 years. They have four adult children and eleven grandchildren. He now serves as the professor of Exegetics (II) and Old Testament History at the *"Theological Seminary of the Assemblies of God of Spain"* as well as other academic-administrative responsibilities. They travel frequently and receive invitations to participate in conferences and church services worldwide.

KJV
GNB
MSG
Amp
ASV
NIV

CPSIA information can be obtained at www.ICGtesting.com
Printed in the USA
BVOW04s2054180614

356760BV00002B/5/P